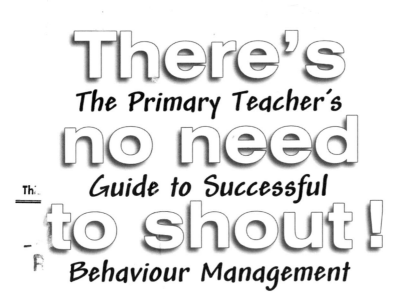

There's

The Primary Teacher's

no need

Th...

Guide to Successful

to shout !

R

Behaviour Management

Ol...

2

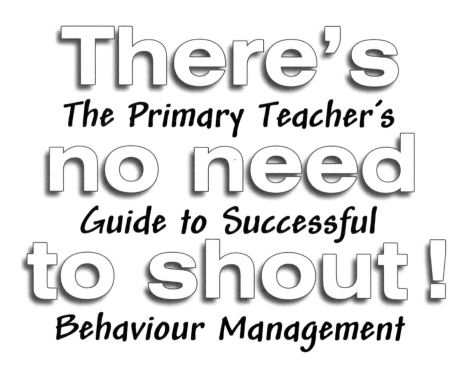

There's
The Primary Teacher's
no need
Guide to Successful
to shout!
Behaviour Management

David Wright

Published in 2005 by:
Nelson Thornes Ltd
Delta Place
27 Bath Road
CHELTENHAM
GL53 7TH
United Kingdom

05 06 07 08 09 / 10 9 8 7 6 5 4 3 2 1

A catalogue record for this book is available from the British Library

ISBN 0 7487 9360 7

Illustrations by Clinton Banbury
Page make-up by Florence Production Ltd

Printed and bound in Spain by GraphyCems

Dedication

This book is dedicated to my family, Maureen, Sean and Jamie,
for their patience and support while I was writing it.

I would also like to express my thanks to Geoff Wroe. I learned so much about
teaching and leadership while working with him. Truly a great head teacher.

CONTENTS

ACKNOWLEDGEMENT

Page 130: Assessment Framework from *The Framework for the Assessment of Children in Need and Their Families* (Department of Health, 2000). Crown copyright material is reproduced with the permission of the Controller of HMSO and the Queen's Printer for Scotland.

PREFACE

Primary schools can be remarkable places. The way the curriculum is planned and delivered, coupled with the commitment of the staff to really want to make a difference for every child, results in a really positive atmosphere for learning. Parents tend to be very interested in their child's education and want the best for them. When the school and the home are working in partnership the effects can be startling.

Every so often a glitch can occur. It may be because of a child with particularly challenging behaviour, or perhaps a group of unruly children; or even a teacher with a lack of experience or knowledge in managing behaviour. Whatever the reason, the effect can be far-reaching in the school, with whole classes of children suffering. Prevention is better than having to deal with the fall-out and that is where this book becomes a must for every teacher and learning support assistant working in a primary school.

Too often the title of a book promises so much to the reader but then the text disappoints. Well, have no fear with this particular book. It has been written by a skilled teacher who knows exactly what the inside of a classroom is like and the difficulties that the pupils can cause. This book is packed with workable ideas that have been tried and tested and proven to work. They are based on the principle that children need to learn to take responsibility for their own behaviour and that they should be given choices. All choices have consequences. Poor choices lead to negative consequences. Applying a consistent and fair approach will enable your pupils to learn to make the right choices and you will have no need to shout.

INTRODUCTION

I get calls from head teachers about students who are becoming so challenging that they are nearing permanent exclusion. The class teacher has tried everything she can think of. The educational psychologist has offered advice and suggested reasons for the child's behaviour and the behaviour support team has been in and worked with the staff, but none of the interventions seemed to have worked. The parents are at their wits' end. Home life is in turmoil, with chaos and disruption virtually every night. It is a plea for help and the head teacher is desperately hoping that I will be able to provide a solution. I take children that are very challenging and try to 're-engineer' their behaviour. For some of the children, success is hard and no matter what we try to do to help, it doesn't happen. My team of staff are not magicians.

The children's emotional difficulties are so complex, ingrained and interlinked to wider issues within the family and the community that we can only scratch the surface and make a little progress. Children who have experienced significant traumas such as sexual abuse, domestic violence or neglect or who are victims of war will develop barriers in their minds that have far-reaching effects on their ability to function normally. Most schools will have some children with these kinds of experiences. The children will be on the far end of the behaviour spectrum and will create enormous problems for their teachers. The classroom can become so distressful and unbearable that the teacher begins to feel they cannot manage. Help is often too slow in coming or too little to have any real effect.

This is not the case for the majority of teachers or children but I feel it is important to make it very clear that there are vulnerable children in mainstream schools and we are not always successful in helping them. When a difficult child finally leaves a class and is referred on to an agency or another educational provision in an effort to help them, the teacher will feel a great burden lifted from their shoulders. At the same time, they may also feel that they have failed and that is why it is important to recognise that we cannot get it right with every child.

Today's schools can be challenging places to work in. They are very different to the schools of my youth in post-war Britain. For decades, teachers were regarded as pillars of the community, professional people held in high regard. If you stepped out of line in a lesson, a wooden board rubber would come flying across the room and just skim past your head, hitting the wall with a chilling thwack to remind you of who was in charge. Be caught messing around and you might find your ear being held and twisted while you dangled from the hand of the teacher scolding you. The really naughty kids would be publicly punished with a sharp swipe of the slipper, T-square or board ruler. The ultimate punishment was a caning from the head teacher. Many believe that those days were good and claim that it never did them any harm. I am not going to take up that argument here. It was a different era and things have changed.

The rock and roll years of the 1950s heralded the arrival of the teenage phenomenon. The war began to fade into the past, along with the austerity of rationing and making ends meet. Increased production required larger labour forces that in turn led to people having surplus spending power and manufacturers looking for new markets. For the first time in our history, young school leavers discovered they had money to spare. The manufacturers were quick to identify them as a potentially enormous market. The 1960s became a decade of wealth and consumption and the teenage market became a major force because young people did not have financial responsibilities. Teenagers in Britain and the United States did not have the demands on their income that their parents or grandparents had endured. By the end of the decade there was a general feeling of being well off, which brought with it a sense of freedom that was typified by a tide of liberal opinion sweeping the nation. Old values were questioned, challenged and rejected. Social rules and class divides were disintegrating. The strict Victorian attitudes towards sex and marriage that had pervaded began to disappear with the emancipation of women in the workplace and the home.

The advent of the contraceptive pill liberated women and allowed them to decide who they would have sexual encounters with. The sexual revolution enabled men and women to become more sexually active before marriage. This in turn led to the questioning of the value of marriage itself and young people began to take partners and even live together outside of marriage, something that would have been unheard of a decade earlier.

Children were encouraged to question the way things were. They were allowed to be freer. In school the move was away from the strict regime of didactic teaching in classrooms with rows of desks. Examinations divided children into 'those that could' and 'those that couldn't'. Primary education became experiential. Teachers encouraged children to discover and learn for themselves through project-based activities. Subject boundaries started to get blurred and lesson structures faded as the children were given opportunities to see what they could find out about a topic. Interestingly, secondary education did not go down that route of educating the 'whole child' using the new, quite innovative but untested methods.

It was not only the curriculum that changed. The architecture of the primary school evolved to accommodate the new liberal approaches. Walls were knocked down between classrooms and corridors. Movable tables and chairs were arranged in islands rather than rows and replaced traditional fixed desks and benches. Children were even given the freedom to move from one area to another. Carpet time was introduced so that the class could sit round the teacher for some activities to offer a more homely or relaxed experience.

In the 1970s the political trend was towards more central control. Governments began to recognise the economic value of education. A chilling realisation dawned that the population as a whole was not being well educated. Levels of numeracy and literacy were poor, which led to significant changes that have put their stamp on the contemporary landscape of education.

The high regard that the profession was held in by the general public has been undermined by the teacher-bashing activities of the popular tabloid media. Attacks on teachers are commonplace whenever standards drop, yet when they rise it is because the tests are allegedly getting easier, not because the teaching and preparation have improved. The regular negative reporting about teachers in the 1980s and the early 1990s has opened the floodgates for criticism at all levels. Now it is considered acceptable for parents to speak to teachers rudely or threateningly when they feel their child has been treated unfairly. I do not support unprofessional or poor practice but equally I believe that teachers have rights like everyone else and there are proper channels that can be used. The harm is done when a parent decides to launch into a tirade of shouting and abuse in front of the child. This undermines the teacher's position with the child and condones shouting and abuse. The repeated talk of student and parental rights coupled with the complaining, compensation culture must have had a detrimental effect and harmful influence on the teaching profession and a teacher's ability to do the job.

The second major change has been the programme of educational reforms. This includes the introduction of the National Curriculum and testing, GCSEs, the reduction of local education authority powers, Ofsted, and numeracy and literacy hours. More recently, it includes workforce reform in the shape of *Excellence and Enjoyment*, which is almost a government U-turn back to some of the thinking behind the liberal approaches of the 1960s, and wrap-around schooling to enable working parents to access childcare. The effects of these changes remain to be seen as longitudinal studies are still incomplete, but from a personal perspective the continual removal of power from the profession as a whole can only lead to deskilling. If a government repeatedly puts out publications that direct teachers on what to teach and how to teach it, it will inevitably end up with a compliant, servile workforce. The problems occur when a government changes its mind, which seems to be quite often. This destabilises the system. Teachers begin to think they are wasting their time, because as fast as they understand the latest initiative, a new one replaces it. Planning the curriculum has become an annual task because teachers never know whether it will be the same next year.

Uncertainty leads to problems elsewhere. Teachers who are desperately trying to keep abreast of the curriculum and new initiatives will find that their lessons are not as good as they could be, because they do not have the opportunity to review and evaluate them as they would like. Their time is eaten up with research and reading, and then incorporating the new government guidelines into their lessons. Behaviour of the students becomes an afterthought and lessons may not be as good as they could be, so students get bored and switch off.

Change is necessary and in most cases has benefits, so we should embrace it. We have an excellent track record over the past two decades for doing just that, maybe more so than any other profession. Change also brings with it disadvantages that need to be managed and solutions found. The major difficulty many teachers are currently experiencing is the issue of inclusion. I do not know anyone who would argue against the idea, because everyone has the right to be a member of the community, to contribute to it and to benefit from it. Our job is to find ways to include everyone in the mainstream education system as long as it is in their best interests.

Teachers are struggling with problems caused by students behaving in ways that could have been avoided. They call me in to help and what I invariably see when I arrive is a child unable to cope because the teacher is not using an effective method of classroom management.

The idea for this book first came to me near the start of my career in education. I entered teaching after a number of jobs. I began working in further education colleges teaching photography and video. The principal asked me whether I would like to take a class of 15 year olds and teach them video production. They were all truants and many had not been to school for over a year. The local education authority had set up a Back to Education course for them. It had six modules consisting of numeracy, literacy, IT, business, video plus art and design, and science. The principal was very honest with me. She told me all about their backgrounds. I knew exactly what I was letting myself in for. These guys would be difficult. They did not view school as useful and teachers were not on their list of people to respect. They had reputations on the streets and could not be messed with.

I was really into my subject and just wanted others to get the same amount of enjoyment from doing it as I did. The project we did included paper engineering and programme making. The kids learned how to make pop-up cards and then produce a short piece for a children's television programme on how to make them.

The attendance for my sessions was a hundred per cent over the eight weeks. I later found out that the other teachers had not had such a good response. One of the reasons behind my success was the intrinsically interesting nature of the subject. The other reason was good teaching combined with well-planned activities matched to the abilities of the class.

Several months later I began to think about that class of kids and started wondering what would have happened if things had gone differently. What if the behaviour had deteriorated in the lesson? What would I have done? I realised then that I hadn't got a clue. I would have had no idea how to handle things and would have probably ended up with a riot on my hands.

Later I moved into the secondary sector and the rude awakening of the fact that many of the students were not going to behave without some kind of intervention by me. Suddenly I was in the front line of mainstream education and the daily problem of maintaining order. I had not been trained to deal with recalcitrant children.

The years have passed since those early, quite frightening days and I have learned a lot. The ideas and methods in this book are the product of learning the hard way. The case studies that I have used have either happened to my colleagues or me and provide a wealth of material to analyse and evaluate in an effort to find solutions.

The ethos behind the methods described in this book is simple and easy to understand: (1) the children take responsibility for their own behaviour; (2) this is done by helping them recognise that they have choices and are in control of them. Everything that I have suggested stems from these guiding principles and the aim is to help the children reach them. Gender references are used simply to help the text flow. Boys and girls are equally capable of behaving in ways described in this book. All names used in this book are fictitious to protect the identities of individuals featured in the case studies.

1 What kind of teacher do you want to be?

The teacher holds a powerful position. You can shape and influence the hearts and minds of your pupils by what you say, what you do and how you do it. Your expectations can ignite a passion for learning in a child that can determine their life chances and launch them on to great things. Alternatively, you can extinguish their enthusiasm, dampen their hopes and dreams and turn them off the path of learning. Such power to influence and motivate has been recognised for centuries, which is why the teacher holds such a revered position in many societies. Good teachers are respected in a way that other professionals are not.

The learning process is a complex one. How it takes place is becoming better understood in terms of what can be done by the teacher and the pupils to make it more efficient. For example, adopting a particular teaching style or linking information to familiar objects or ideas can help the pupils make better sense of the new and remember it over time. What is only just starting to be understood is how the brain functions during the learning process. We know little if anything about how we comprehend and process something like $2 + 2 = 4$.

Recent advances have pinpointed where in the brain the activity is taking place when we try to learn something. We are also aware of which areas of the brain have become specialised for specific kinds of learning, such as visual stimuli and physical skills like playing a musical instrument or executing a complicated movement.

One of the most important factors in the learning process is the mental state of the pupil and this has been known for some time. It is obvious really – if we are not ready to learn, we won't. So what are the barriers to learning that pupils experience? How do they arise and how can they be overcome? Maslow's hierarchy of needs (Figure 1.1, overleaf) offers us a model that represents all our individual needs as a pyramid, with our essential physical requirements at the base (Maslow, 1998). These must be satisfied before we are able to consider others. Next comes our personal safety. If we are under threat, the body's biological defences are activated, producing hormones that prepare us for either fight or flight. Once safety needs have been satisfied, we can begin to consider ourselves and our position within a group or community.

The classroom environment can be matched against the pyramid. If a pupil is not secure in the lower levels then the higher levels, including learning, will become difficult. There can be many barriers to learning. Here are some examples:

- The room is too cold, hot or cramped, so the pupils cannot apply themselves to anything other than the discomfort.
- The pupil is thirsty, hungry or ill, so they need to do something about physical needs immediately.
- There are distractions such as noise or something unusual or interesting inside or outside the room.

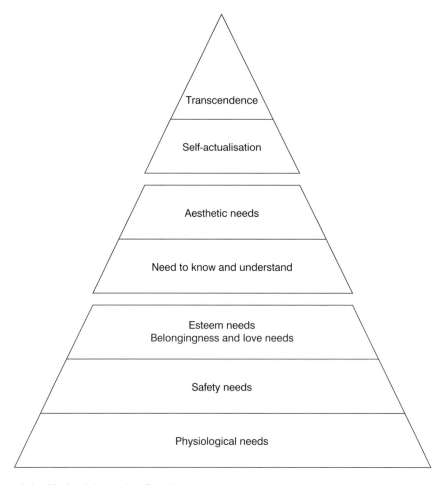

Figure 1.1 *Maslow's hierarchy of needs*

- The teacher has made the pupil feel scared, angry, embarrassed or useless in the way they have spoken or acted.
- The teacher's expectations are unrealistic or too low and the pupil feels unable or unwilling to try because they feel unsupported.
- The pupil may be experiencing some kind of difficulty outside the classroom, such as bullying, or at home, such as parents arguing, divorcing or being violent. There may be illness, crime or poverty in the family or they may be moving home.
- Another pupil or group of pupils in the class may be putting an individual down every time they try to answer, speak or do something in the lesson.
- The pupil may have difficulty concentrating due to a medical condition called attention deficit hyperactivity disorder (ADHD), which is characterised by an overactive brain.
- The pupil may be on the autistic spectrum and find it impossible to move on from a problem because they cannot bear to have an unresolved aspect of the subject they are studying.

The teacher has to be sensitive to the needs of the children. This means assessing whether barriers exist and, if so, helping a child over or around them. As you can see, the teacher can cause some of the barriers, so care must be taken to prevent them. Many teachers are skilled in avoiding them and newly qualified teachers need to develop these skills.

Many of the barriers to learning are due to incidents and events happening beyond the classroom and the school. The ones within the school can be avoided. Your presence in the classroom will determine how successful you are. Your ability to manage the pupils, the resources and the room will be the important factors. Teachers do this by being reactive, proactive or inconsistent in their style. The reactive teacher can be aggressive, domineering and oppressive or the exact opposite by being weak, passive and lacking authority and presence in the classroom. The proactive teacher will pre-empt problems and plan for good behaviour by using an assertive style backed up by fair rules and a consistent approach. The inconsistent teacher is perhaps the hardest one for children to understand, because they veer between being reactive and proactive.

REACTIVE STYLES

The aggressive teacher

Characteristics of the style

The aggressive teacher (Case Study 1.1) very rarely teaches the pupils how to behave. They take on the responsibility for behaviour, as they believe a good teacher is one who has complete control over the class and can command a healthy respect from them, based on fear. The pupils will do exactly what they are told because they know what is coming if they don't. They do not make any real attempt to involve the children in constructing the rules. The pupils are there to do as they are told.

Case Study 1.1

'Last week you behaved terribly when we went to assembly. I am not going to have a repeat of it this week. I have my eye on you, Mark, and as for you, Nathan, if you so much as utter a word, you will stay back during lunchtime for a week. Let that be a warning to you all. Do you hear? I said, do you hear?' The children said 'yes' while keeping their eyes downcast to prevent getting into her sights.

Ms Torrington did not believe in endearing herself to the children. She demanded good behaviour and always got it. In the 15 years she had been teaching at the school, every child had developed a dislike for her. When they saw her outside the school, they darted into the nearest shop. Even the parents had come to dislike her.

The class moved off down the corridor and turned towards the hall. Alex was a lively young boy who was not totally oppressed by Ms Torrington. He was devious and quite clever at going against her orders without getting spotted. But today was not his lucky day. He thought he was beyond her view, so he hopped out of the line, lobbed a ball of screwed-up paper in the air and drop-kicked it over the kids in front. It landed neatly in the middle of an oncoming class.

'Alex Collins, stand where you are!' 'Oh dear,' he thought as his heart sank. The children nearby cowered sideways against the wall and stared at the ground. Ms Torrington came striding up. Her face was a frightening sight. She reached Alex and looked him straight in the eyes. 'You've gone too far this time, Alex Collins.' She paused for a moment then turned to the boy standing in the line near her. 'So you think it's funny do you, Raj? You two can stand aside and wait until last.' When everyone had gone in, the shouting began. The rest of the class couldn't help hearing Ms Torrington as she gave the two unlucky boys a real earbashing. 'I warned you I was not going to tolerate poor behaviour any more. You will do a week of lunchtime detentions.'

The style is one of a bygone age of corporal punishment and military-style oppression. It has been caricatured in countless books and films and is typified by Wackford Squeers in Dickens' *Nicholas Nickleby* and Ms Trunchbull in Roald Dahl's *Matilda*. Thankfully the teaching profession has moved on but there are still teachers using this style in our schools today. They get their results by fear and oppression. Their authority is rigid and unquestioned. The classrooms and the school are battlegrounds where daily skirmishes are fought with naughty children who, they believe, don't know how to behave.

Their style requires a considerable amount of shouting and bellowing of orders and a significant investment of emotion, usually in anger or contempt. The teacher believes she has the right to get what she wants but has little understanding of the rights of the children. In fact, she believes they should not have rights, because it will lead to discipline problems. The pupils have to know who is in charge and nothing should be questioned. They have several ways of dealing with pupils who break rules or question their authority. They show their anger, and short of getting physical, they will shout, threaten and abuse them, using a raised voice until the pupil backs down out of fear about what might happen. This also sends out signals to other children that should they misbehave it will be at their peril.

The teacher may resort to sarcasm in an effort to force the child to back off by making them appear stupid in front of the others. They will use phrases like these:

'It's about time you finally started acting your age.'

'If you are going to behave like a baby, you'd better go back to the nursery class!'

The other children may laugh, but they also know that it could be them next and so the atmosphere is not one of relaxed humour, more nervous laughter.

Belittling the children is a very common ploy of this teacher. The object is to make them a target of ridicule, but the result will be to seriously damage their self-esteem. This is where the aggressive teacher runs into difficulties. Fifty years ago she would have got away with it. The pupils would have accepted their fate and not questioned it. They may have expressed their dislike within the confines of their own peer group, but they would never have stood up to the teacher. Times have changed and everyone is far more aware of their rights. Children have become used to expressing their views publicly, even the very young ones, and teachers have had to come to terms with this.

The aggressive teacher does not seem to have evolved with the times and she believes pupils should not answer back. When they do, it is perceived as a direct challenge to her authority and leads to a conflict situation. In many cases the challenge develops into a battle of wills and becomes an issue connected to secondary behaviour rather than the original incident (Case Study 1.2).

Case Study 1.2

It was registration on Monday morning. The class were always rather more excitable because of the weekend. Everyone wanted to talk about what they had done, where they had been and what new things they had got. Two girls at the far side of the class by the window were looking at something under their desks. Once the register had been called and the dinner money collected, Patricia started her countdown.

'Okay, you have ten to get out your pens and literacy book. Ten, nine, eight . . .' The children buzzed around. There was a flurry of activity then a gradual calming down as they finished the task and sat with their arms crossed until everyone was ready. The two girls had done what she wanted and then resumed playing with their game, or whatever it was, under the desk.

Patricia was tired. She had spent a good part of Saturday marking books and planning. On Sunday she had worked her way through the washing, cleaning and shopping, so by the evening she was exhausted. Come Monday morning she was far from refreshed. When she saw the two girls messing about she tackled them.

'What are you two doing under there?'

'Nothing, Miss.'

'I can see that. You should be paying attention. Now put that thing, whatever it is, away and face me.'

One of the girls switched off the game and put it in her pocket. As she did, she tutted rather loudly.

'I heard that, Zahra.'

'I didn't do anything, Miss!'

'Yes you did, you kissed your teeth.'

She had risen to the secondary behaviour and was making an issue out of it. The rest of the class were starting to get fidgety but were enjoying the show.

'I didn't do it, Miss, I was just trying to move my brace back because it came loose.'

'Don't get cheeky with me,' sighed Patricia. 'You had better stay back when the rest go to break.'

'That's not fair, Miss, I didn't do anything.'

The attention has moved away from the low-level original incident of playing with a game during lessons to a much higher-stakes conflict about the girl's response. Patricia has to come out of this as the winner, so the girl has to stay in as a consequence for arguing back. Patricia has ended up using a heavier response to a quite insignificant incident because of the way she mishandled it. The teacher managed to move the attention from something low-level like being off task to a major battle over a secondary response.

The aggressive teacher does not consider giving the pupils the opportunity to take responsibility for their own behaviour. She retains control, offering little or no choice, only ultimatums. The decision about what happens next remains with the teacher because she believes she can control the class and make the children do as they are told. She is confident that she can force them to do what she wants because she will follow it up with threats and punishments. The pupils resent this kind of treatment and some children retaliate. What ensues is a power struggle, and in a battle of wills the teacher knows she must not lose face at any cost. The children will lose because she regards them as the underdogs and employs her full armoury of sarcasm, aggression, abuse and physical presence to ensure she triumphs. On no account can there be a win-win situation. The children will not be given a means of saving face. The only result for them will be damage to their self-esteem caused by the humiliation they will suffer. It may come immediately or it may be via a threat of revenge in the future (Case Study 1.3).

Case Study 1.3

'Neil, what's that you've got there?'

'Nothing, Sir, I was just looking at my watch.'

'I wasn't born yesterday, Neil. You were playing with those stupid game cards, weren't you?'

'Yes, Sir, but I have put them away now.'

'I don't care, give them to me.'

'No, Sir!' Neil had only just got the cards. They were a present from his dad. He spends alternate weekends with him and he always gives Neil a packet of game cards just before he goes home to his mum. He didn't want to part with them that readily.

'Give them to me, now!'

'No, Sir, my dad only just gave them to me.'

'You know the rule about game cards, so give them to me immediately or else!'

'Or else what? You can't make me.'

'Oh yes I can and I will, then you will be sorry.'

Many teachers do not want to be aggressive but feel they have no option, especially when things start to get difficult. They have little experience of dealing with non-compliant pupils except to exercise their status in a forceful, threatening manner.

When they do, the relationship in the class changes quite dramatically. Teachers who use these tactics on very rare occasions do not usually experience any problems, because the pupils recognise that they have pushed them too far. They are not normally aggressive. After all, it is sometimes necessary to show you have teeth, so the children know you are capable of something more that you keep under control. Overuse of it will end with the children fearing you, making it impossible to develop a positive, productive relationship with them.

The effects of this style

The most significant effect of this style is the absence of respect. Obviously the teacher does not respect the children and they do not respect him. His negative expectations rub off on them and they end up acting in the same way. They believe that they are not good enough and that it is not worth making any effort, because the teacher will not notice. The message he sends is that he does not like them.

Pupils who misbehave become his targets. He puts them down directly with his actions and communicates to everybody else that they are in the wrong. He will blame the class, parents, friends and other teachers for the poor behaviour. In fact, he will blame just about everyone except himself. He will go through his career with this fixed view and will be unable to contemplate the idea that he is wrong and there could be another way of managing behaviour that does not require an aggressive stance.

Teachers who use aggressive tactics may end up feeling guilty when they lose their temper. The process is self-destructive because once they show they are aggressive, the children put up their guards and become wary on future occasions. It will be very difficult for them to develop relationships with the teacher if they are always suspicious and on edge in case there is another outburst.

A teacher who is continually aggressive in his approach will be regarded as an enemy by the class. They will see him as unfair and resort to illicit means of coping with his lessons. They will lie, cheat and make up excuses to get themselves off when he blames them. They will feign illness and make up appointments to get themselves out of the room and away from him. In the end, they may even vent their frustration on their own classmates by passing the blame or bullying. The net result will be a climate of fear and the children will become completely turned off the school. They will go home and tell their parents of their grievances. Then the parents will side with them against the staff unless the trend is reversed.

The passive teacher

Characteristics of the style

The passive teacher (Case Study 1.4) is generally uncertain about his role. He understands the importance of being the adult and leader in the classroom but confuses the various qualities that a good teacher needs to have. For example, the purpose of the teacher is to teach. To teach is to help and he believes those in need of help will naturally welcome it. In reality, those in need of help may not realise it and may regard themselves as beyond helping or see the offer as an insult.

The passive teacher lacks the self-belief that he can lead and manage the pupils. He is aware that there are teachers with different styles to his own, teachers who seem to be far more extrovert and have the knack of getting the best out of their pupils. This awareness has an oppressive effect and renders him helpless to change. He will readily acknowledge that he is not in the same league and resign himself to the fact that he cannot perform any differently. He puts the abilities of more successful teachers down to some kind of natural, innate gift that he has not got and cannot learn.

Case Study 1.4

Theresa was quite good at managing her classes. She could normally keep them in line, but then they had always been nice infant groups. The little ones were always so keen to learn and they were so cute. They would come up and hold her hand in the playground or stroke the material when she wore a silky top. She really didn't have to try.

Then the head told her there was a new girl joining her class. Her name was Annette and she could be a bit of a handful. 'Don't worry,' Theresa said reassuringly. 'We will make her welcome and I am sure she will soon settle and make friends.'

The next day Annette arrived. She was a little girl with a sweet face and a lovely smile. Theresa took her hand and led her to the classroom, where she showed her the coat peg with her name on and her tray. Everything went well on the first day until halfway through the religious education lesson, when Theresa asked the children to turn over the page and write the date in their books ready for the next task. Annette did not want to start a new page, so she dug her heels in.

'Come on, Annette, hurry up and start a new page.'

'I like it here,' said Annette, pointing at the previous page.

'Oh all right, you do it there then, there's a good girl.' But Annette wasn't being a good girl; she was not doing as she was told. Anyway, she did start work but as Theresa walked away she had a bad feeling about this girl. Annette was challenging her and she had allowed Annette to get away with it but she did not really know what she could have done.

The same thing happened in the history lesson. She refused to do the work unless she could use a red pen. Theresa didn't want to have a scene with her, so she let her use one. As she moved back to the front, she heard Annette say, 'Perhaps I won't do it after all.' Then she put the pen down, folded her arms, pouted and looked upwards in a prissy, flouncy sort of way.

'Come on now, Annette, I would be very pleased if you would get on with your work.'

Theresa had moved on to shaky ground, because Annette was not bothered whether she was pleased or not. What had happened was that Annette had tested Theresa and found she was weak. She had won the first challenge so she had tried again. To her surprise she won again and resolved in her mind that she could do anything she wanted – Theresa was not going to stop her.

Some teachers are confident in what they do and get satisfaction from doing the job well regardless of whether they will be popular. They do not seek acknowledgment or favour from the pupils. What usually happens is the pupils recognise they have a teacher who is supportive and who is encouraging them to be individuals and take responsibility for their own learning and development. They understand that order is part of the process and that the teacher is in charge. This gives them a feeling of security, so they feel confident to extend the boundaries and push themselves beyond their own limits. The passive teacher does not possess a very good sense of self-confidence. He is at heart insecure in what he does and so he seeks recognition and affirmation of himself as a person rather than from the job he is employed to do. He needs to be liked and seeks popularity by avoiding making unpopular or difficult decisions. He will shy away from confrontations and be cautious about challenging pupils when they misbehave. He will endeavour to ingratiate himself with the pupils, staff and parents rather than be assertive when a boundary is under pressure, a decision is in question or an action is disagreed with.

His feelings will be fragile and exposed in his quest to be accepted and liked. The slightest criticism will cut deeply. The need to be liked will become the priority and he will be quite hurt when a pupil makes a remark like these:

'Mrs Cooper is much better, she lets us do it in pen.'

'You're not as good as our usual teacher.'

'Mrs Brown always makes it seem so easy.'

Such remarks are often a ploy by the pupils to manipulate the teacher to get them to do things that they want.

The passive teacher reacts to situations. He does not work proactively to control or use them. He does not pre-empt situations by planning how he will manage behaviour, yet he will plan lessons in detail. He may even have a behaviour code but he will enforce it poorly. He will probably miss incidents or only become aware of them once they have happened. He will be unclear about how to deal with them and appear erratic because of his lack of preparation. Most people who face new situations without having prepared themselves beforehand will be anxious and have to think on their feet. The passive teacher will feel threatened by misbehaving pupils, because he has not worked out his response. He will let incidents go unchallenged because he is afraid he will make himself unpopular. Pupils who get away with behaving inappropriately once will start to get confused. They will test the boundaries to try to find out just what they can and cannot do. The passive teacher will find that incidents increase and he will feel that he is fire-fighting all the time. His opinions about the pupils will be tarnished because he believes that they should respect him, even though he does little to command it.

A great deal about a person is communicated by their tone of voice. It is not what you say but how you say it. If you sound like you do not really mean something, then people will ignore you. There is a difference between quietly asserting yourself and being timid and shrew-like. The passive teacher will endeavour to persuade, request or plead with his pupils. The way you look conveys meaning too. A resigned expression, outstretched arms and a detectable stoop are the body language of a defeated person. He will use phrases like these:

'That's not fair.'

'That's not what I would have expected from you.'

'I would have liked you to . . .'

'If you cared about me, you would . . .'

His efforts to appeal to the pupils' better nature may work with some but not all. Many will be ready to exploit this weakness once they discover it.

The passive teacher will assume the role of the victim when things go wrong. He will wonder why it always has to be him. The other teachers do not seem to have the problems he has. He may feel isolated during stressful times and the result will eventually be an outburst of emotion. If it comes as aggression, he will immediately feel guilty and wish he hadn't lost control. The pupils will be confused because he will not tell them why he is angry. He will harbour aggression until it has to escape somehow and when it does, it will be unrelated to the original reason for his feelings.

The pupils will quickly get the measure of this kind of teacher. They will realise that he has weaknesses and some will even try to dominate him. The room will become a place for slanging matches between the pupils and the teacher. When pupils do behave for him, it will be because they choose to, not because the teacher is asserting his will. The class are in control and free to change their behaviour in an instant.

So where does the passive teacher go wrong? He fails to assert his presence and status as the adult in charge. He confuses the pupils by giving directions that are unclear and he is erratic in dealing with them when they break the rules. His fear of the pupils not only prevents him from challenging them at the time but also stops him following up at a later date. He is easily swayed and gets drawn into secondary issues. His overriding hope is that they will be better next time.

The effects of this style

There will be a growing resentment between the teacher and the children because they do not behave responsibly and of their own accord. The children will resent the teacher for his failure to keep order and manage the class. The children who are behaving well will despise the teacher and feel they are losing out. They will also be frustrated because the recalcitrant children are getting away with things. They will want the help of the teacher but it will be taken up by the disruptive children. Eventually they will realise that the only way they can get the teacher's attention is to misbehave as well.

Praise is sometimes used as a bribe along with the rewards already available. The passive teacher will give the least deserving children rewards in an effort to curb their poor behaviour. The better-behaved pupils will see this as unfair because it undermines the behaviour code and devalues the rewards at the same time. Some of the children will feel that their efforts go unnoticed because only the most able and the poorly behaved get rewarded.

The passive teacher's style does not result in the children learning to make choices about their behaviour. They are not helped to develop their own internal checks and accept their responsibilities. Ultimately the teacher's abdication of this key role becomes the pupils' loss. Furthermore, if the teacher does not change and push back, he will find himself retreating into the corner, failing in his efforts to teach and feeling more and more stressed when he goes home. When a teacher reaches this point, depression and illness eventually become the outlets for their feelings. Patchy absence and a tired, washed-out view of the profession develop.

THE PROACTIVE STYLE

The proactive teacher (Case Study 1.5) is assertive and able to get what she wants in the classroom. She is confident of her ability to manage the children and is committed to creating an environment that will help them feel safe, secure and liked. She states what she wants using unambiguous directions and communicates her expectations clearly to the children. She will back up what she says with appropriate actions, reassuring those who lack confidence, praising those that do well and challenging those who try to test her boundaries. She recognises her right to teach the class and achieves it through the creation of a learning climate that is in the best interests of the pupils.

We can choose which style we want to adopt as teachers. The positive, assertive teacher makes the effort to communicate to her pupils that everyone can succeed if they try. She knows it will not be easy and some children will find it harder than others but she will do her best to help when things get tough. She will be pleasant, kind and understanding and at the same time provide very clear guidance on what is acceptable behaviour. She will exercise her right to lead and teach in a friendly but assertive manner without resorting to threats. She will not need to shout, because the children will know that if the task requires them to talk, they can do so in a normal way. When a group of pupils start to raise their voices, she will check them in a firm but friendly way and if they go off task, she will bring them back by redirection and reminding them of the rule for group work.

Case Study 1.5

Connie's Year 5 class were studying the Tudors. They had already found out a lot about the kings and queens and the battles. She was helping them to find out about the lives of ordinary people. They were looking at sailors and explorers who went to the New World. Connie had organised the class into groups to consider what things they might take from the Old World to trade and what things they might want to bring back from the New World. The class was divided in half. One half were in groups discussing what they would take with them to trade. The other half were looking at things from the New World. At the end, each group had to send an envoy to a group in the other half of the class to gather up ideas and complete the picture of trade items. During the discussions, one of the groups began to get a bit louder, so Connie went over to them.

'Have you swapped your list of trade items, Martin?' she enquired, picking on the child who seemed to be making the most noise.

'Yes, Miss.'

'Good. Will, can you tell me the thing you think would be the most desirable for the Indians to trade?' directing her question at the other loud member of the group. She told him she would want potatoes and explained why. Connie listened intently, nodding, smiling and affirming Will's choice. She asked a few more questions then suggested that they put the things in order of desirability. 'Remember, it should be a group decision, so you will all need to agree,' directing them back to the task. 'I want to remind you to keep your voices down, because you were getting rather loud and disturbing the others. Thank you.' Connie reminded them of the rule and finished with a smile.

'Okay, sorry, Miss.'

Connie made a point of talking to the whole group but addressing her comments to the two loudest children. She cleverly refocused them by skilful questioning, listening intently to their replies and then reminding them of the directions in a calm, assertive way.

The low-level disruption in Case Study 1.5 calls for a different level of assertion than would be needed to remove a very disruptive child from the room. Keeping response levels in proportion is essential. Careful modulation of the voice will communicate your expectations. Teachers who use their very assertive voice for the small things like wandering, being off task or chattering will find it harder to deal with extremely stubborn behaviour.

The proactive teacher will establish her behaviour code by first agreeing a set of basic rights for staff and children. Everyone will be aware that it is their own responsibility to reinforce and support those rights. Fairness is one of the key factors of a positive, proactive style. The proactive teacher will ensure that she is consistent in the way she deals with all her pupils. She will help them make their own choices but will not try to persuade or influence them. She will explain the consequences of their actions and then it must be up to them to decide. In this way, she will be helping them to learn to make their own decisions. Eventually all the children will know where they stand, that the rules are fair and that their actions will be followed up by the teacher.

No one can be right every time. We all have our off days. It may have been a late night or a domestic crisis, but whatever the cause, there will be times when our patience is short or our tolerance low and then our ability to handle the children is impaired. The proactive teacher knows her pupils will not always be able to behave well. She also understands that there will be incidents she has not experienced, so she will plan for them by considering her response in advance. She will work out what she says and does for a range of incidents to ensure she is fair and has no need to shoot from the hip.

The proactive style is based on the recognition of good behaviour. The saying 'catch them being good' is a useful one because we should try to be on the lookout for children doing the right thing rather than just reprimanding those who cannot follow the good example set them. Praise is essential in building self-esteem so the more of it we can give, the better (Case Study 1.6).

Case Study 1.6

Lee was a lively boy and could be a real handful during some lessons. Rachael, his teacher, had been working with him for over a term on helping him remain seated and focused on what he should be doing. She had tried a number of things and had eventually found something that motivated him. It was quite by accident actually. They were sitting in the room after school waiting for his mum to collect him because she had been delayed. During the conversation, the subject of football came up. She knew Lee was interested in it but had never really found out about his team and the players he liked. It turned out that he was very keen on the local team who were up for promotion to the Premiership. She had a friend who worked at the club and she often got to go to games and different events where the players were present. When she revealed this to Lee, his eyes lit up and from that day on their conversations usually ended up with her telling him about this player or that player or something going on at the club. She used this as a motivator together with the occasional souvenirs that her friend gave her.

She was teaching a science lesson one afternoon and Lee had been very good up until then. The class were split into small groups carrying out investigations into which objects were conductors of electricity. She noticed that Lee was recording results for his group and stayed in his seat during the whole task. He was paying attention and really seemed to be concentrating. She moved around the groups and kept her eye on him. When he looked up she gave him a discreet thumbs-up sign, smiled and then moved on to the next group. He beamed at her then went back to work.

Later that day, Rachael was able to call him over for a quiet word of praise. 'You did really well during the science lesson, Lee. I noticed you recording the results and you stayed in your seat for the whole time.'

'Yes, Miss. Did you know that electricity can pass through a spoon?'

'Really, is that something you found out today?'

'Yes, Miss. It's a conductor.'

'That's right, Lee. By the way, I saw my friend last night and she has arranged for me to take a class of children to tour the stadium. I think you could be in that group now you have started to follow directions. What do you think?'

'Yes please, Miss. Will we go to the players' changing room?'

'You will.'

Her brief exchange and praise sent the message that he had done well and she was pleased. They were able to share what he had learned in a friendly way that reinforced their relationship. The reward trip sealed it and gave him a real boost of confidence that he was doing things right.

The proactive teacher uses non-verbal communication to send signals to the children that she is in charge but not a threat. She does not point her finger at them. She respects their personal space. Her posture is open and she will speak to her pupils face-to-face in a relaxed way. Her expression will convey the calm of a person in control through a smile and direct eye contact. Her tone of voice will reinforce her position and convey warmth that children will interpret as friendly and helpful. Cold, curt, aggressive remarks will not feature in her repertoire of day-to-day comments. When there is an opportunity to use humour or when she finds something funny, she will use it to defuse difficult situations and restore calm.

Her overall presence in the room will convey to everyone that she is in control and well organised. She will be smart and well groomed, decisive in her actions and her classroom will reflect these qualities in its orderliness and stimulating resources. None of these qualities will be accidental or innate. She has worked hard to develop them and she will continue to hone them as the children change and bring new challenges.

Putting it all together

Think first. The best way to manage is to plan your approach, work out your responses and pre-empt potential problems by communicating your expectations to the pupils and by teaching them how to make good choices. When you direct a child, use *I* statements like these:

'I want you to stay in your seats during this activity.'

'I am the adult in charge in this room.'

'I want you to follow my directions.'

Be clear about what you want and state it:

'Stop talking and fold your arms.'

'In two minutes you will stop the discussions and go back to your own seats.'

Say the pupil's name so they know you are addressing them:

'Samira, I would like you to work with Michael.'

'Sally, all four legs on the floor, thank you.'

'Kallum, nice work.'

Avoid getting caught up in the child's own agenda through getting sidetracked by their secondary behaviour. Refocus them on your original direction.

A common mistake that teachers make is to ask a question that has nothing to do with what they want the child to do:

'Why are you talking?'

'Why are you out of your seat?'

'What are you doing?'

Each of these questions can be rephrased in a way that is far more direct and prevents the child being cheeky or arrogant:

'Put your hand up if you have something to say.'

'What was the direction for this task?' 'It was stay in your seats.' 'Good, then go back to your place and raise your hand if you need something.'

'I can see you haven't made a start.'

Some rule reminders are best phrased as questions, such as the pupil out of his seat. It helps the child to focus on the original direction or rule and not get into explanations about why they are not doing what they are supposed to.

'Martin, what is the rule about Game Boys?'

'No Game Boys during lesson times, Mr Wright.'

'Good, put it away in your bag or on my desk, thank you.'

Finally, do not confuse your opinion of the behaviour with your opinion of the child. It is the behaviour you do not like. Make a point of saying that to them. We need to reassure our pupils that we like them. That way, we are able to support them. If a child feels you dislike them, they will not make the effort.

The effects of this style

The classroom will reflect the proactive teacher's personal views. It will be orderly in its layout of desks and furniture. Getting this right is fundamental to the effective management of behaviour and delivery of the curriculum. The resources will be carefully organised and stored in a way that gives the children access. The wall space will be used to display work in progress as well as supporting material to stimulate the children. The displays will invite interaction through questions, puzzles and hands-on exhibits. The work on display will be a celebration of the achievements of every child in the class.

Eventually the children will get used to a culture of respect that has been cultivated by the teacher. They will defend the rights of everyone and in doing this they will create a room where they can all feel safe, secure and able to learn together. The whole class will know what to expect from the teacher and what they are expected to do and how to behave. The teacher will have worked hard to build their self-esteem so that they value themselves and feel confident. With confidence will come the ability to accept responsibility for their behaviour. The proactive teacher does not try to control the behaviour of her pupils. She helps them manage it. Her goal is for them to grow into responsible people. In adult life they will need to be independent, so they will have to make responsible choices. She will guide and support them at the start of this journey.

The proactive teacher tries not to react to situations, especially new ones she has not encountered before. When she is in doubt about what to do next, she does not act. She tells the child she wants to think about the incident before coming to a decision. This will serve several purposes. She will have time to calm down if she has become stressed. The children will also calm down. She can mull over the facts and seek a second opinion if she needs to. The children will develop a higher opinion of her because she obviously wants to make the right decision and is prepared to take time to do that.

FOOTNOTE

There is another teaching style, probably the worst for children to experience. The teacher is inconsistent and does not adhere to any particular way of working. One day he will be assertive and seem very fair and in control. The next day he may be assertive and fair again or he may have changed and be very aggressive and snappy or very weak and passive, letting all sorts of behaviour go without comment. The children will become so confused that they will keep their heads down. Any chance of a productive relationship will founder. They will become defensive and uncertain, sticking to behaviour they know will keep them out of trouble.

This book is about acquiring and developing the skills to become a proactive, assertive teacher. The methods and procedures are used to create a positive atmosphere where children and teachers can do their best, learn without limits and feel safe and secure. The starting point will be your own perceptions and expectations. The next step will be to create a learning environment where your expectations can become a reality. Good management of behaviour is crucial in this process. It does not necessarily come first but needs to be perceived as having equal importance as the teaching of the curriculum. The two go hand in hand. Children who can behave well give themselves the best chance to get involved in their learning. Interesting lessons will engage the child and then they will not feel the desire to misbehave.

SUMMARY

- Barriers to learning can be caused by the teacher within the classroom. It is in their power to make the classroom a positive learning environment.

- Teachers can be reactive or proactive in their style of behaviour management.
- Aggressive teachers and passive teachers generally have a reactive teaching style. They tend not to plan ahead but respond passively or aggressively to incidents as they occur.
- The proactive teacher adopts an assertive style to uphold their own rights and the rights of the pupils.
- The assertive teacher ensures that she is the leader in the classroom and teaches the children the boundaries of acceptable behaviour.
- The assertive teacher communicates her expectations to the pupils.
- Self-esteem and confidence are important and nurtured by the assertive teacher through praise, positive reinforcement and choice.
- Children learn that choices are accompanied by consequences. They know that when they make a poor choice there will be a consequence to it. The teacher does not try to control or persuade the children to behave, because she believes they need to learn to be independent.
- The proactive teacher plans ahead so she is prepared to deal with problems in a rational way rather than reacting to them as they occur.

2 THE FOUNDATIONS FOR GOOD BEHAVIOUR

The room is full. There are thirty energetic children occupying it. They share the space with a teacher and a learning support assistant, seventeen tables, thirty-four chairs, as many bags, coats and lunch boxes all hemmed in by piles of textbooks, several computers and an atmosphere of excitement, heat, hunger, humour and for many a desire to be somewhere else, somewhere freer. This enforced captivity will end when they are finally released by the school bell and the conclusion of the school day. The experience of school is over five hours of this punctuated by changes of lesson or movement from one room to the hall or dining room.

It's unnatural, yet we put our children through this day in, day out with the hope that they will go on to a good secondary school and ultimately find a career. For some the journey is fraught with obstacles. They not only have to survive the daily routines but also the added problem of fear. During their school life, some of them will be bullied and oppressed by teachers and their peers until the experience becomes unbearable and they seek a release. It may be truancy, school phobia, aggressive behaviour or, in the most extreme cases, self-harm or suicide.

The timetable of predominately language-based activities such as reading, writing, copying from the board, dictation, note-taking and written examinations and tests forms the backbone of the curriculum; it does not suit everyone. Alternative approaches based on visual, auditory and kinaesthetic (VAK) teaching methods may well suit a large proportion of pupils much more than linguistic methods. Teachers who understand this will plan lessons to accommodate a variety of styles and will probably find they have more success and fewer problems with behaviour than those who do not. The experience of school becomes less mundane and those children likely to encounter problems with behaviour, learning or both will be less likely to end up turned off or in trouble because their boredom has led to incidents in lessons.

It is not surprising that behaviour becomes an issue for many teachers. Children and parents no longer regard the teacher as a paragon of society, someone to hold in high esteem and respect. Forty years ago teachers had a control over children that was not questioned. When a pupil was disciplined, the parents would support the school and not question the authority or decision of the teacher. Things have changed. Children feel they can answer back and parents feel they can go to the school and dispute the action taken by a teacher. We now need to be very careful how we respond to children who behave inappropriately. Teachers who use a coherent set of rules and directions backed up by rewards and consequences that are administered in a fair and consistent way will find that they can explain their actions confidently and clearly to parents and pupils who feel the need to challenge decisions. Teachers who act irrationally will find themselves on shaky ground because a parent or a child will spot the inconsistency and argue strongly. Eventually the teacher will have to concede because they will know they do not have a watertight case to fall back on.

Establishing a strong foundation for your behaviour plan will be a vital first step. Rogers (1994) outlines four elements that contribute to a well-balanced system that goes beyond simply managing behaviour in the classroom. These elements form the cornerstones to a means of developing responsibility, respect, self-esteem, confidence, fairness and opportunity for all the pupils in the group:

- Prevention
- Correction
- Consequences
- Support.

You will need to get the balance right between them if you are to manage and develop responsible behaviour within your groups. The only way is to roll up your sleeves and assert your position as the teacher in order to establish yourself and be able to introduce your methods. The children will not give up their position freely, so you cannot expect to walk into a new class and get started. You will have to show them that you are in charge and expect them to listen and act responsibly. Many children will do this and accept your behaviour code willingly. Those who do not will become the focus of it. So what is involved in each of these cornerstones?

PREVENTION

Many teachers will argue that it is natural for children to test the limits of authority. Part of growing up and the circle of life is a desire to be independent and to break away from parents and the rules and systems imposed by adults. Children need to find their own identity that separates them from their parents. The uncertainty that comes with the changes at the onset of puberty causes adolescents to look to their peers for support, so they feel a strong sense of belonging to that group. Children are maturing earlier, so all these changes are happening at a much younger age.

The order and authority that might have existed in schools several decades ago is now one of the targets to be challenged. Teachers need to be far more active in putting preventative measures in place to help children learn the limits of authority in a safe way. Their search for an identity should not be crushed in an aggressive regime. It is possible to let them develop their own personalities by firmly asserting some boundaries that should not be transgressed, while allowing less important ones to be crossed for the sake of their learning. Mistakes are part of this process and need to be made in a supportive culture so the benefits can be gained without damage to the child's confidence and self-esteem.

The most irritating distractions for teachers tend to be the low-level, minor ones that occur regularly. More serious disturbances are less common but do need to be prevented as well. Therefore the first step is to list the most common disturbances and sort them into minor and major ones. This can be done as part of in-service education and training (INSET) by having a session to develop a behaviour plan for the whole school. Here are some of the minor disturbances you might come up with:

- Calling out
- Leaving their place and wandering around the room
- Note passing

- Arriving late
- Not bringing the correct books and equipment to lessons
- Eating or chewing during lessons
- Not wearing the correct uniform
- Wearing jewellery
- Chatting during silent work
- Being too loud during group activities
- Bickering while entering the room
- Taking another child's things
- Kicking and throwing bags or lunch boxes
- Writing on the board
- Sitting in the teacher's chair
- Defacing displays and writing on desks
- Wanting to go to the toilet during the lesson
- Feeling sick
- Passing wind
- Mobile phones going off in the lesson
- Loud noises in the next room
- A wasp in the room
- A pupil outside the room distracting your lesson
- Forgetting homework or not doing it.

And here are some major disturbances:

- Swearing directly at a teacher
- Swearing at another child
- Hitting a pupil
- Hitting a teacher
- Having a tantrum by throwing things and shouting
- Making sexual or racial comments or being abusive
- Theft or alleged theft
- Leaving the room without permission
- Bringing a knife or other weapon into school
- Vandalising school property
- Vandalising property outside school during school time
- Bullying.

The aim is to draw up plans that will minimise the effects of these disturbances. Some preventative measures will be outside the remit of the class teacher, but thoughtful and careful planning will reduce the likelihood of most of them occurring. This is achieved by establishing a behaviour plan with the help of the children. It should contain rules that will apply at any time, one of which should be to follow directions. It should also detail the rewards and consequences that you are going to use.

Another useful exercise for an INSET session is to consider what questions a newly qualified teacher might have about classroom management in the school. Preparing a list of questions will enable you to put together guidance on how to prevent obvious problems in a practical way. For example, too often teachers have not considered whether they trust pupils or they have felt pupils are trustworthy and then found their valuables have disappeared from an unlocked drawer or bag. It is far better to remove such temptations to begin with. So what are the questions? Here are some that staff may come up with:

- Should the children line up outside the room or go in and wait until I arrive?
- Should the children stand behind their chairs and wait until I tell them to sit down?
- Should the children sit where they choose?
- Should they call me Mr Wright, Sir or by my first name?
- Should I allow them to go to the toilet during lessons?
- Should I give out the books or let a child do it?
- Should I be in a classroom or storeroom on my own with a child?
- To set homework, should I tell the class, write it on the board or give out a sheet?
- What will happen if some pupils arrive late?
- Should the children leave as soon as the bell goes or should I dismiss them when I am ready?
- Can I trust the children or should I lock my bag away?
- Should I use physical force on a child?

Some of these questions will almost certainly involve putting together a set of directions. Activities like getting changed for physical education (PE), doing group work and taking Standard Assessment Tests (SATs) require their own sets of directions. It can be extremely useful to work out sets of directions in advance so the problems can be anticipated and preventative measures planned. Sometimes you may not be aware of a problem at first. It may take something shocking to reveal an underlying problem that you need to address (Case Study 2.1).

Case Study 2.1 *Stephanie*

I had always wanted to be a teacher for as long as I could remember. I loved the feeling you got when the children did something that you had taught them. You know what I mean. You work for several weeks on something like a multiplication table or number bonds and then, all of a sudden out of the blue, you realise they are using them to calculate or find the solution to a problem.

I had a mixed-up experience myself at school. I never really tried very hard. Some say I wasted my talents but I disagree. I got out of school what *I* wanted and that was more than just qualifications. I hated most of my teachers. There was one I liked. She was the only one who saw me as an individual. The rest treated me as one of the 'cattle'. It was a faith school and some of those teachers had a strange idea of religion. They were so horrible and nasty to us, and probably to each other as well. Anyway, I was sure that it must have changed now.

I took up my post at a similar faith school and was determined it was going to be a good experience. I knew the school had a strong head teacher and the word was that behaviour was good. It was a bit of a relief, I must say, because I had read books and heard staff tell stories about incidents that had happened and had felt worried in case the same happened to me. The difference was that those things that I had heard about happened in tough comprehensives in what I would describe as rough areas. You know what I mean, predominantly working-class and highly populated places you get in big cities. The school I was going to was totally different. It was a primary school linked to a church in a leafy suburb with a lot of the parents in the professions and management. The kids were scrubbed, bright-eyed and full of life.

The job was great and the class were lovely. I had Year 4 and they were a dream! Everyone was right about the workload though. All along, my friends who were teachers had been telling me that the first year would be hard going. They said, jokingly, that I could kiss goodbye to my social life. I found myself taking home sets of books to mark every night, which was gruelling. That and the planning really ate up my evenings and weekends but I was determined to do my job well, so I didn't object. I just got on with it. I would use the time at the end of school to put up displays. The school was very hot on nice displays. I usually had about an hour I could set aside for displays and getting things in the class ready for the next day. Looking back, I don't know how I got through that time but I did. Then out of the blue the surprise came and it shocked me in a way I hadn't expected.

I was walking across the playground with my class to the gate where the parents were waiting to take their children home when suddenly I heard the head calling out the name of a pupil. The class froze. I had never seen a whole group of children react in that way before. The look on their faces was one of terror. I don't know why they seemed so frightened; after all it was only the head. It would take only a few moments before I found out.

She strode across the playground in such a ferocious way I almost imagined that the ground was thundering. By the time she reached us, the children were leaning away from her in a very defensive way. 'Do up your tie. No one leaves this school dressed like a scarecrow. Do it now!' The boy dropped his bag and lunch box and hurriedly fumbled with the offending item of clothing. But he was so nervous he only managed to pull the knot tighter. He had pulled the wrong end.

'Get back into school and stand outside my office!' she commanded and off he scurried, leaving his bags where they were. I could see tears welling up in his eyes as he anticipated what would happen to him. I felt it was an unfair response by her really, because we had just had PE and he was one of the children I had been working with on doing up ties. But that was nothing compared to the next outburst. I thought it was over and I was just about to get my class moving to the gate when she called my name.

'Mrs Curtis. We have standards here. If you are going to allow the pupils to take off their ties, make sure they do them up. I am surprised you are so lax in allowing them to go home improperly dressed. I would appreciate it if you would check each child before they leave the room in future.' With that she turned and walked away. I was dumbstruck. I never knew she could be like that and I was embarrassed being told off like that in public in front of all the parents. Surely that cannot be right. I quickly said goodbye to the children and handed them over to their parents then went back to my room. Once inside, I broke down in a flood of tears. The bubble had burst. My whole image of the school and the head changed instantly. The woman was so out of order it was unbelievable.

A few minutes later the other Year 4 teacher came into my room and tried to console me. 'Come on, let's go for a cappuccino and try to get this behind you.'

'I've got all this work to do,' I replied. I needed to get the books marked for tomorrow and a science lesson needed planning because I had only just received the resources to do it.

'Oh leave it, it won't be the end of the world. What's more important is getting you back together. A bit of TLC is far better than a bunch of English books.'

So I did what she said. She is very persuasive and I had had enough. She told me about the head and her erratic outbursts. Some days she could be as nice as pie to everyone. She smiled and was very sweet to all the parents. She would breeze around the school in and out of the rooms without making a comment. But other times she was completely different. I hadn't seen that side before but I could see why the children were terrified.

The problem with this was not obvious at first. The children behaved whenever she came into view. They became quiet and subdued and kept their eyes downcast. Too much contact with her led to real difficulties. It was like the kids bottled things up in her company and as soon as she was gone they would relax their behaviour and get a little out of hand.

I hadn't really noticed at first. I suppose I was preoccupied but now it was obvious. The class behaved according to their contact with her. On the days she did dinner duty, assembly or came into our room there was always a reaction afterwards. There was no system for managing behaviour in the school. The head used her methods and we were supposed to invent our own.

Gradually it became apparent that one or two of the teachers were like her. They did not give the kids a fair chance; they just cut them down when necessary. Well there was no way I was going to be like them and I was not happy about the way she spoke to me.

I decided that my class would be managed in a fair way. I couldn't see myself operating like the head or her sidekicks. The children deserved better than being forced to quiver with fear when she was around. I introduced my own code of behaviour after talking it through with the children. I spent my time helping the children to understand how to make good choices and explained that there should be no need for me to shout, because everyone in the class was going to be responsible for their own actions. Any child in the class who made poor choices would have to accept the consequence but I always talked it through with them after they'd paid it off. By Christmas the whole class were well behaved. I really had to be tight after they had the head because they needed to let out the stressful feelings. It was definitely advantageous to have such good control, because it allowed me to do some useful exercises with the children such as brain gym. I always had brain breaks after the head came through. It helped the kids drive out the negative feelings.

When any of her followers tried to browbeat my class I always intervened and assured them that I would deal with the children who were misbehaving in my own way. I know some of them started to think I was a soft touch, but the children appreciated the new climate in the room and many of the parents gave me their support and told me how much happier their children were because they said I was 'firm but fair'.

And my advice to anyone who is just starting out like me? Take control, set up your procedures for managing the class and be assertive not aggressive.

Thinking through how to respond to the minor disturbances will also help you grow in confidence and your lessons will run more smoothly. It takes time but it's a sound investment, especially if it is shared. A useful activity for staff meetings can be to set aside some time on a regular basis to discuss responses to particular incidents. These can be compiled into a school behaviour management manual that provides invaluable guidance on how incidents can be dealt with using positive, proactive methods. You will need to nominate a group leader who is responsible for timing the session, noting down the suggestions and writing them up afterwards. They should be a keen and experienced member of staff who can separate the suggestions into those that could be useful and those that are not useful. Scenarios 2.1, 2.2 and 2.3 give some examples.

Scenario 2.1: Refusing to begin the task

'Okay, you have five minutes to draft your headline based on our discussions. Remember you are trying to make it snappy, easy to read and short. The reader will need to be struck immediately by it and want to pick up the paper and read the rest of the article.' The class got started but Freddie just sat at the desk digging his pencil into his rubber. Getting started was hard for him but he would do it once he realised you were not going to give him any leeway. He knew that if he wasted time, he would have to stay in at break and finish the work. 'I haven't got a pen, Miss!' he said in a cocky way.

How not to deal with this

- 'Get on with it, Freddie, or I will make you do it at break!'
- 'Get started now or I will call Mrs Holland.' Mrs Holland was the deputy head.
- 'You're always trying to get out of doing the work, Freddie. Will you ever learn?'
- 'Stop digging at your rubber, Freddie. The work won't get done by itself you know!'
- 'What's the matter, Freddie? Are you lost for words for a change? You are normally very good at chatting.'

And this dialogue:

Teacher Get on with it, Freddie.
Child I haven't got a pen!

Teacher	I gave you a pen earlier. What have you done with it? I can't keep giving you pens just to lose. You should take more care of things.

These responses will almost certainly result in the child challenging the teacher and then the low-level incident will become a high-stakes, win-lose battleground that could have been avoided.

The positive, proactive approach

'You haven't started yet, do you need some help, Freddie?' The teacher makes a friendly offer of assistance to ascertain whether the pupil is having problems understanding what he is required to do. He declines the offer, so the teacher leaves and expects him to begin but he doesn't.

'I see you still haven't started yet, Freddie.'

'I need a pen, Miss,' he says smirking. He is trying to delay by finding an excuse that could waste more time or draw the teacher into an argument over the lack of equipment.

She ignores this and holds out some pens, smiling at him. 'Choose a blue one or a black one.' She has refocused him with a limited choice that prevents him thinking up another excuse.

Once he has chosen a pen, she directs him back to the work. 'Now you have a pen, let me just remind you of what you have to do.'

Then she follows through with a rule reminder in the form of a direction. 'Okay, so you have until 10.45. That's just under five minutes to complete the work.'

Finally, she repeats her offer of support in a friendly, helpful way. 'Off you go and remember if you get stuck or need any help, just raise your hand and I will come to you as soon as I can.'

The whole chain of events takes less than a few seconds but results in the child getting down to work and doing as instructed despite his attempts to delay things and cause a disturbance in the lesson.

Scenario 2.2: Arriving late to a lesson

A pupil arrives late and the lesson has already begun. The teacher has called the register, introduced the lesson and is doing a short warm-up activity with the whole class.

How not to deal with it

Teacher	Hi, Samantha, (*sarcastically*) it's nice of you to join us. What time do you call this?
Child	I'm sorry, Mrs Wells.
Teacher	You are over fifteen minutes late and this is not the first time! You need to leave home earlier.
Child	Sorry, but . . . (*beginning to cry*)
Teacher	Well, what's your excuse this time then?

The teacher stopped midway through the warm-up activity, which disturbed the whole class. Every child will lose out and become an audience for the incident. Children love a spectacle and will enjoy the show even more if the teacher is the object of derision or ridicule. Conflicts like this create unnecessary difficulties for the teacher, especially as she seems to have assumed the child was deliberately late and not bothered to ascertain what the reason was. Furthermore, children do not view teachers kindly if they use sarcasm.

Some children use lateness to gain attention and cause a great deal of disruption.

Child   Sorry I'm late, Miss. I forgot my lunch box and had to go back and get it.

Teacher   That's okay, Jordan. Try to be on time in future. Now go to your place and take out your things.

Jordan swaggered across the room, poking the children as he went and then sat down in a loud way by scraping the furniture. The teacher resumed her lesson and was immediately interrupted again by Jordan tapping his pencil on the table.

Teacher   Stop that, Jordan! You are disturbing everyone and I am sure they would prefer not to have been given this exhibition of silly behaviour.

Child   I bet they would, Miss. Shall we ask them?

The teacher let Jordan disturb her lesson by being late. Directing him to his usual place allowed him to cause further disruption. Jordan's attention seeking was finally successful when the teacher responded with a rhetorical question rather than redirecting him. Jordan took up the gauntlet at the end by suggesting that the rest of the class should be asked whether they wanted to be distracted or not. The teacher seemed to have lost sight of the fact that her lesson had been disrupted and the pupil had gained control of what was happening.

Some teachers invest too much time on lateness.

Teacher   You're late, Aaron!

Child   Sorry, Miss, I had to see Mrs Gunn in the office to give in my dinner money.

Teacher   Well I've just about had enough of this. You lot don't seem to realise how important it is to be punctual. Furthermore, you are wasting valuable time and we have the SATs in a month. I am going to have a word with Mrs Gunn and you can stay back at break to make up for the wasted time.

Once again, the teacher is adopting a confrontational stance that is totally unnecessary. She is showing the whole class that she can get wound up by a child being late. She is overly concerned with telling them about her worries to do with the Standard Assessment Tests (SATs) and seems oblivious to the fact that the lateness may not have been the fault of the child. She is blaming Aaron when all he was doing was what his mum had told him to do – give the money in as soon as he got to school and not lose it.

The positive, proactive approach

Pupils arrive late for all sorts of reasons. Some are legitimate and some not. Whatever the reason, it can be disruptive and parents are expected to get their children to school on time. That may be difficult if they are working and have to get more than one child ready, especially if they go to different schools. The teacher should not be talking to the child about lateness, they should be talking to the parent.

We have two objectives: to find ways of incorporating latecomers without disrupting the flow of a lesson and to establish the reason for the lateness so the necessary action can be taken. Most teachers allocate their children places. A late arrival will interrupt things if they cross the room to get to their usual place. To avoid this you may be able to leave a couple of spare seats near the door. When a child is late, direct them to the spare seats as unobtrusively as possible.

Child   Sorry I'm late, Miss.

Teacher   Good morning, Jane. Please sit there for the time being (*pointing to the seat near the door*) and you can tell me why you are late at the end of the lesson.

Do not attempt to find out why the child is late, because the rest of the class are waiting for the lesson to resume. A simple greeting followed by a direction and a request to see you later are all that is required. You can find out the reason for the lateness after the lesson and take any action then if necessary. Do not prejudge the child; assume they have a legitimate reason for being late, welcome them into the class then forget about it until the end.

Scenario 2.3: A child passes wind during a lesson

The class have been working on a report about rivers on a recent geography field trip. They have been working silently for five minutes and doing well when suddenly the silence is broken and one of the boys passes wind loudly so everyone can hear. Boys can be quite crude at times and events like this are extremely hard to avoid. When they happen they cannot be ignored. They usually prompt a wave of laughter and feigned asphyxiation. There is little chance of it going unnoticed by the rest of the class, who will take the opportunity to stop work and engage in humorous and silly behaviour. Preventing the problem is very difficult. It is not easy to raise the issue in a serious discussion and you can hardly have a rule like 'no passing wind in lessons'.

How not to deal with this

- 'Who did that? Stand up immediately!' This is unlikely to get a response and will lead you into deeper conflict if it is pursued.
- 'Stand up or I will keep you all in after the lesson until someone owns up.' A whole class detention will always cause problems and you will be seen as grossly unfair.
- 'Whoever made that foul noise and smell must leave the room immediately.' You will probably not even be heard as the class will be laughing and your irate, serious response will become the target of their ridicule. Either way, you

will be on the losing end. You cannot get a child to own up and take you seriously, because they will not want to submit to you. You will need to be cleverer than that.

The positive, proactive approach

There are some preventative measures you can try for these kinds of incidents. Teaching social skills like politeness will provide a way in and can be done during personal, social and health education (PSHE) or during circle time discussions on the kind of behaviour that is acceptable in your classroom. Unsociable behaviour could include sudden outbursts, silly noises, humming, tapping and clicking sounds. The mention of burping and passing wind may provoke a few giggles but you will have made your point. Older boys will pass wind loudly to gain attention. The reaction from the rest of the class will be about the smell and will be overexaggerated. Your response should be quite decisive and as unobtrusive as possible.

Teacher	Robbie, that was very rude. Pack up your things and go to . . . (*choose from your class time-out area or another class you have agreed*).
Child	But, Miss, I couldn't help it.
Teacher	Maybe you couldn't and we will discuss that at the end of the lesson. Now go and I will come and see you when the bell goes.

The child will have to negotiate his return to the group with you and agree to observe the behaviour code in future. Do not enter into any discussions or arguments during the lesson. Alternatively, you may feel you do not want to take it this far, so a simple response with a deferred consequence could be used:

'Robbie, that was rude. See me at the end of the lesson.'

Then turn away. Do not respond to any reply, just continue with the lesson.

Sometimes you will not be able to discover the culprit, so your response should be minimal. Open the windows and tell the children who are overreacting to stop being so silly and continue with their work.

The children who cannot be sensible and quieten down will need to be given an activity that demands attention and concentration such as a short period of note-taking. There is nothing like copying a few notes down from the board to get the class back under control.

Child	Phew! What a stink.
Teacher	I'll open some windows.
Child	You pig! That was evil.
Teacher	Right, this seems to be a good time to make some notes of the key points. Take out your pens and copy them off the board please.

Alternatively, you could try humour as an effective means of taking the heat out of the situation. The children who overreact are obviously not really suffocating, so you could play along with the gag:

'It's windy in here today!'

'Someone overdid the beans at lunchtime!'

'We really must have a word with cook about the dinners!'

'Whoever did that trouser puff is in dire need of dietary advice.'

This will probably defuse the situation, put an end to the play-acting and give rise to general laughter that can then be allowed to die down. You can get the class under control more easily because they will not find your quips as funny as their own show of amateur dramatics. You will still have to deal with the incident if it occurs again but by showing you have a sense of humour you won't have children deliberately doing it to wind you up.

The point of working through incidents like this as a staff is to develop uniform responses that are positive and assertive. Staff with less confidence will feel better prepared and not have to work out what to do at the time. The children can be taught the sets of directions for the activities to eliminate the disruptions that are often caused when changes occur during lessons. They will become second nature as the children internalise the routines. You can then concentrate on rewarding the majority for getting things right rather than spending too much time on negative behaviour with the minority.

CORRECTION

When incidents do occur, they should be dealt with fairly by being consistent and challenging all the children who fail to comply with your directions. This can be very hard for a variety of reasons. The hurly-burly of being a teacher often prevents us from paying attention to the small things children do that have the potential to quickly escalate into larger problems.

Some teachers find certain children hard to challenge because of their size or demeanour. Furthermore, it seems unfair to correct a child who usually behaves very well, especially if a consequence is due. Surely a child should be allowed to make a mistake. Being fair to everyone involves treating all children in the class in the same way, to avoid accusations of favouritism. Corrective measures should be as unobtrusive as possible and consist of the following four things:

- Rule reminders
- Questions about the work or the behaviour
- Redirections with choices
- Support and encouragement.

These can be given using diversions and humour to take the heat out of the situation. They should be made in a calm way with a lowered voice, employing privately understood signals where appropriate. The aim is to help the child understand what they did wrong by using coaching methods to help them avoid the same mistake in the future. Sometimes words are unnecessary because you can correct simply by looking at the child in a particular way, at the right time. Scenarios 2.4 to 2.9 give some examples.

Scenario 2.4: Children talking during lessons

Alison was teaching a science lesson to her Year 5 class. The children were working in groups of three on an experiment to find out what were the best conditions for microbes to grow in. They were putting pieces of bread in bags, tying them up and labelling them. Then they were placing them in the light, the dark, near a radiator and in a box to go in the fridge. Several children were taking advantage of being at the back and having a bit of a chat. The third girl in the group was trying to do the work on her own.

How not to deal with this

- 'You two! Cut the chatting and get back to work or I'll put you in detention.'
- 'I presume you two have finished. If so, I'll give you some more work.'
- 'If you want to chat, you'd better stay in at break and you can chat in your own time!'

All of these ways disrupt the whole class and provide them with a show. They will also embarrass the children and prevent them from appreciating what they did wrong.

The positive, proactive approach

Alison noticed them and stopped talking to the group she had been helping. She caught the eye of one of the girls who was chatting and gave her a very stern look that said, 'I am aware that you are chatting. I do not approve, so stop now!' The girl was transfixed for a few seconds. The other girl realised she had stopped talking and followed her gaze to the teacher. She could see that Alison was not pleased and was looking at her friend. They both turned to the third member of the group and asked her what they should be doing. The whole incident took only a few moments but was an example of how an authoritative look can speak volumes. Another way of getting the pupils back on track is by proximity. This involves moving near to them so they know you are watching what they are doing. Your closeness does not require anything being said, so the other children will not be distracted.

Scenario 2.5: A child is off task

The children always got a bit noisy during technology but things got done and they enjoyed the lessons. Carol had an easy-going style suited to the nature of the work. She expected the children to get the work done but did not insist that they worked in silence. When a child stopped work and carried on chatting, she intervened in a quiet way. You would never hear a raised voice in her room. She knew when a child was having a problem and she helped them overcome the barriers so they would gain success. She had a way with the class that was based on the belief that everyone was going to do the work she set. Some might do it better than others but they would all do their best. She made sure the children knew this. One child was supposed to be working on his slippers but was tangling the cottons into a bit of a mess.

How not to deal with this

The temptation is to tell the child off for making a mess rather than correct him by refocusing him on the task. Here are some typical negative responses:

- 'You can come back at lunchtime and untangle that lot!'
- 'That's school property you're ruining. Do you have to make such a mess?'
- 'I have been watching you waste your time for the past five minutes and I can't understand why you do it. You must be some kind of idiot. You are in Year 6 now and you'll be taking your SATs before you know it. You haven't got time to waste this year.'

The teacher will not get very far with responses like these. Stressing the value of time to Year 6 children will not have much effect. They are unlikely to understand what you are getting at. Time stretches out in an unlimited way at that age. The concept of school property being of value is also difficult for some children to comprehend, so a wanton waste of resources will not concern them much.

The positive, proactive approach

Carol spotted the boy not getting on with the project she had set. She quietly moved over to the area where he was working, checking the progress of various groups as she went. She walked up to the boy and stood close to him but looked away at what some other children were doing. The boy felt her presence and realised he should stop what he was doing. He looked up at Carol, who was still looking in another direction, then picked up a slipper and started threading the needle ready to sew up the back. Carol registered his return to work then turned and made a comment about aligning the two edges. She gave the boy a few reassuring words about the quality of his work before moving to the other side of the room, where another child was also going off task. Groups of children can be remotivated in a similar way (Scenario 2.6). A direct intervention is required and the ringleaders should become the target of your attention.

Scenario 2.6: A group is off task

It was a beautiful summer day, so Sarah decided to take her Year 6 class outside and do some drawing. They were working on a project about landscape and a sense of place. The children were instructed what to do, given boards and materials and then off they went to their various positions in the field. Sarah toured the groups to check progress and give advice and assistance where necessary. She noticed a group of two children who did not seem to be engaged in the work.

How not to deal with this

Teachers often feel they are doing the class a favour by letting them go out to the field to draw. The children do enjoy it but some will take advantage of the freedom and misbehave. The teacher will then feel betrayed and respond in an emotional way:

- 'Right, you two, pick up your stuff and follow me. I'm not having you wasting time misbehaving over here.'
- 'I don't get it with you two. You never do as you're told. I give you an opportunity to do something different and you take advantage and spoil it for the rest.'
- 'Show me your work. You haven't even started. How do you expect to complete the work this lesson with half the time gone already?'

And this dialogue:

Teacher	Okay, you two will stay in over lunchtime for mucking about!
Child	But we don't know what to do, Miss.
Teacher	Of course you do. We have done this before. It is exactly the same.
Child	That was in class and we did it from imagination.
Teacher	Stop making excuses. I have been watching you and you haven't even made an effort.

The positive, proactive approach

When Sarah got to the children, she directed her first question at John, the boy who had clearly done the least.

Teacher	John, where are you going to put that tree in the picture?
Child	I was thinking of here, Miss. (*John draws it lightly.*)
Teacher	That's probably about right, because there is more of that building showing on the other side of it from where we are sitting. Now work out where the door goes and let's see if you can start to rough in the other buildings.

She guided John back to the task with some specific questions and useful tips. Then she turned to Paul, who had been throwing grass.

Teacher	Paul, you have drawn in the main buildings but no detail yet. Show me where the railings will be around the hall. (*Paul draws in the details.*) Do you know how to draw the windows using the perspective method? Remember they will get smaller as they get further away from you.

Sarah had Paul engaged. Then she returned to check how John was getting on. Once she was satisfied they could both do the work, she reminded them of the target for the lesson and told them she would be back later to see what they had managed to do.

Careful correction combined with support and assistance had been all the boys needed. She did not need to resort to scolding and reprimanding them for not doing their work. All they needed was the personal touch. They were finding the work difficult but when she showed them what to do they settled down.

Directing questions at children who do not seem to be giving their full attention invariably wakes them up and forces them to refocus their minds. It will also bring in children whose minds were wandering, because they do not want to be caught out with a question they cannot answer.

Scenario 2.7: A child falls asleep during the lesson

The history class had just finished watching a video about the Victorians. Some of the pupils were sleepy by nature. Kelly knew some of them stayed up late at night and were slow-witted in the lesson the next morning. She was drawing their attention to the main points in the video to make sure they had noted them down, when she noticed a boy slouched in his chair with his head down. He was not looking at the front or taking notes. It was hard to tell whether or not he was asleep, but it was clear he wasn't paying attention.

How not to deal with this

Many teachers will just move in and disrupt the flow of the lesson. They may feel indignant that a child seems to be falling asleep in their class. They will assume this is the reason without attempting to find out.

- 'Wake up, Martin! This is not a bedroom. Go to bed earlier.'
- 'Would you like me to dim the lights and get you a pillow, Martin? You look very uncomfortable trying to get to sleep like that.'
- 'Come on, Martin. I don't want you falling asleep in my lesson, it can't be that boring.' This comment will probably give the child an opportunity to tell you it is, even if other children don't find it boring.

The positive, proactive approach

Kelly was very good at handling whole group activities. Her use of open questions combined with reassuring comments helped her bring everyone into the discussion. She would carefully structure her questions in a way that would enable any child to answer at their level of understanding. If a child was not particularly knowledgeable, she would begin with a fairly basic question and then get the child to amplify what they had said with further probing questions rather than ask a different child the next question. She believed that getting one child to talk about something for several minutes aided their understanding and the rest of the class also benefited by listening. They knew their turn would come eventually and everyone got used to it.

Kelly ended her explanation about the huge differences between the ordinary people of that period and today and then directed a new line of questioning at Martin.

Teacher	So, Martin (*pause for Martin to lift his head and give his attention*). You remember the point that was made on the video about the way the Victorian houses were designed. Can you tell me where they usually had their baths?
Child	(*woken up and ready to answer*) In front of the fire in the kitchen, Miss.
Teacher	Well remembered, Martin. What other differences were there between their houses and ours?

Martin went on to show what he knew about the absence of good sanitation and the toilet being outside. He also added that many people only bathed about once a week, if that. Her strategy had got Martin back into the lesson without having to break the flow of thinking in the rest of the class.

Sometimes it is necessary to challenge the children to help them back on the correct path. A break or distraction is unavoidable but it serves another purpose. It shows the rest of the class that you do mean what you say. The procedure of correction should aim to help the child recognise where they are going wrong, and you may not always have to give a consequence; a small reminder of the rule may be sufficient to refocus them on the task.

Scenario 2.8: Children calling out during lessons

Jill liked the students to contribute to the lesson but had difficulties with them calling out rather than waiting to be invited.

How not to deal with this

The aim is to keep control without crushing the children who are trying to participate. Avoid statements like these:

- 'Put your hand down, Steven. We know you know the answer.'
- 'Stop calling out, Michael. You are preventing the others from answering.'
- 'If you call out once more, Sajit, I am putting you in detention.'
- 'For goodness sake, Ollie. If you're going to call out the answer, make sure it's right.'

The positive, proactive approach

The objective is to control the situation as soon as you begin asking questions. This is easily done in several ways and removes any conflict, calling out or the need for put-downs.

Teacher	Michael, what do we call the process that plants use to manufacture food using light?
Child	Photosynthesis, Miss.
Teacher	Thank you, that is right.

The teacher focused the question solely at Michael, so the rest of the class knew they were not being called on to answer. Alternatively, you can begin with an instruction like this:

> 'Put your hands up and wait for me to ask you to answer if you can tell me the main features of a square.'

The teacher waits for the children who know the answer to put up their hands then she selects one of them.

Teacher	Yes, Milly, can you tell me the main features of a square?
Child	It's got four right angles and four equal sides.

This could be turned into a game: I am going to ask you a question and if you know the answer, you must wait and do nothing. Then when I say 'now' everyone who thinks they know the answer puts their hand up. I will pick the person with their hand up first and invite them to answer. If you put your hand up or call out before I say 'now', you will be disqualified for that turn.

Some children will still ignore your directions. It may not always be deliberate but they will need correcting.

Teacher What was the name of Queen Victoria's husband?
Child (*without being invited*) Prince Albert!

The teacher has a number of options but should make sure the child does not feel he is being put down in front of his peers simply because he was eager to give his answer. The teacher should tactically ignore him by choosing someone else with their hand up:

'Thank you for putting your hand up and waiting, Shelley. Do you know his name?'

The first sentence is a rule reminder. The teacher is reinforcing the behaviour she wants and ignoring undesirable behaviour. The correction is indirect but often just as powerful, because the children who are keen to answer will soon learn the right way and put up their hand. The direct approach is different in that it requires an immediate response.

Teacher Colin, what should you do when you want to speak? (*rule reminder*)
Child Put up my hand and wait, Miss. (*correction*)
Teacher That's right, so in the future I would like you to do that. Okay? (*redirection*)
Child Yes, Miss.
Teacher Thank you. (*repair*)

Sometimes the correction is better deferred to a more suitable time when you can have a one-to-one conversation.

Scenario 2.9: The child who cannot seem to settle

Chris was finding it hard to settle down. He seemed to want to do other things. He was looking out of the window, tapping the desk, and repeatedly putting his hand up and asking for paper, pencils, a textbook, a compass, etc. The teacher finally warned Chris that he needed to get down to work and stop wasting any more time. Chris returned to his work but a few minutes later he was turning round and chatting again.

How not to deal with this

- 'Turn round, Chris. I've given you a warning but you seem to be dead set on ignoring me, so you can stay in at break. You won't be able to ignore me there.'
- 'That was your last chance. You can stay in during lunchtime.'

The positive, proactive approach

The purpose of the intervention is to get the child back on task and to correct him. If he has failed to follow directions, a consequence is due but should be deferred until later to minimise the disruption.

Teacher Chris, I have already given you a warning for chatting during silent work. What is the rule about talking? (*rule reminder*)

Child	No talking during silent work. If I need to talk, I've got to raise my hand and wait for you to give me permission. (*rule reinforcement*)
Teacher	That's right. Now, I gave you a warning for talking and you carried on.
Child	Sorry, Miss.
Teacher	That's okay. I accept your apology, Chris, but you chose to chat after being given a warning, so you know you have a consequence. We will discuss what it will be at the end of the lesson. (*deferred consequence*) Right now, I want you to get on with the work with no more interruptions. (*redirection*) Do you need my help or can you get going alone? (*support*)
Child	I think I need your help on this bit, Miss.
Teacher	Okay, let's have a look at it together. (*repair and rebuilding*)

Chris has been challenged, corrected, given a deferred consequence and helped to get back to work without wasting unnecessary time in the lesson discussing the incident.

CONSEQUENCES

Sometimes it is necessary to go further than just correcting the child, as we saw with Chris in Scenario 2.9. The child that breaks a rule will need to learn from *you* that they have chosen to do so and therefore they are choosing the consequence as well. This is an essential area of your response. The proactive teacher sets out to help children learn to manage their own behaviour. Part of this is the understanding that when a rule is broken a consequence will follow. Consequences can be immediate such as a time-out, moving places or being sent out of the room, or they can be deferred such as detention or loss of privileges. They should be linked to the behaviour (Chapter 5) and in proportion to the incident. Scenarios 2.10 and 2.11 give two examples.

Scenario 2.10: Children damaging school property

On her way to the classroom, Lisa noticed two children drawing over a poster in one of the rooms. They didn't see her because she was outside the building in the playground and they had their backs to the windows.

How not to deal with this

- She could have gone in all guns blazing and rapped on the window. 'Oi, you two, cut that out and get to the head's office now!' Some children would feel intimidated and actually do what was being asked. Kids who deface displays are more likely to run for it, and then the opportunity is missed.
- She could have tried going to the room and pleading with them. 'Now come on, boys, that's not a very good use of your time.'
- 'A lot of time and effort goes into those displays, lads. You are spoiling them and probably upsetting the teacher and the children in her class who did the work.'

None of these strategies will help the children to understand that they have done wrong and should make amends. There has been no talk of consequences and putting things right.

The positive, proactive approach

Lisa thought that they should make amends but she did not teach them and felt it was a hard one to prove because when she got to the room they were sitting down chatting. The children were not allowed to stay inside unless it was a wet break, so she used the rule as her way in.

'Hello, boys, you're aware of the rule about being in the room during break?'

'No,' replied one of them cheekily.

'Well let me remind you,' she responded confidently. She went on to reiterate the rule and while she did it she surveyed the room and displays for any evidence of damage. If it had been negligible, she would have talked about the amount of effort that goes into displays. When she spoke about preventing deliberate damage, she engaged the boys in direct eye contact to communicate that she knew what they had been doing.

'I was walking past this room a few minutes ago and I saw you two doing something you probably shouldn't have been doing.' Making eye contact, she continued, 'It reminds me of a display that needs changing. I would appreciate it if you would both help me with it.'

Lisa did not actually accuse them because she was not sure they had done any damage. Instead she chose a tack that would enable them to see how much work was involved and gave them some ownership of a display board.

When the damage is obvious you should challenge them and get them to own up.

Teacher	(*pointing to the damage*) As I passed this room a few minutes ago I saw you both at the back by this poster.
Child	It wasn't us, Miss.
Teacher	It was someone. This damage is deliberate. Those cartoons have been drawn during break. We can easily prove it wasn't either of you by comparing the writing on the poster with a sample of your handwriting and the pens that you have. Do you understand what I am saying? (*making eye contact again*)
Child	Yes, but it wasn't us. We were just looking at them.
Teacher	Maybe you were, so I am going to offer you a choice. You can empty your pockets and then we shall compare the pens with the drawing on the poster. If it proves to be yours, we shall call your parents in and discuss what you have done. I am sure they will be furious if they see the damage you have done. Alternatively, you can own up to it now and I won't say anything to them.

The teacher uses parental disapproval and the punishment the children may receive at home as a threat to get them to admit they did it. Once they have owned up, she can start working with them on repairing what they have done. The consequence could be helping to put up a display and then letting them take responsibility for it. This way the consequence fits the incident. The children will have to give up their time but in return they may take pride in their work and be less likely to repeat the offence.

The essential aspects of this area of behaviour management are choice and enabling the children to realise it is their behaviour that is undesirable, not them as people. They will sometimes make the wrong choice but that does not make them bad people. We are all entitled to make mistakes and that is how we learn. It is the handling of mistakes that matters. An opportunity to help the children see where they went wrong could be lost if it is handled wrongly. Sensitive handling will help the children learn from their mistakes. Then the relationship between child and teacher will grow and self-esteem will be enhanced. The children will become more independent and responsible for their own behaviour and aware of the consequences that accompany their choices.

A sense of fairness is an important element. The children need to feel that the teacher is making balanced judgements and treating everyone in the same way. Teachers who do not do this will damage the confidence of their pupils.

Scenario 2.11: Fairness and consistency in dealing with children who are chatting

Susanna was taking a class in the computer room and the pupils were working in pairs on a webpage design. Two of them decided to take advantage of the teacher working on the other side of the room; they started talking and surfing the internet. When Susanna returned to her computer she could see on her screen that they were not doing the work.

How not to deal with this

Susanna was fed up with the kids messing about. She felt they should feel lucky doing information technology (IT) and so they should concentrate. She called across the room, 'You two, be quiet and get on with your work.'

The two pupils stopped for a few seconds, then they resumed their surfing expedition once she had looked away. Susanna started to get angry and a little paranoid that they were deliberately winding her up and trying to test her. She stopped what she was doing and went over to them. She scolded the two children then addressed the whole class, 'I don't know what's the matter with this class today. Perhaps it's because it's very windy or maybe because we have moved to the computer room. You all seem to be unable to settle. You two can do a detention at lunchtime and anyone else who misbehaves can join them.'

The class settled back down to their work but one or two children continued messing about and fiddling with the screen wallpaper. Susanna felt that they were deliberately challenging her authority. She was getting angry and confused about what she wanted. This was partly due to the difficulties she was having with the computers. Several had frozen and the printer had got jammed and she had to clear it herself. When she looked up after fixing it, several students were sniggering about something and she thought it was directed at her.

'That's it, I warned you. You two have spoiled it for the whole class. Clearly you can't get on with things on your own, so you will all stop what you are doing, log off and come and sit at the desks until the end of the lesson!'

'But that's not fair, we weren't doing anything wrong,' pleaded a couple of girls who had been trying to get on with their work.

'I don't care. You will have to take that up with the two boys who were.'

'But, Miss, you said that if we did not behave right, we would get a warning first. You didn't give one.'

Susanna was on shaky ground. She could not argue because the girl was right, but she had already said it and she did not want to do a U-turn. The class were very upset. They felt they had been treated unfairly and conned. Susanna had introduced the behaviour code and wasn't sticking to it.

The positive, proactive approach

Susanna seemed like she was having a bad day and that is when a good behaviour code usually comes into its own. It will only be of use if you stick to it, but Susanna seemed to have forgotten and was letting her emotions take over. It was a straightforward case of dealing with the kind of distraction that happens in every lesson. Her approach should have gone as follows. She should have wound up her discussion with the children she was helping by saying, 'Okay, see how you get on with that. If you need any more help, just raise your hand and I'll get back to you as soon as I can.'

Then she should have moved on to the boys who were chatting, stood near them and given them a look to say, 'I am watching you and I expect you to stop talking and get on with the work.' If a more direct approach was required, she could have said, 'The work is to be done in pairs. I notice you are not doing the work and making very little progress. If you are stuck, you should raise your hand and wait for me to come over. Otherwise you should be working and if you need to talk, keep your voices down.'

The children will realise she has rumbled them and will probably get back to work but if they stray off task again, she will need to speak to them in a calm, unemotional way: 'I have already spoken to you but you have chosen to ignore me, so I am giving you a warning to get on with the work and get it finished. If you use the internet any more in that way, you will be choosing a consequence, which will be to wait after class for one minute. You will also have to do the work in your own time if it is not finished.'

Notice the rule reminder about consequences. The children are given a chance to decide and the consequences are made clear. The rest of the class can carry on working without being involved. This places the responsibility with the children. Sometimes children just cannot behave well. When they make poor choices, do not feel you have failed. Providing you give them a chance to decide and make the consequences clear to them, you will be doing your job well.

SUPPORT

The final area of behaviour management is support and encouragement. It is vital to the whole process because it can have a disproportionate effect on the progress of the pupils. Feeling that you are doing things right is important to everyone. Praise and feedback are important in affirming that feeling. A lack of acknowledgement can make your class feel that you do not really care or that you have not noticed their efforts. The end result will be unmotivated children. Critical feedback given sensitively can have a profound effect in helping children identify where they went wrong and how to improve. Giving this kind of feedback needs care and practice. It is best begun with something positive:

'I really liked the way this table got down to work. You got all your things quickly and quietly. That saved a lot of time that could have been wasted.'

Then move on to the constructive criticism:

'What you could do now is to take turns measuring each other's feet so you get to practise using the tape measure.'

The pupils will feel that you are genuinely trying to help and treating them in a fair way; this will contribute to fostering a positive relationship. Children who begin to experience difficulties with their behaviour will need a particular kind of support to ensure that they do not end up losing control and getting excluded. Many schools have a framework for supporting children with behaviour difficulties that includes:

• Peer support
• Behaviour recovery plans and mentoring schemes
• Anger management courses.

The aim is to curb the frequency of incidents and prevent children getting trapped in a spiral of repeating consequences where they feel they are always doing something wrong. The methods employed should be practical. The solutions are not obtained by producing a written plan with targets and dates. The child needs help, not a piece of paper. The written plan is for recording what everyone agrees should happen, but it will not be sufficient on its own. The child will need coaching in order to change habits and eliminate poor behavioural traits. Time needs to be set aside and specific methods need to be used that will include role-play, drama, empathising and customised exercises for specific difficulties. The coach will need to work with the child on a regular basis so that new ways can be properly learned and internalised. There is not enough space to describe these methods in depth but 'trust the teacher' (next section) is a typical activity and will give you a flavour of what might be done.

TRUST THE TEACHER

A common problem that exists in primary schools is the pupils' lack of trust in the teachers to sort out their difficulties. The usual route that children go down is to respond to an incident directly rather than take it to someone in authority. The reason is partly due to the lack of trust and also a lack of personal control. The child gets angry and then retaliates. The result is trouble for all the children concerned. In many cases the retaliation is perceived as the worse offence as it is often out of proportion to the incident that provoked it. For example, a boy bumps into another aggressively during a game in the playground. The second boy turns around and says something to him, often an abusive reference about his mother, and he takes offence and lashes out. Before you know it, a fight has broken out and the boy who started it will be in deep trouble. The other boy who took umbrage goes unpunished. The aim of this activity is to help the children to understand how to deal with these kinds of day-to-day conflicts in a controlled way using the teachers as arbiters. Scenario 2.12 is an example.

Scenario 2.12: The stolen pen

The lesson had just begun and the teacher was in the middle of a warm-up activity involving a question and answer session with the whole class. Tony had taken out his pen and textbook and placed them on the desk ready. He was listening intently and raising his hand each time he knew an answer. The teacher looked in his direction and nodded for him to speak, but Tony was not sure whether it was for him or the girl behind. He looked round to see and realised it was for her. When he looked back to the front he noticed that his pen had disappeared.

Activity 1

The children tell you what they would do and you challenge each suggestion by asking them to consider what the consequence might be. Here are some questions for the class and their possible responses:

Teacher What would you do?
Child Call out, 'Who's got my pen?'
Teacher What would the consequence be?
Child I would probably get told off by the teacher for interrupting or getting aggressive during the lesson.

Activity 2

Describe how you would like them to respond and then help them to role-play it to practise their response. You will want to help them with how they report to the teacher because the obvious response from most children will be that the pen has been stolen. However, it may have fallen on the floor or in a bag. Conclude by showing them how you will respond to their report:

'Thank you for telling me that, Tony. I will deal with it at the end of the lesson. Can I lend you a pen or do you have another?'

This defers the whole incident until later and prevents the lesson getting disturbed. The offer of a pen ensures Tony can continue and gives him something different to think about. It is all about making good choices, and the four areas of behaviour management will enable you to support your pupils in taking on that responsibility.

SUMMARY

- The positive approach involves responding to the four key areas: prevention, correction, consequences and support.

- Plan to prevent conflicts and problems by communicating your expectations in advance to the children.
- Consider the whole experience of the children, including room layout, work partners and pace of lessons. They may contain triggers for poor behaviour.
- When correcting, tackle children in an appropriate way using rule reminders and redirections.
- Wherever necessary, use assertive instructions with choices rather than emotionally driven orders.
- Consequences must follow when rules are broken. They can be immediate or deferred until later.
- Dislike the behaviour not the child.
- Consequences must be fair and in proportion to the behaviour.
- Repair the relationship after the consequence is given.
- Coach children who make the wrong choices so they do not repeat the mistake.

3 THERE'S NO NEED TO SHOUT!

Children may be used to teachers shouting at them. There is nearly always one who barks instructions and reprimands children in a loud voice. Some schools become dominated by that culture and the pupils get used to it. Shouting is not the same as projecting your voice in a loud way that allows you to be heard. Shouting above the hubbub in an assembly or the dinner hall may seem the only way, and there lies the problem. Good management of behaviour prevents the problem to begin with. There is no reason why the noise level should be high in an assembly if classes are well managed by their teachers and the understanding is that the children whisper or remain silent. Equally, dining halls can be a cacophony of noise if staff allow children to shout, call across tables and behave in ways more appropriate to a football field. Children should be allowed to relax, chat, socialise and meet with their friends over lunch but control is needed with any activity in a school where large groups come together.

In the first chapter we looked at the styles that teachers could adopt when managing behaviour. The focus of the second chapter was on the four main elements that go to make up the foundations of good behaviour management. The next step is to consider how you can develop a proactive style. This entails thinking about how the teaching space will be used, personal appearance, language, and the use of humour and anger so that you make positive, formative interventions that enable the children to learn and grow from the experience. The essential ingredient in the process is modelling the behaviour you want to see from the children. Setting a good example through demonstration is the most effective way forward and this chapter provides useful insights into how this can be achieved. The overall objective is to manage the behaviour using positive, assertive methods so that the classroom is a calm place, conducive to learning, and you remain confident and relaxed and do not need to lose your temper.

THE TEACHING SPACE

The room is the theatre for your lessons, the place where you will teach the class, so make it yours. This can be done in several ways. The noticeboards and displays can be used to support your lessons and celebrate the children's work. You should try to stamp your identity on it and present a wide variety of visual materials. Then get the children involved by putting them in charge of the boards and contributing to what goes up.

The ownership of the room is an important issue. Children know their space is at the desks and the teacher has the area up front around the board. You can subtly assert your authority in any room by changing things. This is particularly important if you are new or covering a colleague's lesson, because the pupils will perceive you as outside their normal group even though you are employed by the school. A useful analogy is a herd or pack of animals in the wild. The members of the pack recognise their leader, the usual teacher, and the authority he holds. They know their position in the pecking order. A new buck who enters the pack will not have any power at first.

To gain authority you must assert your position and dominate the space. When you enter a room, greet your class and start to change things immediately. Here are some examples:

- If the lights are off, switch them on.
- If the windows are shut, open them.
- Clean everything off the board and write your name.
- Move books, etc., off the teacher's desk.
- Open your bag and place your things on the desk.
- Move the teacher's chair and sit in it or put your coat on it to show it is yours.

If you can get into the room before the term starts, rearrange some furniture, alter the angle of computer monitors and put up one new display. What you are doing is making the environment yours.

INCREASE YOUR SPACE

During the lessons do what the children least expect. Make a point of walking around the room and down every aisle and between every island of tables. Show you are not afraid to venture forth from your 'teacher's space'. You are making a statement: this is my room and I can go where I like and do what I want. Teaching outside your space will increase what is yours. Move to the front while you do whole class activities and even conduct them from the side of the room.

Impose your will by seating the children where you want them, rather than letting them choose where they want to sit. This may not be necessary if you are only covering one lesson, but any longer and it is essential. It can be done alphabetically, boy and girl or in groups to maximise cooperation. Explain that you are doing it to learn their names; use it to assert yourself even though changing seats takes time. Do not respond to their protests.

The subtle signs you will give will show that you are now the authority figure in the room. This will enable you to command respect and cooperation without even needing to say anything. The signals are strong and even primeval. Our natural instincts run deep and it is worth drawing on them in situations like these.

LANGUAGE

Body language contributes significantly to the overall communication process. It can convey much more than can be said. For example, when we first meet someone new, we make immediate judgements about them from their clothes, expressions, mannerisms, facial features and posture. Much of the decoding is instinctive but it can be useful if we understand more about this means of communication. Such skills could contribute greatly to our ability to manage a class well.

We pick up visual cues about people almost instantaneously, so appearance is a vital part of our armoury. The pupils have expectations about what their teachers should be like and will typecast you depending on their first impressions. The male teacher who is well groomed, wearing a neutral-coloured shirt and tie, together with a suit will send out the message that he means business. He is dressing for the position he is aspiring to and recognises that others will expect him to dress in that way as well. The converse is the man who lacks confidence. He wears the right clothes but it looks like the suit is wearing him because he hunches and stoops.

The same is true for women. A smart businesslike outfit and a well-groomed appearance confer a level of status that the children expect and understand. Too much attention to fashion will distract from this image. On the other hand, do not ignore attention to detail. A teacher who stumbles into a classroom with a mountain of books under her arm and dumps them on the table only to see them slip and slide every which way does not create a good impression. Try not to carry too much; if you have a lot of things that need to be taken to a room, ask some children to help you. It avoids you struggling with the load and it will create the impression of someone in authority. You may need to carry a bag, so choose one that will reinforce your status such as a briefcase but do not pack it too full. Definitely avoid plastic carrier bags.

Much depends on how you address the children and what you say. They are more likely to pick up what you are saying if you use phrases that tune into their preferred learning styles. For example, visual learners may tune into you more quickly if you use phrases like these:

'Let's have a look at . . .'

'Can you see what I mean?'

'That looks good.'

'I want you to imagine in your mind's eye . . .'

'What does success look like to you?'

'Try to picture this.'

Here are some phrases for auditory learners:

'I hear what you are saying.'

'How does this sound to you?'

'That rings a bell.'

'Ask yourselves what you would do if . . .'

'Do you hear what I am saying?'

'What will people say when you get it right?'

'Tell me about your experience.'

And here are some phrases for kinaesthetic learners:

'I can follow what you are saying.'

'That touched a nerve.'

'What does success feel like?'

'I want you to get to grips with this.'

'Can you change your position on this?'

'What will people do when you get it right?'

'Where do you stand on this?'

Teachers tend to talk a lot. We give instructions, directions, explanations, praise, criticism, advice, support and when there is time we chat to the kids. To get across your messages effectively, avoid long explanations before giving directions, because the children will be poised for action. When an intervention is required it is best to be brief and precise. Begin by naming the child and making eye contact with them to ensure they are paying attention:

'Chantelle, (*make eye contact*) remember the direction about walking.'

Allow a pause so the child can engage with what you are saying, then give the direction in an assertive tone. Finish with a smile and a thank you, then turn away expecting it to be done.

'Peter, (*pause*) put the chewing gum in the bin please (*spoken assertively*). Thanks.'

Some children will have a tendency to switch off and go deaf when they think they are being lectured to about their behaviour, so avoid lecturing. They do not need long explanations about what they did wrong. A simple rule reminder followed by a redirection will be enough. Explanations should be left till later to avoid disturbing the lesson. Do not discuss a particular child's behaviour in the presence of the class or their peer group, because it may well fuel their need for attention. Furthermore, the rest of the class love a show between a child and the teacher.

Long sets of directions can be confusing for some children. You will need to know what they are capable of and gauge how much each one can take in at a time. Low-ability pupils generally perform better when the task is broken down into smaller steps with discrete instructions that can be given separately. The objective for a step should be clear so the children will recognise when it is complete and judge whether they have been successful. Securing success is one of the keys to good behaviour. Children who feel they are failing will often become troublesome.

Ignoring the child who is behaving inappropriately can sometimes be a powerful strategy. They will quickly realise that they are not getting your attention and figure out why (Case Study 3.1).

Case Study 3.1

Teacher	I want you to put your hand up if you can tell me the name of one of the wives of Henry the Eighth. (*Joe calls out without raising his hand.*)
Joe	Anne Boleyn! (*The teacher physically changes his position and turns his shoulder towards the child. Then he points to someone with his hand up.*)
Teacher	Thank you for raising your hand and waiting for me, Matt. Can you tell me the name?

Matt	Catherine of Aragon.
Teacher	Good, now can anyone tell me how many wives he had? (*A number of children put up their hands, including Joe.*) Thank you for putting up your hand this time, Joe.
Joe	He had six wives.
Teacher	Thank you. (*Joe realised the teacher had deliberately passed him by the first time because he had called out instead of raising his hand, so the next time he did as the teacher asked and was rewarded by being chosen.*)

Eye contact is crucial to engaging attention. By looking straight at a person, you show that you are addressing them. Our eyes are our most important means of communicating. You can tell a lot about how someone is feeling and the sort of mood they are in by the look in their eyes. Children will read your expression and see disapproval, happiness, displeasure, humour and compassion. Learn how to control and use these expressions to your advantage. Direct eye contact is essential to ensure the children pick up your feelings. Very often a child who is being reprimanded will try to break eye contact because they are ashamed, angry or trying to control the situation. When this happens, you should regain eye contact to maintain your authority (Case Study 3.2).

Case Study 3.2

Layla was fast becoming a cause for concern because she had started behaving in a very annoying way that wound up the other children. She was indiscriminate about who should be her next target; it really didn't matter, she would go ahead and irritate anyone. Usually it was by kicking a chair, poking or pinching them or muttering abusive things about their appearance. Mark could see what she was up to; she was deliberately kicking the underside of the chair of the girl sitting in front of her. The girl turned around several times and told her to stop but she just smiled. Layla knew she was irritating the girl and this pleased her. Mark gave her a very clear warning to stop or there would be a consequence. Layla waited until Mark had turned to talk to a group of pupils on another table and then started again. He guessed she would and turned around just in time to catch her giving the girl's hair a sharp tug.

'Layla, I warned you to stop or there would be a consequence. Move to the time-out table. I will talk to you in five minutes.'

There were no more incidents for the rest of the morning, so just before lunch Mark called her to him and said he wanted her to stay back for a short chat. When all the children had left the room, he started to talk to her about her behaviour. She listened but kept her eyes downcast, not attempting to look at him. She fiddled with the edge of the table and the chair next to hers. She gradually changed her position until she had her shoulder turned and was no longer facing him. Her body language showed she was not prepared to listen to him and was trying to blank him out.

'I can see you are not happy but I want you to turn and face me while I am talking.' Layla did not move and Mark could see this was going nowhere. He needed to get through quickly. 'I

will wait until you are looking at me. It's your lunchtime so the longer you take, the less time you will have to play with your friends. I cannot continue until you are looking at me.'

Eventually she decided to turn round. He knew she would because she was wasting her own time. Mark finished talking to her about her behaviour during the lesson. He did not get embroiled in the rudeness of her efforts to block him. He had offered her a choice and she had chosen wisely in the end. If she had looked like she was not going to turn around, he would simply have kept her waiting and got on with what he wanted to do in his classroom. She would have had to sit until he finally let her go. Her turning back and facing Mark had redressed the balance of power. Mark regained control and could conclude what he wanted to say.

The tone the teacher uses can convey to the pupils how they feel. Try different ways of saying some of your regular directions and listen to the effect:

'Come here, John.'

'Sarah, put the book in the tray, thank you.'

Change your tone of phrase so it is friendly, polite, angry, sarcastic, indifferent, assertive, pleading and joking. Notice how they sound. Try to imagine someone else speaking to you in these ways. Put yourself in your pupils' position and consider how you would feel. How would you want to be spoken to? Most people prefer to be spoken to in a decent way. Obviously there will be times when urgency is required and a more assertive, louder tone is necessary.

The difficulty that teachers face is the underlying 'them and us' assumption that immediately sets up a conflict situation. It is very easy to make this assumption rather than treating people in a friendly way. Calling the register provides a simple illustration. Surnames can be used:

Watson. Here.

Willis. 'Ere.

Wright. Here.

First names can be called:

Helen. Here.

Michael. Here, Miss.

David. Here.

Or first name and a greeting:

Morning, Helen. Morning, Miss Brooks.
Hi, Michael. Hi, Miss.

Hello, David. Hello, Miss Brooks.

This way may take a little longer but it sounds friendlier and helps the children to be polite and well mannered.

Different situations need appropriate responses. A fluffy, soft approach would be totally impractical in the playground when two well-built Year 6 pupils are trying to knock the stuffing out of each other. Instead it requires an assertive response in the form of a command (Case Study 3.3).

Case Study 3.3

Meg was dashing to the office to quickly photocopy something she needed for the next lesson when she noticed a couple of Year 5 boys squaring up and shouting at each other. One of them had actually kicked a ball at the other, so he felt he needed to get a bit tough in front of the girls nearby. Meg could see it getting nasty and one of the boys had been in a fight last week, so something needed to be done and quickly. Playgrounds are noisy places and there was little chance of Meg being heard if she shouted at them to stop; she was quite a long way off.

She moved quickly towards them until she was in earshot then called out in a commanding tone to get their attention, 'John! Leon!' They stopped and looked over to her. 'John, over there!' She pointed to the far end of the playground. 'Leon, over there!' She pointed to the other end. Once she had them separated, she was in with a chance. She sent a responsible child to inform the deputy who was on duty that she needed help. Then she turned to John and asked him what was going on. 'Nothing, Miss.'

'Okay, go in and wait outside Mr Wilson's room and cool off. I shall be in to talk to you both in a few minutes,' she said in a very authoritative voice. Then as she turned to Leon, the deputy arrived, so she changed the tone of her voice – a loud, assertive approach was no longer necessary – and explained what had been happening.

ANGER

The chief priority in any positive approach to behaviour management is maintaining personal control and not revealing emotional feelings, like anger, that will obviously occur from time to time. There will be occasions when you need to show displeasure but these will be rare. Then, when the children do experience your anger, it will have far more effect, because they rarely see that side of you. Overuse will diminish the impact and change their perception of you as a teacher from someone who is reasonable and in control to a fierce, grumpy person who is always barking and shouting. Some teachers believe they should show their anger at least once to demonstrate they have teeth, so the children do not misjudge them as easy-going.

Anger is an emotional response and may result in negative feelings after an incident, especially if you are trying to handle conflicts in the way this book describes. Getting angry does not lead to a rational set of actions. Harassment, abuse and overreaction are the usual kinds of response, and it can be difficult to control them when you're seeing red. You may find that not only have you said things you did not mean, but you've said them in a way that was harmful. Devastating damage can be done to relationships when tempers are lost and that is why it is better to avoid losing your temper. Ask for assistance or postpone making a judgement until you have calmed down and can think more clearly.

When are we most likely to get angry? That is an interesting question and will vary depending on your personality. The common trigger is when a child becomes defiant, rude, belligerent, consistently annoying or abusive. Try to find out what makes you angry in your work and consider how you have been dealing with it. Do you get sucked in emotionally then fly off the handle? Does your anger get directed at a child, resulting in outbursts like this?

'You make me so angry!'

'I am really annoyed with you.'

'That's it. I've had enough of you.'

This is unproductive. If you need to express your feelings, direct your anger at the child's behaviour:

'I am very angry because of your comments.'

'Your behaviour has made me extremely cross.'

'Calling me that has made me very angry.'

This enables the child to see how their behaviour has caused your reaction.

Anger is a powerful emotion. If you bottle it up, it will leak out eventually in a way that causes damage to people who were not involved. Controlled anger is different and can be a very potent force when used sparingly. If you do get angry, consider carefully how you plan to control it. By far the best option is to give yourself time to cool off. Things always look better the next day (Case Study 3.4).

Case Study 3.4

John was small for his age. He was very cute when he smiled and the teachers thought he was a real sweetie. He had a darker side and it only came out at certain times. His life had been a mess. His parents had been living apart for quite some time. He had lived with his mum and her partner for as long as he could remember. He had three older brothers and an older sister. The two oldest moved out several years ago because of problems with the police. Well that's what his mother had told him. The other brother was always out at night and eventually things came to a head.

John remembered being at home one afternoon and some people came to visit. He didn't know who they were but by the end of the visit they had told him that he would be going with them. His mum helped him to get together a few clothes and one or two of his favourite toys. She told him she would pack up the rest and send them on. She had tears in her eyes but was telling him to be good and she would see him soon. He moved to a new area and a new home with new parents. He called them Uncle Sam and Auntie Susan. They were very nice but did not let him go out to play in the evenings. John gradually got used to his new life and things settled down.

Carol was John's new teacher. She had been teaching for just over a year and felt she was getting into it. The only problem she had was remaining calm when the kids behaved badly. She had read the books and been on the courses run by the local education authority (LEA) on behaviour management and felt confident she could manage the classes most of the time. Occasionally her temper frayed when she got frazzled but she had been developing some strategies.

Last night Carol's mum had called and asked if she would like to come over for tea. She had lessons to plan and a set of books to mark and felt that she couldn't afford the time even though the break would be welcome. A huge row broke out between them, with her mum getting very upset and saying that she never bothered to go round anymore. She was always going on about her sister and what a good job she had at the travel agents. She got loads of perks like free tickets to nice places, an office and she was always home by 5.30. Furthermore, she never took her job home. She always seemed to have time for her parents. Talk about making you feel inferior. Carol struggled through the marking but was feeling really miserable by the next morning.

She didn't know what was up with John that morning but whatever it was, he needed to cut it out otherwise he would be in trouble. He was clearly in a mood and it was probably because he had visited his mum the previous night. It often unsettled him and on this occasion he was worse. When Carol asked him to start the maths they were doing, he dug his heels in and refused, saying that she wasn't his mum and couldn't tell him what to do.

Later in the lesson he decided to get up and go and stand by the window. Carol directed him to return to his seat but he ignored her. She gave him one minute of take-up time then made it an official warning, recording it on the behaviour sheet. He stared at her defiantly as she started the timer for a further one minute that would lead to a yellow card. Then he blew. He turned and made a beeline for the door. She moved to intercept him but he kicked her in the shins as she tried to block his way. Carol knew she shouldn't take this but she was feeling low because of the incident with her mum.

'John, stop or you will regret it,' she warned.

'No!' he shouted and pushed his face hard up against the glazed door. Then he turned round and ran across to the side of the room; he knew he wasn't going to get the door open with her leaning on it. He crawled under the bench against the wall and lay there with his back to everyone. Carol realised she was getting angry and decided to stop. She turned to the support assistant and asked her to get Ms Stevens, the deputy.

A few minutes later, Ms Stevens arrived and took over dealing with John. She managed to get him to come out from under the bench and go to the office with her. She talked to him about his visit to his mum and managed to calm him down. Then she changed the subject to mortorbikes, something she knew he was interested in. Within minutes he was talking animatedly about his uncle's bike. Eventually she concluded the discussion by helping him see that he had done wrong. He apologised then went back to the classroom and said sorry to Carol.

On reflection, Carol felt she had handled the incident very well. Admittedly, she should not have threatened John and that was something she still needed to improve, but when it came to pulling herself back and sending for help, she felt she had done the right thing.

WHEN SHOULD YOU RAISE YOUR VOICE?

When you shout you condone shouting. If you do it to get attention, that makes it okay for the children to do it. It can be a challenge to find other ways of getting attention in a lesson where a healthy level of discussion is required. There are various ways depending on the age of the pupils. You could count down:

'Three, two, one, stop. Pens down. Look at me.'

You could give a signal like calling out 'one minute', ringing a small bell or perhaps putting a large card on the board. Raising your voice to reprimand a pupil will lessen the effect when you really need to use a loud command to prevent a serious incident or break up a fight. Only use a raised voice when you really need to and then only to gain the attention of a pupil. As soon as you have got their attention, lower your voice back to normal and adopt a more controlled tone.

Voice control is a useful exercise to try at home. Say something loudly then follow it with another sentence said quietly:

'Martin, put the hammer down!' (*say it loudly*)

'Now come over here please.' (*say it quietly*)

Simulated anger can have its uses in your repertoire of responses in order to emphasise a point. Again, it should be used very sparingly to maintain the effect. The secret is to raise your voice in the same way as if you are angry:

'Throwing your bag is wrong!' (*say it loudly*)

Then modulate your voice back to normal:

'Now go and pick it up and bring it to me.' (*say it normally*)

This shows that you are still in control and have not succumbed to your emotions. Teachers who have a problem dealing with their own anger will find it a useful skill to help them with their self-control. Ultimately, the aim is to use an assertive voice instead of losing your temper.

HUMOUR

Some people believe that teaching is like acting. The classroom is the stage, the lesson is the script, the pupils are the audience and the teacher is the actor. Collectively they become the performance. This is a useful way of viewing one aspect of teaching. The upfront, whole-class part of the lesson can indeed become a performance. This is not all that a teacher does but it enables you to develop a rapport with your class.

Humour can be a key part of the performance because it helps break down barriers. A funny story or silly sound effect can turn a mundane piece of work or potentially tricky concept into a memorable event that children will retain. A well-placed comment or joke can take the heat out of a difficult situation (Case Study 3.5).

Case Study 3.5

Max was keen on football and had put himself forward to organise and run the football skills club after school. He also organised small games for any of the boys and girls who wanted to play at break time. He found that it helped him to manage their behaviour during the other times of the week and it had certainly helped him to develop better relationships with the children in his class. He got a group of children together to work out the teams and was talking to them about their tactics when one of the boys stood back and exclaimed, 'Phew, your breath smells, Sir!' Max was quite taken aback and for a few seconds he was stunned into silence. Eventually he responded in a very quick-witted way. 'I'm sorry, I was taking part in the International Curry Championships last night and some of the dishes were explosive!'

Finding humour helped to lighten the situation and showed he had the capacity to make fun of himself. It also gave him the chance to get away behind the smokescreen of laughter and he felt better even though they had levelled a harsh personal comment at him. Imagine how it might have gone if Max had taken offence and got angry about the comment. He might have spoken to the boy in a harsh way, told him not to make personal comments or reprimanded him for something he was doing wrong as a means of getting back at him. The boy would have felt a sense of injustice, because the teacher's breath did actually smell. What the boy did wrong was to speak to Max as though he had equal status.

Children tend to like teachers who can share a joke with them and are confident enough to laugh at themselves. Deliberately doing something wrong then getting the children to find the mistake and explain why can be a very useful and enjoyable way of checking for learning. Ridiculing personal characteristics or possessions also helps to build bridges: 'Is that your old crate in the car park, Miss?' 'Do you mean the blue, metallic hatchback, 0 to 60 in five minutes, not bad eh?'

Making light of things that children do can be a good way of showing you do not get wound up by the small stuff. For example, a child aims a screwed-up piece of paper at the wastepaper bin but misses. The teacher says, 'Let me know when you are ready for a trial for the basketball team, Shelbey. Now come and pick it up and put it in the bin, thanks,' followed by a smile.

Not all teachers see themselves in the role of the performer and capable of using humour in the classroom. You may feel your personality does not fit with the extrovert role. But you need not be an extrovert to use humour. It's about acting like an extrovert and going into a role for the duration of the lesson. It requires you to step outside your own self-image and be someone else (Case Study 3.6).

Case Study 3.6

Alex had been teaching Year 6 classes since he joined the school two years ago and was really enjoying the work. He was not an outgoing person but was pushing himself to try to do more teacher-led activities. He had recently read about hot seating, a method that involved the teacher going into role as a character from the lesson being taught and then answering the children's questions as that person. He really liked the idea because he could be someone he wasn't and it didn't matter. The class could get more from the lesson and he was sure they would enjoy it.

He was doing an art project about people in action and was going to introduce Pop Art. One of the artists he wanted to include was Jackson Pollock, the American action painter. He came up with the idea of combining action painting with music. The children would create pieces of work using the beat of the music as the stimulus and film themselves painting. They would edit the clips to produce a short film of the class in action making their paintings. This would then become the artwork. Action painting is great fun and can be exhilarating to produce and watch being done.

Alex told his children that next lesson there would be a visiting artist coming. He got himself some American-looking gear and prepared to be Jackson Pollock. He produced a special flyer that announced Jackson Pollock would be visiting the school and named the class and the teacher. The flyer gave useful background information that the children would need to know. It also included some colour reproductions of Pollock's most well-known pictures. On the day, Alex got a support assistant to begin and end the lesson so he could go and change. He made his excuses to the children and explained that he had a meeting to go to but Jackson Pollock, who was in the UK for a week gathering inspiration for a new work, would be staying with them for the lesson. He did not tell them that Pollock was dead, because they would see it was him after a while. A few minutes later he returned to the room dressed in an old sweater, baseball cap and shades.

He introduced himself in an American accent and explained his action painting technique. The beat of the music would inspire the mark-making process. If they heard slow music, they should make lazy, undulating, open marks; with a medium tempo their marks would be thicker and more angular; and a fast tempo would give rise to harsh, jagged, aggressive lines in bold colours. He also explained the filming process and the need to download and rough-edit the pictures and sound by the end of the lesson. When he had finished talking, the class got going. The camera was a simple design for primary school children. It had its own software to make editing a very quick and easy process that could be done in minutes. At the end he set up a session to preview the film and allow the whole class to discuss the results and ask questions.

Eventually he left and Alex returned. He used the plenary to get the children to tell him what they had been doing, show their pictures and film and talk about Jackson Pollock. This worked brilliantly because the children were so absorbed. They had so much to say and none of them let on that they knew Alex was Pollock. They kept up the act and colluded with Alex. He thought that was rather nice. The lesson was a resounding success and they said they really enjoyed it, especially doing the action painting.

Alex was pleased, as he had done something that was difficult for him. He was not usually outgoing but as Jackson Pollock he felt he had really become a different person. He had done and said things that he wouldn't have imagined doing as himself.

MODELLING GOOD BEHAVIOUR

Modelling good behaviour is a powerful means of securing the behaviour you seek and making sure the children know how you want things done. The children will use what you do and how you do it as their standard, so if you value good manners then you should demonstrate good manners. This means avoiding examples of bad manners:

- *Scrawling on work*: having taken a child's book to look at, the teacher might scrawl corrections all over their work.
- *Thoughtlessly changing what a child has done*: a child may have been writing a poem in a brief style to give a staccato feel when read aloud. Unaware of this intention, the teacher may tell the child to use longer, more complex sentences.
- *Touching a child*: some children may not want their teacher to touch them while commenting on their work.
- *Ordering children around*: this is common in many schools, especially when larger numbers are involved. If a group of children are not queuing for lunch and a teacher starts ordering them to get in line, in twos, etc., they might reply that the teacher is not being very polite. This will allow them to shift the emphasis from their inability to queue to the secondary issue of manners.

The best approach is to use basic manners with children of all ages. Model good behaviour with 'please', 'thank you' and requests rather than orders:

'Can I see how far you have got please?'

'Please may I read your introduction?'

'Would you like me to read through and make some notes on the work or on a separate sheet?'

It is well worth explaining your marking policy and how you will correct their work during the first week of taking a new group so that everyone in the class is aware of how you like to do things. Try to draw attention to the children who are behaving in the way you want them to. Sitting, waiting patiently, putting bags away tidily, whatever it is, praise good behaviour wherever you can. Any children who are not showing this good behaviour can then learn from the situation.

PRIMARY AND SECONDARY BEHAVIOUR

The skill is to address primary behaviour and ignore secondary behaviour; secondary behaviour will draw you into side issues:

'We have a rule of following directions, Harry. The direction was only two at the sink at once.' (rule reminder)

'It is not your turn yet, so go back to your seat please.' (redirection)

The teacher turns away to attend to the needs of the other children. Harry is expected to do as he is asked and is given some take-up time, as children do not always respond immediately they receive an instruction. Some need more time than others to process the request.

There will always be some children who will ignore the redirection and answer back:

'I thought Simon had finished and was drying his hands.'

There will be the temptation to rise to the bait and over-service a comment like this, but you need to refocus the child back to your direction:

'The rule is only two at the sink. Return to your seat and I will tell you when you can go to the sink and wash your palette.'

Secondary behaviour includes the way a child acts and their tone of voice as well as what they say. An arrogant or deliberately defiant posture can be infuriating but the important thing is to stay calm and unaffected. You may think 'How dare he act like that?' or 'Who does she think she is talking to in that way?' but reacting to those thoughts will only make the incidents messy. The children will get the attention they are seeking and a shift will take place from the rules, in your control, to the uncertainties of individual personalities, not in your control.

A common cause of secondary behaviour comes when a teacher is too much of an authoritarian and issues orders. Most of the class will probably follow the order but there will usually be one or two who do not like being told what to do or are looking for a means of expressing their frustrations as an outlet for other problems in their lives. They will defy the teacher in a challenging way that usually results in a conflict over their rudeness or something they said, not the original reason. The child ends up digging themselves into a hole and the teacher cannot offer a way out (Case Study 3.7).

Case Study 3.7

Sam was a Year 2 pupil with a mixed-up home life. His mum and dad had separated and now he had a stepdad. His grown-up sister had married and had a baby but things had gone wrong, so she had recently moved back with them. Sam saw his real dad every other weekend and really enjoyed his time with him. His dad doted on him and would often buy him a toy during his stay. This caused all sorts of problems at home because Sam would get very attached to it and wanted to take it everywhere. He would bring it to school and usually put it in his tray but the last time he did that, another child took it out to look at and broke it.

So this time he put it on the table in front of him. The teacher noticed it and called across the room, 'Sam, where should we put things we bring in from home?' Sam knew it should go in the tray but he wasn't going to do it. This was special. It was a Teenage Mutant Hero Turtle with all the weapons and if you pressed a button on the back, it did a somersault and landed back on its feet.

'In the tray, Miss Norton.'

He picked it up and made as if to do what she said. She turned and carried on dealing with the absence notes and marking the register. A few minutes later, when she had finished, she noticed the toy on his table again. 'That toy should be in your tray. I have told you once!'

'I don't want to put it there. Someone might steal it.'

'Of course they won't. Now be a good boy and put it away quickly.'

'No, I want it here.'

'I am waiting.'

She stood over Sam and glared at him. He did not like the way she did that, so he turned around and stared at the wall. Miss Norton did not like his response. It was disrespectful. 'Do not turn your back on me, Sam. That's very rude.'

'I can if I want.'

'Turn round now! Don't be so rude.'

The teacher is getting dragged into an unnecessary conflict. Sam has dug in and has no way out. Soon he will be removed and the deputy head will have to deal with him. The teacher had no way out either, because she had gone down the win-lose route by insisting that Sam obeyed her orders. She could have explained to him that the toy would be safe and if necessary put it in her drawer. If he continued not to trust her, there would be a consequence later. Then she could have left him to think about his options and make his mind up. The conflict would have been avoided and she would not have got involved in his secondary behaviour. Sam may even have decided to comply once he had some time to think about it.

Take-up time allows the child to reflect on the situation, to weigh up the consequences and calm down. This will ensure the child doesn't use it as a means of wasting time and getting out of doing the work. Whatever method you choose, lost time needs to be made up and this is something you should discuss with the child once things have calmed down. Take-up time also allows some space for the child to look for a way of saving face. When they choose to comply, there will be less damage to their pride because they are not being made to give in. Resolving any conflict depends on minimising damage to the child's pride. This is even more important once they move on to secondary behaviour.

WHEN TO INTERVENE

There are several schools of thought on when to intervene. One is that the teacher uses their judgement and tactically ignores minor disruptions to maintain the flow of the lesson. Praise and positive affirmation are given to the pupils who are behaving in the desired way at the same time as a child who is being tactically ignored. The child will learn from his peers who are modelling the correct behaviour. The flaw in this method is the inconsistency. A child who is spoken to about a specific incident may plead that the teacher did not do anything when another child did the same thing earlier.

The other option is to pick up every incident when it happens. In that way, the children will know that they can never get away with anything. The difficulty in this approach is that the teacher has to be extremely vigilant and there will be times when they will miss incidents. It is also very demanding and may turn out to be time-consuming, especially with difficult classes.

The decision must lie with each individual teacher. Sometimes teachers may have extra members of staff in the room with them if the class is very difficult or there are children with special needs. In this case the second method could be more advantageous. Teachers in pupil referral units may use this method because the children need retraining, so a tight consistent model is essential. For most other types of class, the teacher's judgement will be the most practical solution. The rest of this section will be based on this approach.

Minor distractions such as tapping, leaning on a chair, chatting and chewing should be dealt with unobtrusively to prevent the flow being disrupted and avoid attracting attention from the rest of the class. Wait for an opportune moment when the class are engaged in the task then have a quiet word with the child followed by a thank you; turn away expecting it to be done. When words are not enough, a warning or consequence should be given with the minimum of fuss. It is very easy to get cross with a child and show you are angry by saying things like this:

'Right! That's a warning!'

It is far better to remain calm, put a tick on the behaviour sheet and address the child in a normal voice:

'Lawrence, you were talking during silent work, so I am giving you a warning.'

'Lawrence, you have a warning for talking during silent work and have chosen to continue to talk, so you need to go to the time-out desk for five minutes.'

The intervention is made in a direct way. There is no ambiguity and the child is expected to comply. On the occasions when he doesn't, the teacher must ignore the secondary behaviour and avoid saying things like:

'How dare you ignore me!'

'Who do you think you are?'

'That's no way to speak to a teacher.'

Just refocus the child back to the rule that has been broken and remind him of the consequence for not complying. Children do not like to be threatened. Make your challenges unthreatening by being polite and assertive (Case Study 3.8).

Case Study 3.8

Ellie had been dreaming of her birthday for weeks. She was counting the days on a calendar at home, crossing off each one at bedtime just before she turned out the lights. The big day finally came and she got her present, her pride and joy. The new Barbie doll was finally hers. She brought it to school to show her friends because she was so proud of it and wanted the others to share in her pleasure. She knew the rule was that no toys were allowed in school but she was so carried away with talking about it and letting her friends take turns to brush its hair that before she knew it, she was in the classroom. Besides, it didn't seem right to leave it outside in her tray.

When Sharon came in and saw the doll on her desk, she was rather angry because she had only just told the class that toys were not allowed. There had been so many problems with toys and jewellery that the head had decided to ban them.

A letter had gone home telling the parents of the change and asking them to support the new rule. The assumption was that they would be able to get their children to comply without any difficulty.

How not to deal with this

The head had the authority and was able to get a child to give up a toy or take out an earring but the rest of the staff didn't always have that success. Some of the children could be extremely stubborn and would not part with their possessions. Sharon walked over to Ellie's table.

Teacher   Ellie, you know the rule about toys.
Child   No, Miss, what is it?
Teacher   They should be left outside the room in your tray.
Child   I didn't want to, Miss. She will be lonely.
Teacher   No she won't. Now give it to me.
Child   No, I don't want to. I want to keep her. I got her for my birthday.
Teacher   I'm not going to ask you again. Now give it to me!
Child   You're always picking on me. I'm not doing anything wrong. Leave me alone.
Teacher   You'll have to go to Mrs Beaumont if you don't give it to me now!

Sharon has failed. She got dragged into a conflict and the child ended up trying to imply that she was picking on her. The end result was that the teacher had to pass the matter on to Mrs Beaumont, the head.

The positive, proactive approach

Teacher   Ellie, will you come here please. You can bring your doll. I need to talk to you. What's her name?
Child   Barbie, Miss.
Teacher   That's a lovely outfit, have you got any others?
Child   Yes, Miss. I've got an evening dress for her as well.
Teacher   I bet it's beautiful. Now will you put it on the table and let's talk.

At this point, the child may object but you should be insistent. Explain that you want to talk and you are not asking her to put it in the tray yet. Eventually, with persistence, this will happen because the child knows she has broken the rule.

Teacher   Now, Ellie, what is the rule about toys?

Let her explain the rule to you then ask her what she should do in the future, e.g. put it in her tray or leave it at home. Slowly stand up while explaining why you have the rule – to prevent it being stolen, becoming a distraction, etc. Go to where the toy is and pick it up. Reassure and praise the child for getting it right and tell her that she can collect it from you at home time. This prevents a clash and is a very effective way of dealing with toys, phones, jewellery, cards and games. You could also telephone or send a note home to the parents explaining the rule and what you have done and requesting their support to help avoid this problem in future.

The other important factor in determining when to intervene is whether to defer dealing with the issue. Some incidents can be dealt with by telling the child you are aware of their behaviour, noting it then dealing with it later on. This allows the lesson to continue and gives you time to think about the incident. Making a note will ensure you do not forget. Incidents that may cause serious injury or endanger another child must be dealt with immediately.

DEVELOP A BEHAVIOUR CODE

The scenarios included so far often depend on a well-thought-out behaviour code that includes clear rules backed up by rewards and consequences. Developing the behaviour code is the next step in managing behaviour. It should be done with the children to ensure they know why it is needed and are prepared to support it. Chapter 4 begins this process by considering what the rules should be.

SUMMARY

- Developing a positive style involves a range of factors, including the teaching space, personal appearance, specific modes of address and non-verbal communication.
- Tailoring your language to match the preferred learning styles of the pupils will enable better communication and more effective learning.
- Model the behaviour you want the children to learn.
- A powerful way of teaching the children how to behave involves tactically ignoring them when they do not follow your directions and praising them when they correct themselves.
- Helping a child to build their self-esteem is very important. Give praise and reassure the child that they are doing something right to reinforce their confidence.
- Humour can be used to take the heat out of potentially difficult situations.
- Feigning anger on rare occasions will show you have teeth and are in control of your emotions.
- Becoming a performer will enable you to adopt different personas during whole-class teaching sessions, and this will enhance the learning experience.
- Focus on the primary behaviour and do not get sucked into responding to secondary issues. Timing is crucial. Knowing how to intervene and when to challenge a child is essential in maintaining the flow of a lesson.

4 THE BEHAVIOUR CODE

WHY HAVE A CODE?

Surely you cannot plan how a class will behave? Anything could happen. A child may talk during silent work, throw something, hit someone, set off a fire alarm, etc. A badly behaved class is one of the crosses we will probably have to bear at some time in our career. Or is it? Of course, we are not able to control the children completely so that incidents like these never happen but we can reduce the likelihood of them occurring. Furthermore, and more importantly, we can plan how we will react to incidents. We can choose to respond assertively and fairly, or we can be irrational and unfair. The behaviour code is a carefully thought-out set of guidelines and responses that will help children to choose responsible behaviour leading to greater self-esteem. Just as lesson plans enable you to deliver the curriculum, a behaviour code helps you to manage the children. It's a sort of game plan.

Teaching is a very challenging job that often requires us to make thousands of on-the-spot decisions every day. We deal with the needs of up to thirty children during a lesson as we endeavour to teach them new things. A great deal of time and effort is spent planning how we will teach particular subjects, topics and new concepts. But how much time have you spent thinking about how you will help your pupils behave appropriately? Have you thought about how you will tackle the disruptions and conflicts that hinder you from teaching and the children from learning? The successful teacher plans lessons with teaching styles that reinforce the desired behaviour. This is achieved by teaching the rules and positively acknowledging good behaviour through what is said, together with activities that carefully match the range of preferred learning styles of each child.

The behaviour code is a means of communicating exactly what you expect from your pupils and what they can expect in return. It lays down the parameters of responsible behaviour and details what the consequences will be for a child who steps over the line. The purpose of the code is to achieve a classroom that is an orderly, organised, safe and happy place where everyone can learn. A behaviour code will vary according to the groups you teach and will be the blueprint for your own style of classroom management. It will help you plan your approach in advance by

- Being positive and using encouraging language and actions
- Sharing your expectations when you introduce it into your lessons
- Working out your responses to common problems in advance.

Thinking through each of these points and developing your own style will help your pupils learn to choose the right behaviour. It will also help you become more confident in what you do as a teacher.

THE SCHOOL APPROACH

A measure of a good school is the way the behaviour is managed. It may be that you work in a good school with a well-disciplined environment and the children understand what is required. Even so, you may still encounter very challenging behaviour from time to time and will need to use the procedures. Try to imagine what it would be like without a system that supports you. You would feel isolated and left to your own devices (Case Study 4.1).

Case Study 4.1

Karen was a new teacher to the school. She had been teaching for two years in another school. When she saw the post of literacy coordinator advertised, she jumped at the chance because she could take on more responsibility and put some of her own ideas into practice. She spent the rest of the summer term tying up the loose ends in her current school then went off on the summer break with an excited feeling about the new job.

She was able to go into the school and prepare her room during the holiday, so she got a lot done before the start of the term. This enabled her to concentrate some more of her time on the coordination work. The first day of term finally came and her new Year 6 pupils filed in full of holiday chatter. Things went well for the first two weeks then she sensed a change happening. The pupils seemed less responsive to her directions. In fact, she felt some were almost defiant.

Her responses did not seem to have any effect. She began to get depressed about the situation and found she couldn't sleep. She tried sending pupils outside but it got to the point where one boy just refused to budge and Karen did not know what to do. Sitting at home, half-heartedly marking books, she broke down and burst into tears. By half-term the class was completely unmanageable. Parents were ringing up and coming to complain. She found she was having to defend herself from quite aggressive criticism. She did not know what to do or who to turn to. A terrific burden of failure bore down on her and she wished she had never come to the school.

Karen needed support but she did not know how to obtain it. The other teachers had all been at the school for quite a while and did not have problems, so all they could offer were tips on what to say and the tone of voice to use. A school is only as good as its weakest link and if situations like this are to be avoided, the links need to be stronger. There needs to be an induction programme to support new teachers. A proper staged response needs to be available. Karen needed a behaviour code that would help her to deal with the incidents in her class before she had to refer them to a more senior member of staff.

THE CODE AND ITS OBJECTIVES

What will a behaviour code do for you and your pupils? A behaviour code will help you establish the right atmosphere in the classroom so you will be able to teach. Children in a school environment will often try to test the rules to find out where the boundaries lie and what they can get away with. They will put considerable thought and energy into thinking up creative and elaborate schemes to go off task or evade lessons. Read *Learning to Labour* (Willis, 1977) to get an insight into this. We need to think about how we will deal with these events in a positive, assertive way. Children should be redirected to the task in a calm, considered way. If you do not have a code, you are forced to think on your feet. You will have to decide what to do when it happens. You will find yourself reacting to the situation instead of using a preplanned set of responses designed for that incident. On-the-spot reactions may lead to inconsistencies in your approach and there is also the risk of irrational action. The children will be quick to comment on things they believe are unfair, and if they are ignored, they will become frustrated and possibly angry (Case Study 4.2).

Case Study 4.2

Stuart had been teaching for one term. Things had gone well and he was enjoying what he was doing. However, as the year wore on, the class began to become more of a handful. It wasn't helped by the influx of new children. He had three join his class after Christmas. One was from a traveller family and could hardly read. The other two could barely speak any English and did not have any support in the room to help them understand what was going on. Their needs obviously stretched Stuart to his limits but he was just managing. The two Russian children were picking up some bits of language and he had managed to teach them some rudimentary words using books he had borrowed from the nursery.

It came to a head one day in February while he was doing some textiles work with the class. One of the boys called John had got up to get some coloured threads. On his way across the room he caught his leg on a chair, or that's what it looked like but he claimed later that he had been deliberately tripped by the traveller boy, Ewan. John turned and thumped Ewan, which made him fall and prick himself with a needle.

At this point, Stuart intervened. 'Go back to your place. I did not give you permission to get up.'

'Yes, but I needed some more thread and that little **** tripped me.'

'No I didn't, you four-eyed git.'

'Right, that's it. You are both in detention this lunchtime.'

'That's not fair,' protested Ewan. 'I never went anywhere near him and he called me a name.'

Stuart was getting very impatient and did not like the way Ewan had challenged his decision. The rest of the class had stopped what they were doing and were enjoying the show. One of them called out, 'I saw it, Sir. Ewan put his foot out just as . . .'

'Don't interfere.'

'But . . .'

'Right, you can join him in detention this lunchtime.'

The whole incident was escalating. Stuart was beginning to act irrationally and letting his emotions cloud his judgement. His temper was preventing him from being fair to his pupils. He had failed to set up the rules for his class and it had resulted in a pupil wandering and

causing an incident that needed a decisive response. He had done the right thing in placing them in detention but he was probably shocked by their outburst and his adrenalin level was high. It resulted in him giving a consequence to another child that was completely out of proportion and possibly even unjustified.

What Stuart needed was a behaviour code that communicated his expectations to the pupils. He had no systems for dealing with the incident and had failed to use a staged response at the end.

THE BEHAVIOUR CODE WILL HELP YOUR PUPILS TO LEARN

Children do not come to school trained in how to behave properly. Many will come from homes where the expectations are not clear. Parents have different standards and levels of authority in the home environment. Sometimes they may appeal to the school for help because their child is out of control at home. So assume that your pupils will need to be taught how to behave in your room. They should learn the rules and adhere to them if you are to maintain an orderly class. A well-behaved class is the bottom line. You cannot teach effectively and your pupils will certainly find it hard to learn if they are distracted by one or two individuals. Every child has the right to learn and when one child misbehaves, he is infringing the rights of the other children (Case Study 4.3).

Case Study 4.3

Marion was given the task of teaching mathematics to the bottom set of Year 5. She was trying to improve her teaching of numeracy and this seemed like a great opportunity. The class was fairly good but there were one or two boys who were certainly going to be a handful. They already had a reputation from the other class and last year their form teacher had found them challenging but had managed them well. Marion was having trouble after a few lessons and couldn't seem to find a way of getting them to settle. They would begin the work and then find a reason to start talking and mucking about.

Marion found she was calling for assistance more and more, and the other children in the class were getting fed up with the disruption. Eventually the parents started to complain. They would come in and insist on talking to Marion. She seemed to be meeting a parent every day and her time was being eaten up. Instead of preparing for lessons, she found herself fending off one criticism after another. It was very stressful and she often came out of the meetings feeling angry, fed up and sad. This had an adverse effect on her teaching. She did not prepare her lessons as diligently and her patience diminished.

Marion needed a much clearer classroom code, a code based on agreed rules with rewards and consequences that every pupil had contributed to and accepted. This would help her respond to their behaviour fairly and dispassionately. The consequences could be staged depending on the seriousness of the incident and she would be able to keep control of herself and prevent things from escalating out of proportion.

THE BEHAVIOUR CODE WILL LEAD TO A SAFE ENVIRONMENT FOR EVERYONE

Put thirty children together in a room and you have a potential problem. Some of them will probably not want to be there but know they have to. They will not always get on with each other and will disagree. Some will wind up others for the sport. You may not notice friction occurring until it is too late and the flashpoint has been reached. How can this be avoided? Your code will communicate the rules clearly to the class, offering them a safe, calm environment in which to learn. Fighting, swearing and bullying are unacceptable and your plan will reinforce that. Your pupils will know that everyone's safety and well-being are being safeguarded.

A behaviour code will enable you to gain the support of pupils, parents and other staff. It shows you have thought how you are going to manage behaviour in your lessons. Parents will be more supportive because they will know you are endeavouring to help their children. Colleagues will be prepared to offer assistance if they know you have exhausted your own strategies first and they will realise the situation must be getting serious.

WHAT DOES THE BEHAVIOUR CODE ACTUALLY LOOK LIKE?

The behaviour plan consists of three elements:

- Rules and directions
- Rewards
- Consequences.

These elements will vary according to the age of the children and the conditions you work under. However, the basic principles remain the same. Figure 4.1 shows a typical behaviour code.

Behaviour Code for Infant and Junior Pupils

Rules
Keep hands, feet, objects to yourself
No teasing or name-calling
Follow directions at all times
Speak in a nice voice

Rewards
Praise
Stickers, house points, credits, etc.
First choice during choosing time or free time
First in line for break, lunch, end of school
Made a monitor
Postcards and letters sent home to parents
Telephone call home to parents
Have lunch with the teacher

Consequences
The first time a pupil breaks a rule
    Warning recorded in the behaviour log
The second time
    Five-minute timeout away from the group
The third time
    Last in line for break, lunch, home or choosing time
The fourth time
    Stay in during break or lunch or 5 minutes after school
The fifth time
    Teacher calls parents
The sixth time
    Sent out of the room to the next stage in the hierarchy, e.g. head of the key stage, deputy or head teacher
Serious incident
    Sent to the head teacher

Exclusion from class
A pupil who is sent out of the class must apologise and state what s/he will do to put things right and how s/he will behave in the future. A letter will also be sent home explaining why the pupil was internally excluded

Figure 4.1 *Behaviour code for infant and junior pupils*

WHY DO WE NEED RULES?

Why do we need rules? The reason is very simple. Rules enable us to live in peace together. They allow us to go about our daily business, safe in the knowledge that we are free to do as we please as long as it is within the law. The rules protect our rights. The same applies in schools. Every child has the right to enter a classroom without fear of being teased, called names, racially abused, etc. The rules in your classroom protect these rights and make it clear to everyone where the boundaries are. The rules will also protect your rights as a teacher. Yes, you have rights too. You have the right to carry out the responsibilities of a teacher in safety. You have the right to teach and direct what goes on in your lessons. Fair rules are part of an orderly, well-managed classroom.

Children have their own perceptions of what is acceptable. They may differ from yours, so you will need to communicate your rules. Generally, children want to know what they can and cannot do and will respect the teachers who set fair rules and enforce them consistently. Do not assume that the children will behave when you take on a new class. They will see you as a challenge, someone to test to find out whether or not the boundaries can be pushed back. In the worst case this could develop into a battle for supremacy (Case Study 4.4).

Case Study 4.4

Ann had started out as a learning assistant. She enjoyed working with the children so much that she decided to train as a teacher once her own children were in secondary school. After several years of studying on an access course and teacher training, she finally reached her goal. She was looking forward to her new job and had been given a Year 4 class that enabled her to get some experience without having to worry about Standard Assessment Tests (SATs). The term began and she was full of enthusiasm for what the future would hold.

Everything went according to plan; she learned the names of all her pupils and started to get to know them. She soon settled into the routines and rhythms of the school and started to plan ahead for Christmas but things did not go as smoothly during the autumn. A number of pupils began to misbehave and her responses were to tell them to sit down, be quiet, turn round and get on with their work, but they did not comply. One group of boys took to entering the room each morning chanting 'Arsenal' and clapping their hands loudly. She felt she was losing control and didn't know what to do.

The teacher in the room next to hers was very nice and tried to help by explaining how her own behaviour code worked. Ann tried the consequences but gave up after two days. She was becoming depressed and knew the pupils were getting the better of her. The children in the adjacent room were distracted by the unruly behaviour and shouting that came from Ann's class. Some of them even asked whether there was actually a teacher in there, because they couldn't believe that children could act that way during lessons.

Ann had assumed that her class would behave. She underestimated the class because they were only Year 4. She thought she could handle any problems easily and decided not to commit valuable time to establishing the rules within the room. Some of the pupils put Ann to the test and discovered that she did not have the authority a teacher would normally have. Things deteriorated as more and more pupils strayed off task and lost respect for her. Unfortunately, this is typical of many situations teachers find themselves in. They assume that behaviour will not be an issue then find they have problems because they have ignored the establishment phase of putting rules and expectations in place.

HOW DO DIRECTIONS DIFFER FROM RULES?

Rules remain in force through the whole day. For example, if there is a rule of no swearing, the children must abide by it whatever they are doing. Directions vary according to the activity or context. You cannot have a rule that says 'no getting out of your seat' because it would be impossible to enforce. Children need to collect and return resources in some lessons. You need a specific direction instead, e.g. 'raise your hand and wait for permission if you need to leave your seat'. This will enable pupils to leave their seats and you can control when and how many at a time. Directions are given at the start of each lesson and the children should learn them. One of the class rules is 'follow directions'. Therefore any child leaving their seat will have broken the rule and face the consequences outlined in your behaviour plan. Directions enable you to introduce a range of working methods and still manage the class effectively. Rules and directions used together will help children understand the boundaries you have set.

INTRODUCING THE RULES

Pupils should be involved in deciding the rules so they can have some ownership of them. Then they will be more likely to take responsibility for their behaviour. Rules provide a structure that can be very liberating for children. Once they know the boundaries, they can be more motivated to behave, which in turn will raise their self-esteem. Children will be more inclined to learn the rules and use them if there are not too many. Three or four are about enough. Make sure they apply at all times and to every activity.

There are lots of rules in schools and you will adopt them in your classroom. Here are some typical school rules:

- Uniforms must be neat and tidy.
- Line up in twos outside the room.
- Walk in the corridors.
- Do not leave the room without permission.
- Address the teacher as . . .

Canter and Canter (1992, p. 51) describe these as 'observable rules' because the behaviour can be seen clearly. Children who see the correct behaviour are much more likely to understand the rule and adopt it. Rules like 'no unnecessary talking' or 'be kind to other pupils' are very good goals to aim for but are vague and ambiguous, making them difficult to enforce.

MAKE THE RULES CLEAR, POSITIVE AND FAIR

Rules need to be easy to understand and not open to questioning. When you begin to write your rules, state what behaviour is acceptable or what is unacceptable:

- Keep your hands and feet to yourself.
- No swearing.

Frame the rules positively wherever you can. 'Keep your hands and feet to yourself' means no hitting, pinching or spiteful contact.

Rules are designed to help you manage your class, but unjust rules lead to resentment. Encourage the children to suggest some rules. Many children will have a good idea how to behave and will enjoy the opportunity to contribute. Write their ideas on the board as they think of them, discussing why each one is important.

CAN YOUR RULES BE ENFORCED?

Can your rules be enforced? Of course they can, as long as you avoid rules that cannot be maintained. Teachers often start out well, helping the children put together class rules and publishing them on the wall. Then they fall into disuse because the teacher discovers they are difficult to enforce at all times, e.g. 'stay in your seat'.

What happens when a child needs to wash a brush, get a sheet of paper or compare notes with someone else? You could find yourself breaking off from an explanation with a group of pupils to attend to a request for something trivial. The aim is for the class to develop responsible behaviour. A well-managed class should offer children some freedom to attend to their own needs. You may want to control movement around the class during the establishment phase. Eventually the children will know what you expect and you can relax some of the directions.

Rules apply at all times so they can be consistent. How do we deal with the specific behaviour required for certain activities?

GIVING DIRECTIONS

Directions are instructions and are specific to the activity the class is doing. They vary with the activities, so they cannot be enforceable all day. Rules are absolute and should be adhered to whatever is going on, e.g. 'no swearing or name-calling'. Directions are given at the start of each new activity, so do not assume the children will know how to behave for different activities. Give children clear instructions and keep them brief.

WHAT DIRECTIONS ARE NEEDED?

Begin by thinking about the lesson and what you want the class to do. List the routines and practices specific to the activities, e.g. a test. You will want the children to be silent, keep facing the front, eyes on their own papers and hands up when they need something. Here are some of the activities you may want to think about:

- Teacher-led lessons where you stand at the board
- Work done in small groups
- Envoys working between four and five groups
- Practical sessions with pupils working alone or in pairs
- Hot seating involving the whole class
- Class tests, written and oral.

How will you want the children to behave? There are several options, so you need to take control. If you do not assert yourself, the kids will. So tell them. Make it perfectly clear what you want. There are also many routines before the start of your teaching. Here is a list of things you could focus on:

- Lining up
- Coming into the room
- Getting ready for the start of a lesson
- Responding to questions
- Working with other pupils
- Using resources, apparatus and equipment
- Using a computer
- Cleaning up after practical subjects
- Moving to the carpet area and back to the tables
- Leaving the room.

Consider every activity the children will be doing and make sure all activities are included. Your aim is to help the children recognise the need for rules and directions and adopt them in their daily routines. Then they will be able to behave well whatever they are doing.

Keep directions simple so they are easy to understand. Have only a few directions so that everybody will remember them. Imagine you are doing the activity yourself and be alert for when poor behaviour could occur. Then spend some time listing the directions for the activity. Here are some examples.

Lining up outside the room

1. Stand still in single file.
2. Face the front.
3. Talk quietly or no talking.

Entering the room

1. Wait outside in line until you are told to enter.
2. Hang up your coats, put lunch boxes away.
3. Go straight to your place and take out books, pens, etc.
4. Sit with arms folded.
5. No talking.

Registration

1. Sit in seats facing the front.
2. No talking.
3. Answer 'good morning', 'good afternoon' or 'present' when your name is called.

Teaching an upfront, whole-class lesson

1. Put everything away except pen and paper.
2. Look at me. Silence.
3. Raise your hand and wait till I give you permission if you wish to speak.
4. Listen while I am speaking or while another pupil is speaking to me.

Working in groups

1. Stay in your seat; raise your hand if you need something.
2. Do not shout; talk quietly to each other.
3. When I give the signal to stop work, put pens on the desk and face the front.

Art, science or technology activity

1. Stay at your place; raise your hand if you need something.
2. Only one person at a sink, power tool, etc.
3. Clean and put away all the equipment, tools or paints you have used.

Class test or examination

1. Enter the examination room in silence. Do not talk until the teacher gives you permission.
2. Leave bags and coats outside or at the front of the room.
3. Sit facing the front, eyes on your own paper.
4. If you need something, raise your hand and wait in silence until a teacher comes to you.
5. Leave in silence.

Walking in corridors

1. Walk quietly, no running.
2. Walk in single file and keep to the left. (It could be the right in another school.)
3. Do not touch displays on the walls.

Assemblies

1. Enter the hall in single file, in silence and sit in class seats.
2. No talking during assembly.
3. Leave the hall in single file. No talking.

Changing for PE or swimming

1. Enter the changing room quietly. Put all clothes in your PE bag, put socks in shoes placed under the bench.
2. Line up quietly at the door in single file. (It could be in pairs at another school.)

After PE or swimming

1. Line up outside the changing room in single file. (It could be in pairs at another school.)
2. Enter quietly and go to your place.
3. Only *n* pupils in the showers at once. (Choose a value for *n*.)
4. Get dried, changed and line up before the bell.

Computer work

Schools will obviously have their own specific user instructions. These directions will ensure pupils behave appropriately in the room:

1. Stay in your seat.
2. Raise your hand when you need something. Do not call out.
3. Close programs, return to the desktop and log off.

PUBLISH YOUR RULES

Make sure you get as much support as you can by publishing the rules. Put them up on the wall in the classroom and draw the pupils' attention to them. You may want to produce a class booklet as well. Write home to the parents introducing yourself and enclose a brief description of the plan, detailing the rules, consequences and rewards you will use.

SUMMARY

- Rules should be posted on the wall and they are in effect all through the school day.
- Keep the number of rules to a minimum.
- Directions apply to specific situations and activities.
- Directions vary according to the age of the children and the requirements of the activity.
- Keep to three or four directions for each activity.

5 Rewards and consequences

Do I need to give rewards and consequences?

Young people learn through their experiences how and why things are done. Actions that lead to pleasurable experiences are repeated. The teacher who encourages pupils to behave appropriately by rewarding them when they do things right will reinforce the behaviour (Case Study 5.1). Giving rewards has several advantages:

- Children are motivated to do well.
- Attention can be shifted from bad behaviour to good behaviour.
- Self-esteem can be boosted, leading to a positive atmosphere.
- Children of all abilities can gain recognition.

Case Study 5.1

Jill came to the school near the beginning of the summer term as an agency teacher. She enjoyed it and liked the school, so when the head offered her a permanent position she jumped at the chance. She had a Year 5 class and the kids were really nice. They would offer to help her after school and they showered her with presents at the end of term. The parents were really grateful that their children finally had a teacher who was staying for the term. The rest of the year had been a mishmash of cover teachers doing bits and pieces. The poor kids never knew who they would see the next day. The problem was the location – an inner-city residential area in the East End of London. The transport connections were awkward and it was not safe to walk along the streets at dusk or early morning, so women teachers found it complicated to get to work. Male teachers were at a premium and had the pick of the schools. Teachers' salaries were not high enough to support good accommodation, so they had to work further out.

Towards the end of term she heard she would be getting Year 5 again in September. The new cohort was quite different to the current Year 5 and the class already had a reputation for poor behaviour. A couple of her colleagues started scaremongering in a jokey sort of way. They described the class as 'wildcats' because there were one or two who seemed untameable. 'You'll have some problems with that class,' they warned but Jill was not ready to be beaten. She decided she needed to do some work with the class before she took them in September. Firstly, she wrote to all the parents to introduce herself and set up a date in the last week of term so they could come in and meet her face-to-face. Her aim was to get them on her side and outline her approach to behaviour management. She would also give them the information about the curriculum for the autumn term. The school had a Meet Your Teacher day that enabled the pupils to go to their new classroom and spend some time with their new teacher. This was Jill's starting point with the kids and she wasn't going to waste it.

The other important part of the preparations was observing the children around the school and building up a profile on each of them. For most, it was mainly their likes and dislikes, friendship groups, etc., and she did this by having occasional chats with one or two of them when she was out on duty. The known troublemakers became her main focus of attention. She discussed them with their current teacher and the special educational needs coordinator (SENCO). The information she obtained helped her work out the obvious things, such as which children should be sat apart and who would be better sitting at the front. She also began planning activities that would suit the interests and needs of specific children.

Jill noticed a number of useful things about the behaviour of the more challenging children. They liked to wander around the room and that normally created problems. The teacher had highlighted this but did not offer any of her strategies. Jill wondered about this and decided to begin by working on the basics, establishing how she wanted things to be done in her room.

The start of term finally came and Jill met her class in the 'welcome back' assembly. She knew she would probably get a honeymoon period in the first few weeks and that would be her window for change. She explained her behaviour code to them and outlined how she was going to run things. She told them quite unequivocally that she expected them to behave and detailed what she meant. Then she introduced her secret weapon. 'I know this will be hard for some of you because you will have become used to a different way of doing things, so I am going to make a point of noticing when you do things right and then rewarding you individually.'

The class were attentive at this point. She continued, 'You see this clipboard. I will have a sheet on it. I will record the names of everyone who does not follow my directions. If your name is not on my sheet, you will get a point. I will divide up the lessons into twenty-minute sections so you can earn three points. I will also give extra points for those who are exceptionally good or do extra jobs.' She went on to explain how the points could be used to earn rewards. She was very fair and stressed that she did not expect them to get the maximum number of points to begin with. Some pupils would find it hard at first, so the rewards would be achievable for everyone but the number of points required would change after three weeks. Then they would have a class meeting and review how things were going, and she would let them know what the new tariffs would be. All the children were enthusiastic about it but she knew some would find it difficult.

The class were fine for the next few days but she was prepared for the change. It came on Monday of the second week. Will decided he wanted another pencil, so he just got up and went to fetch it. Jill saw him and called to him, 'Will, we have a rule about leaving your seat. You need to put up your hand and ask.'

He ignored her and carried on walking, then he muttered, 'I don't want to.'

Jill could see this was going to be tricky but she wasn't going to be deterred. 'Go back to your seat and put up your hand.'

'No, I never had to ask Ms Collins.'

'We have a class rule which is to follow directions. The direction at the moment is to stay in your seat and put up your hand if you need anything.' He ignored her and leant against the table. 'I am giving you a warning and one minute to return to your seat then you will be on a yellow card.' This was her staged response of 1–2–3 and a consequence.

She started the timer and returned to the front of the class. He watched the yellow sand running through and then returned to his place just in time. He had made the right choice but on his terms. He was taking responsibility for his behaviour but making use of the time. She was not unduly worried about that, because her objective was to get him to do as she directed. The rest of the lesson went by without further distractions.

A similar incident occurred after break. Will did not respond so readily and got as far as a consequence of spending five minutes at the time-out table. He began this then decided to wander again. She challenged him and re-explained the rule. Then she gave him another verbal warning and the one-minute timer. He ignored it, so she issued him with a yellow card and started the three-minute timer. He ignored that too, so she served him with a consequence of a one-minute detention at the start of lunchtime.

The rest of the class were watching closely to see what would happen. They could see him challenging her but they could also see that she was adhering to the behaviour code. Will was pushing Jill's boundaries but she was holding firm. He continued to do this for several days and ended up with consequences on each occasion. What Jill found interesting was that none of the other troublemakers joined in. She had noticed Will trying to get another boy to follow him, but he refused and told him that he did not want to lose any of his lunchtime.

Will's distractions gradually became less frequent and whenever he had a period of following directions she positively reinforced it by awarding him his point and praising him for doing the right thing. It was hard going but success with Will would probably clinch it with the whole class. She stuck to her procedures and made a point of sending home letters of praise to those that earned them. When the parents received them they were very pleased and the children came into school buzzing with excitement. Some parents were very surprised to receive a positive note from the teacher, because their children were always getting into trouble. The children chatted away at break about the extra rewards their parents had given them after receiving Jill's letters.

Jill contacted Will's parents each evening and kept them informed. She stressed that he was able to improve because he was capable of making the right choices. He had shown that when he returned to his seat before the time was up. After a further three weeks she was starting to have some success with him. Eventually he earned his letter as well and came in the following day with a different look on his face. The weeks up to half-term were less arduous now he was not continually distracting her. He seemed to be working really hard to earn his rewards. Most of the children made the occasional mistake but that didn't matter because they had learned to turn their behaviour around. By the end of term, Jill had managed to turn the class into one of the best-behaved groups in the school. The parents were pleased, the other teachers were impressed and the children were happy with the new order and structure in their class.

MOTIVATE YOUR CLASS TO DO WELL

In Case Study 5.1 Jill knew she was going to have a hard ride, so she invested time and effort in the early stages of the relationship between herself and the class. She found out about them, read their files, watched them at play and worked out what made them tick. She got right to the heart of the problem – the class lacked structure. Jill found a reward that they valued and made it possible for them to earn it. She explained what she expected and did not aim for perfection first time, although it was her ultimate target. She kept their interest by changing the rewards. The children who behaved well got their rewards and this prompted the others to join in. The power of peer pressure motivated them. They did not want to be left out.

INCREASE CHILDREN'S SELF-ESTEEM

All too often we ignore children, only giving them attention once the situation has deteriorated. Do not let this happen. Get in there early; notice good behaviour, work and actions. Give out some positive recognition and praise the children four times more often than you reprimand them. We all like to be told we are doing things right. Jill began her lesson on a positive note and made it clear that the children could earn her attention by being well behaved. When parents received her letters they were surprised. Jill had done what she said; she had kept her word and parents were pleased to hear some good news for a change. They supported her efforts by giving their children more tangible rewards. The letters helped the children feel good about themselves and their parents' praise boosted their self-esteem. The potentially challenging ones discovered that they could get the attention they wanted without having to misbehave. The outcome was a class of kids who felt good about themselves and were more likely to learn than those with hang-ups and poor self-images.

CELEBRATE SUCCESS

Make a point of rewarding children in front of others. This will be part of your overall plan to model the behaviour you want. If you acknowledge their efforts, they will do the same for each other. The result will be children who boost the self-images of others around them.

Telling children they are doing things right can be a powerful force in bringing the others in. This is useful during lessons when you want to streamline your activities:

'Well done, John, for raising your hand.'

You can even give out tangible rewards at the end of the lesson:

'Atif, you have earned twenty points, so you get your early lunch pass. Well done.'

'Okay, Ross, you packed up quietly, so you can go first.'

There may be opportunities to present rewards in assemblies.

PROVIDE OPPORTUNITIES FOR EVERYONE TO EARN REWARDS

Positive recognition is for everyone. Make it possible for all your children to succeed. Jill in Case Study 5.1 knew her class would not change their ways overnight, so she set achievable targets where the majority could experience success. The really difficult children could not manage the whole lesson but were able to get it right during some of the twenty-minute sessions. Jill praised them and encouraged them to try again next lesson. Eventually she cracked it with all the class.

Sometimes one or two children simply cannot cope. Do not give up on them. They probably need even smaller periods of time. Try five-minute intervals, or perhaps you could reduce the target to four ticks in a lesson. Treat behaviour in the same way as you would your teaching. Break up what needs to be learned into bits the children can do, and their success will breed confidence.

The use of rewards needs to be balanced. It is easy to give them to the badly behaved to get a quiet class while the well-behaved children get overlooked (Case Study 5.2). They are the 'invisible' ones. Notice them. Give them praise and reward them as well; they deserve it.

Case Study 5.2

Harjeet was a quiet girl in Year 4. She worked hard but did not say much in class. She would always do what was asked of her and her written work was beautifully presented. You couldn't fault her handwriting. She came to school neat and tidy and you could see that her mother took great pride in her daughter's appearance. When it came to volunteering for things, others would always be in front of her. She smiled and looked on but did not compete for things. When she was given a job like going to another class to fetch something, she would do it efficiently and sensibly.

Samira's class had a small group of boys that were often getting into trouble and then being called to the head teacher's office. They needed a lot of attention and were draining her energy away. The head was looking for a solution to the spate of bad behaviour running through the school. She set a survey to find out what the children thought of aspects of the school. When Harjeet was asked, she revealed that a whole lesson might go by without the teacher speaking to her personally about her work. Sometimes the teacher worked with the group she was in but the conversation was often with the other children. She would just look on and smile. She was shy and found it difficult to contribute.

Harjeet was typical of many girls in the school. They came from a culture where women did not push themselves forward publicly. When the head fed her findings back to the teachers, they were shocked. They knew they were overworked, just like a lot of primary school teachers, but they felt guilty all the same. They knew things had to change. The problem they had was that they were putting too much energy into managing the children who were misbehaving at the expense of those who were doing things right. After lengthy discussions, they agreed to shift the emphasis and reward good behaviour much more frequently. They still had to address the poor behaviour but they tried to make more use of tactical ignoring.

After a while they noticed a change in Harjeet and the other quieter children. Harjeet was still very conscientious but she seemed to be coming out of herself. She contributed more, especially when she was given encouragement, and her self-esteem grew as she was rewarded for doing what she had always done. The difference now was that other people acknowledged it.

Not all children are ready to behave and do as you say. Motivating the switched-off children is becoming more and more difficult. If you have any in your class, you will really have to work with them. Some children have little or no respect for teachers and harbour serious hang-ups. You will benefit by getting professional help in dealing with them, but your average 'bored with everything' child is likely to respond to praise and rewards.

Positive recognition and a reward system that is valued by the children will help to reduce behaviour problems and enable you to establish good working relationships with them. By raising their self-esteem, children will become more self-confident and take risks with their learning. They will offer more answers to questions, safe in the knowledge that it will not hurt if they get it wrong. They will also ask more questions and engage with their subjects, rather than being passive spectators who will only give answers when called upon. Follow the rule of praising four times as much as you reprimand.

WHY DO TEACHERS FOCUS ON NEGATIVE BEHAVIOUR?

A teacher's worst nightmare is the class from hell. Have you seen it? Have you been there? If not, have you ever thought about it? Imagine. You walk into a classroom and you find kids sitting on desks chatting, with their backs towards you. Several are sharing the earplugs of a portable stereo. Some are playing catch. One child is sitting in the teacher's chair going through the drawers of her desk, and swearing is coming from a group at the back. You try to call them to attention but there is no reaction. Faced with such a prospect, it is hardly surprising that teachers get anxious about some of their classes. Anxiety is part of the job and we need to manage it. So how do we do it? Have a look at Case Study 5.3.

Case Study 5.3

Megan had come to England for a couple of years because she wanted to travel around Europe. She felt that working in an English school would be a useful experience. She signed on with an agency and started working as a supply teacher. It was hard work because you never knew where you would be from one week to the next. She had heard that some agency teachers had got a bad reputation for commitment but she was determined that this would not happen to her. She read up on the English National Curriculum and the new practices that were being disseminated through the Department for Education and Skills (DfES) 'lunch boxes' that seemed to clutter the staffrooms in schools. Behaviour was not an issue for Megan. She had worked with difficult children and in tough schools. She had spent nearly a year working on an island off the Australian mainland teaching Aboriginal children with serious emotional difficulties and poor language skills. The inner-city primary schools with their diverse cultures did not faze her; in fact, she shone in them.

On one assignment she had to take a Year 5 class from a very poor part of Tower Hamlets in London. The kids were visibly undernourished, unkempt and from very low-income families. As she walked up the corridor to the playground, she could hear noise coming from her

class. They were the last ones left in the yard and the deputy was with them as they chatted and bobbed around. She took charge of them and led them to their room. They lined up and went in, but as soon as she shut the door, the babble and din began. She was not used to shouting and she couldn't shout if she wanted to. She took a deep breath, fixed her gaze on a small group of pupils at the front and whispered in a voice that only they could hear, 'Raise your hand if you can hear what I am saying.' They smiled and put up their hands. She acknowledged them and looked around for another group to work on.

'Raise your hand if you can hear what I am saying,' she repeated. Their hands shot up and so did one or two others near the front. She now had about ten children with their hands in the air, smiling at her. Some of the others around the room started to wonder what she was up to. They ceased their chattering and watched her expectantly. She shifted her attention to one of these groups and repeated herself in a voice that most of the class could hear. Nearly everyone put up their hands. Those that didn't hear looked round to see what was going on. They stared in Megan's direction because everyone else seemed to be waiting for her to do something. All this took place in less than a minute. Megan put her finger to her lips and made a sign for silence. When everyone was quiet, she told them to put their hands down as she had something important to say. She had got their attention and kept calm. There was no need to shout and her anxiety levels remained low.

Teachers have to keep order but when an unexpected incident occurs, they respond to it. For example, a class is working through some sums you have set when something flies across the room. Your anxiety level rises as adrenalin is pumped into your bloodstream. The conflict begins and the chase is on. You need to respond because you know you have to. Your body dislikes stress and is equipping you to deal with the problem. It is a fight-or-flight situation and the adrenalin is preparing you for one or the other so normality can resume.

When things are going well and all the class are working quietly, you have no need to get worried. Your anxiety level is poised in case something may happen but you are fairly relaxed. There are no incidents to respond to, so you do nothing. This should not be the case; there are things you can do during quiet periods to keep your children on task (Case Study 5.4).

Case Study 5.4

Frances believed in positive recognition for pupils who did things well. She had set up a code of behaviour with her class and they had all contributed to it. They had a set of rules that they all felt were fair, and they had rewards and consequences that helped them make the right choices. One of the rewards they said they wanted was praise. They liked it when the teacher told them they were doing well. They also loved getting stickers they could wear on their jumpers and take home to show their parents. The children often worked in pairs and Frances would move around the classroom checking their progress, stopping to give a word of encouragement or help with a problem they might be having. 'You are getting on well, Aileen. Keep it up.' Aileen beamed with pride. 'That's a very interesting introduction, Jason. I can't wait to read what happens next. Good work, girls. Keep it up and you'll both get merit stickers at the end of the lesson.'

In Case Study 5.4 the children were obviously pleased when Frances praised them and they seemed to swell with pride. The behaviour remained good throughout the lesson and the level of concentration and motivation increased rather than decreased. Frances is an example of a teacher who works on maintaining good behaviour even when things are going well. Focusing on the positive behaviour and anticipating problems before they arise are the keys to keeping stress levels down then avoiding irrational and unfair responses to undesirable behaviour.

WHAT REWARDS CAN I GIVE?

There are two ways of giving rewards. You can give them to individual children or to the whole class. Rewards should always be in proportion to the achievement. Valuable rewards should not be given away easily. For example, you would expect children to behave consistently well over a period of time to earn an early lunch pass. Tailoring your rewards to the age of the child is essential. Year 6 pupils would probably like to go for lunch first whereas Year 2 pupils may prefer to earn some choosing time. Rewards need to be given consistently and fairly. Children will compare and question the distribution of rewards, so have clear criteria. Do not use your rewards as sanctions. Avoid giving them out then taking them away later in the day if a child does not behave properly. Try to use alternative consequences; after all, they earned the rewards fairly. There are a wide range of rewards you can give. Here are some examples.

Praise

Praise is easily given and greatly appreciated. Make a point of praising as many children during the day as you can. It is very easy to fall into the trap of expecting good behaviour and effort as a matter of course. The child might need to make a great effort to do something that you regard as normal. Praise costs nothing to give and needs no organisation to deliver.

House points or merit points

Your school may already be using house points or merit points to encourage the pupils. Points are given on an individual basis but are included in a team challenge. Merit points differ as they may count towards special awards such as certificates and privileges.

Free time

Free time can be given to children of all ages. You allocate a set time at the end of the lesson, day or week for the children to choose from a range of activities you provide. They earn free time individually or as a whole class through good behaviour and effort.

First in a queue

First in line for break, lunch or end of school can be extremely effective as it links up with other pleasures. For example, the child who gets out of class first will be nearer the front of the queue for the tuck shop, dinner or the school bus. They will have a longer break and more time. They will be able to meet friends from other classes earlier and they will have a free feeling by getting out first. It is amazing how responsive children can be when getting out first is used as an incentive to behave.

Letters, postcards and phoning home

Letters, postcards and phoning home are powerful motivators for pupils of all ages. Parents like to hear good news about their children and it helps you to establish good links between the school and the home. Writing letters and making calls does consume valuable time and it would be easier not to bother, given all the demands made on a teacher. However, it is a good investment and the children will soon come to value your calls highly. Letters and telephone calls take up more of your time, so you should want more in return. One way they can be used is within a hierarchical reward system that positively recognises good behaviour (Table 5.1).

Table 5.1   *A hierarchical reward system that positively recognises good behaviour*

Action	Reward
First sign of good behaviour	1 stamp* or point
Further good behaviour	1 stamp each time
10 stamps	1 postcard home
20 stamps	1 personalised letter home
30 stamps	1 telephone call home
Stamps are ready-inked with motifs like a star or the words 'Well done'.	

This cycle can be repeated throughout the year. You can keep a record of what each child has received, which may be useful when writing annual reports to parents. Figure 5.1 is an example of a postcard home to a parent.

12 October 200X

Dear Mr and Mrs Brown

I am writing to let you know how hard .... has been working recently. He has made a real effort to behave well in my lessons. You should be very proud of him.

Yours sincerely

Mr David Wright
Class teacher

Figure 5.1
Postcard home to a parent

A personalised letter goes a step further. You have more space to describe how well the child has been doing. You can word-process it and use the 'replace' facility to change the name and the gender words, e.g. his and hers, she and he. Figure 5.2 (overleaf) shows an example. You should aim to send positive letters home by mid-year to most of the parents of the children you teach.

The most prized reward will be the telephone call to parents. Other authors of books on behaviour tend to suggest that the telephone call comes before postcards and letters. This can be problematic and time-consuming because parents are not always easy to contact. You may have to wait until later in the evening, which is an inconvenience. But if you telephone after sending a letter, the parents will be used to hearing good things from the school and the conversation will go smoothly. Case Study 5.5 (overleaf) is a suggestion for a call home to a parent.

12 October 200X

Dear Mrs Brown

I am writing to let you know how pleased I am with Sally's attitude and commitment in class.

I run a scheme to reward children who exhibit the right behaviour and enthusiasm needed to do well. Sally has excelled in these requirements, which has prompted me to inform you because I know how much pleasure it can bring to hear that one's child is doing well at school. I am extremely pleased with Sally's approach and if she continues in this way, she will be developing valuable study skills.

Sally is showing a very conscientious attitude doing her homework. She is working well and I was particularly impressed by the way that she organised her time to get her homework in ahead of deadlines. I hope that reading this letter gives you as much pleasure as it gave me to send. You should be extremely proud of Sally and I look forward to reporting further successes to you.

Best wishes

David Wright
Form teacher

Figure 5.2 *Letter home to a parent*

Case Study 5.5

I really wanted to tell you how well Jane has been doing in my class. She has been making a great effort recently and has produced some very interesting work. She is setting a wonderful example to other children and her efforts have motivated them to try harder as well. I am really pleased with her progress and know that she will go on to do extremely well if she keeps this up. You must be very proud of her. Please tell her I rang.

Privilege pass

Children earn passes giving them special privileges not available to everybody. Here are some examples:

- First in line for lunch
- First choice of games in the IT room
- Seconds at dinner time
- First in line at the tuck shop.

Privileges should be used sparingly by teachers and valued highly by the children. Lunch is a great motivator, as the choice of food becomes limited towards the end. Going into the dinner hall first enables the child to choose their favourite meal. The pass can be used whenever the child likes. Here are some other rewards you could give:

- Certificates
- Extra computer time

- Sitting by a friend for one lesson
- Earning free time
- A special note in the end-of-year report
- Home visits
- Captaincy of a table, team or class
- Helping younger pupils with their reading
- Vouchers for local stores
- End-of-term, out-of-school trips.

CAN I GIVE REWARDS TO THE WHOLE CLASS?

It is useful to have rewards that the whole class can work towards. This encourages the children to work together cooperatively and uses peer pressure in helping them to learn new behaviour. It is a good way of dealing with a particular problem in the class and therefore it is best done as and when needed rather than all year long.

The sorts of rewards that the whole class can earn include free time, no homework one evening, a video (best done at the end of term) or a trip out of school. It is useful to ask the children what they would like to ensure they all buy into it. Once established, make sure the reward can be earned within a suitable time period. Usually the younger children will need to earn it in a shorter time than the older children. Award points and record them on the board or a noticeboard where the whole class can see them.

Rewarding desirable behaviour helps you to shift the emphasis away from the negative response towards the positive. Reinforcing the behaviour you want will turn your classroom into a place where children will want to be. They will learn the appropriate behaviour through being motivated by the rewards. By acknowledging their efforts, you are also helping children to improve their own self-esteem. Confident pupils with good self-images are more likely to learn well.

WHY DO I NEED CONSEQUENCES?

If rewards work and children are motivated by them, why introduce consequences? What is the point? Why punish undesirable behaviour? Case Study 5.6 may help to explain.

Case Study 5.6

Lyn was very interested in developing a positive approach to behaviour management. She had had a negative experience of school when she was young and she was determined not be like the teachers who had taught her. She could see how being positive could make a difference with her current Year 3 class that had some very difficult children in it. By half-term things were getting quite bad and she was feeling fed up. A colleague advised her to introduce a behaviour code, so she organised a system for earning rewards. She explained what they had to do to earn behaviour stars that would lead to the rewards.

It went well for the first couple of weeks and Lyn started to feel happier and more relaxed, but the change wasn't permanent. At times, children may seem to have changed their behaviour for the better but you cannot assume they will stay that way. Some of the boys in Lyn's class decided it would be fun to tease the pupils sitting in the seats in front of them, so they started kicking the undersides of their chairs. Lyn could see what was happening and went across to them. 'Come on now, boys. Stop this and get on with your work. You know that you can only earn points if you follow directions. I cannot possibly give you stars, because you are misbehaving.'

The boys protested and said it was not fair because they had been doing their work. 'Sorry, boys, but that's the way it is. You chose to break the rules.' Lyn kept calm and refocused the boys on the rule they had broken. She redirected them to the task and expected them to stop annoying the others.

'I don't want the stars anyway. I can buy a pack of my own at the sweet shop.'

Lyn turned back and looked directly at the boy who had spoken. 'Right, Eric. I am going to deduct two of your stars for that.'

'Hey, that's not fair. You said we couldn't lose stars once we earned them.' Then he got up, kicked a chair and stomped to the back of the room. He sat next to the book boxes and started to flick through a picture book.

Lyn had done her best within the limits of her experience. She had thought through her reward system very carefully and designed one that would suit her class. All the children had learned what they had to do to earn them. The fundamental weakness with her system was the lack of consequences. Detentions and standing outside the room were too heavy-handed for what the boys had done and Eric may not have reacted in that way if he had known in advance what the consequence would be for his outburst. Lyn had no choice but to redirect the boys and walk away. Eric's insolence pushed her to react and all she could do was deduct stars. The minor incident ended up escalating into a more serious one, leaving Lyn with the feeling that she had failed.

Consequences are choices not punishments. When you construct your behaviour code the aim will be to help your pupils choose the responsible behaviour. The rules establish the boundaries and any children who step over the line choose the consequence instead of the reward. In Case Study 5.6 Lyn was not offering her class a choice that could lead towards good behaviour. Effective consequences have three characteristics:

- *They are something the child chooses*: children know that when they misbehave they are choosing the consequence over the reward.
- *They are dislikable*: the consequence is not a punishment but it is something that children will not want again.
- *They are appropriate to the incident*: the consequence does not need to be really severe for it to work.

IF YOU DO THAT THEN THIS WILL HAPPEN

There are logical consequences when the adult intervenes by making a connection between the behaviour and the outcome. Here is an example:

'If you don't do up your shoelaces, you will trip over them.'

'If you put your hand in the fire, you will burn it.'

There is a connection between the cause and the effect. Parents need to teach their children these basic relationships to keep them healthy and safe. The children learn that if they do something then something else will happen. We can build on this and once the rules are established, there can be an obvious progression (Figure 5.3).

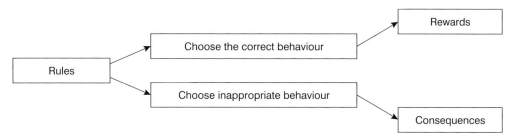

Figure 5.3   *The connection between behaviour and outcome*

As long as you stick to your approach by consistently rewarding the right behaviour and giving consequences for inappropriate behaviour, the pupils will eventually learn how to act and behave in school. They will learn the link between their behaviour and the outcome and they will be in control of the choices between rewards and consequences.

LINK INCIDENT TO CONSEQUENCE

When a child breaks a rule or fails to follow a direction, the logical outcome must be a consequence. In a climate of taking responsibility for behaviour, choice becomes paramount. The emphasis must always be on the children making the choices. It is not you telling them to misbehave, they are choosing to. First you make every child in the class aware that you are helping them to behave properly by giving choices. You are offering them the choice between the reward and the consequence and then it is up to the child. Therefore the consequence must be linked to the behaviour. For example, a child who drops litter picks up litter during break. Using equipment in an unsafe way will result in working without it or doing a different activity. The children will understand these consequences and grow to learn that the consequence is something they choose. Unrelated consequences such as lines in detention or staying back after school in silence in a room will make them feel that you are punishing them, because there is no direct connection.

The most effective consequences are directly linked to the incidents. So if a child is kept back in detention, they should spend the time writing about the incident. They should describe what happened, how they broke the rule and what they will do to fix things. This is a powerful method of putting things right if used sensitively and carefully.

USE PROBLEM SHEETS

It is not always clear who is responsible when an incident happens. While you were working with a group, something may have happened on the other side of the room. An incident may have occurred in the playground and you find yourself having to deal with it. A problem sheet (Figure 5.4) is a very good way of defusing the situation. It enables you to split up those involved and get at the truth through their accounts.

I am upset because	Other people involved	This is what I said
This is what they said	This is how it happened	This is what I will do to fix things

Figure 5.4 *A problem sheet*

Each child is given a problem sheet. They describe how they were upset, who else was involved, what was said and how it happened. They have to consider what they will do to try to fix things and prevent it happening again. This places the responsibility back with the children and enables them to repair the situation by adopting a more sensible approach next time. You can also use problem sheets to compare the accounts and weigh up who was the perpetrator. There is a direct link between the behaviour and the consequence as the children complete the forms in isolation or detention. A problem sheet for photocopying can be found in the appendices.

HOW DO I PRESENT CONSEQUENCES AS CHOICES?

Your skill as a teacher will help you present consequences as choices. Your pupils must see consequences as their choice. They will learn how to behave in your room if they feel they are in control and that is what you want. You are teaching your pupils to behave responsibly, not just to comply with your rules. Compliant behaviour lacks responsibility. You want your children to behave in the same way for other teachers as they do for you, so it is important that they understand what is required of them. Your behaviour code should be in operation whether you are in front of the class or not. Teaching them how to behave will also help if you are away, because the rewards and consequences can be applied by the teacher covering for you. Your aim is to get the children to follow rules and directions in an organised and efficient way. The key is to make sure they know that consequences are inevitable if they do not behave (Case Study 5.7).

Case Study 5.7

Jane has been talking and disrupting the other students around her. The teacher cannot let her continue. Action is needed. 'This is silent work. Either you work in silence or you will have to move to a desk on your own.' The teacher is placing the decision with Jane and it is up to her to decide. She stops for a few minutes then starts talking again. 'Jane, I expected your cooperation but you have chosen to talk, so you will have to move. Stand up and bring your things over here.' The teacher reiterates that Jane has decided to talk and has therefore chosen the consequence.

Giving the children a choice shifts the focus from you to them. You will no longer be the ogre who deals out punishments and the children will cease to be victims. They cannot complain that things are unfair, because they were fully aware of the consequences of their actions. In Case Study 5.7 Jane had to sit at the desk on her own because she chose to talk rather than work in silence. Children who are in control are able to develop and become confident. When they make a mistake, they know it is only a temporary thing and it can be put right. The focus shifts from the child to the behaviour itself.

WHEN SHOULD I GIVE A CONSEQUENCE?

Consequences may be given immediately or postponed until later depending on the circumstances (Case Study 5.8).

Case Study 5.8

Julie came into the room and slumped down, giving off very negative vibes. Amy noted her behaviour but ignored it while she got the rest of the class organised with their swimming kit. Then she went over to her. Amy was taking Year 6 and had put a behaviour code in place. The children had responded well to it and knew what to expect when they did not follow directions.

'What's up, Julie, you don't seem very happy?'

'Nothing!'

'Well you need to get your things and go swimming now. It will be okay once you get going.'

'I don't want to go. You don't understand.'

Amy could see that Julie was in a mood but she knew her well. She often tried to get out of things by making out that something had upset her. She would slouch and pout, looking for attention and Amy knew this. Once she felt confident there was nothing really wrong, she would stop servicing her attention-seeking behaviour.

'The coach is here now so you need to go.'

'I'm not going. Swimming is boring.' She turned to face the wall with her head in her hands and her elbows on her knees.

Amy ignored all the secondary behaviour. 'You may think it is boring but that is what the class are doing.' She refocused Julie to the swimming by agreeing with her.

'I'm not going. I have forgotten my stuff.'

'You know the rule. If you forget your swimming kit, you still have to go and also do a detention at lunchtime. Now do you want me to help you look for your things?' Amy had seen her come in with her swimming kit but was playing along. Eventually they found it and Julie made her way out to the bus because she realised the alternative was not very enjoyable.

In Case Study 5.8 the consequence was applied immediately. Julie would have had to go and sit and watch the class swimming rather than stay back at the school. The other part of the consequence was postponed and she would have had to do the detention later that day.

If you use a 3–2–1 system, the consequence may be deferred. For example, you may give two warnings then a consequence such as being last for lunch. The consequence can be decided at the time or it can be decided later on, giving you time to think about the most appropriate consequence for the behaviour. By calling the first warning a verbal, the second warning a yellow card and the third a red card, you are saying that the child will have a consequence coming without having to spell out what it will be. The pupils know it will be from a range of agreed consequences in the behaviour code.

There will be times when the consequence needs to be applied during the lesson. Breaking the rules of no swearing or fighting, or using up several warnings in the discipline hierarchy should result in an immediate consequence. In Case Study 5.8 the child had the choice and decided to break the rule knowing that the consequence would follow immediately.

SHOULD I EXPECT THE PUPILS TO COMPLY IMMEDIATELY?

Children react to situations differently and respond to directions at different rates. You will need to exercise patience and give them a little time if you want to avoid getting into conflict. Choices need to be considered and children do not always know what to choose straightaway:

'Michael, put the cards away or on my desk.'

The choice is offered. Michael starts to think about his choice. You turn away and continue with what you were doing, expecting Michael to decide. Here are some other examples of waiting:

'Stop talking or come and sit at my desk.'

'Sit down or come and stand at the front.'

'Use the ruler properly or give it to me.'

'Turn round and continue your work or stay back at break to do it.'

Figure 5.5 explains what is happening in all these examples.

Figure 5.5   *Children need take-up time to consider their choices*

You continue to keep an eye on the child in a low-key way, scanning the whole class and checking progress while you are teaching. These examples contain a consequence as a choice – either do the right thing or sit at my desk, stand out front, stay back at break. You allow time for the child to decide then act if necessary. Note there are no warnings. You want the disruption to stop and the children to learn that they are making the decision not you.

HOW DO I PREVENT CONSEQUENCES FROM BECOMING PUNISHMENTS?

Consequences follow from poor choices. The children bring the consequences on themselves. Therefore the consequences need to be suitably distasteful so the children will remember them next time a similar situation arises. Furthermore, you need to guard against getting angry and giving out consequences when you are not in control of yourself:

'That's it! You can sit on your own for the rest of the lesson!'

'Right, you're in detention. That'll teach you!'

'I'm fed up with you. You're going to regret it!'

The children will learn to hate you rather than realising what they did wrong. Consequences should be in proportion to the behaviour. Using a consequence that is too severe will lead to bad feelings:

'You have had your three warnings, Stephen, and you chose to continue talking so you will stay in at lunchtime and write out . . . twenty times.'

The teacher is being too harsh. She may want to keep the child back but writing out so many lines will take a considerable time. Stephen will end up feeling bitter. He did not really do anything serious. Very severe consequences are better saved for serious incidents.

Dropping litter should lead to being a member of the litter patrol. Writing on the walls should lead to cleaning it off. Breaking or damaging school property should be paid for either with the child's own money or by doing jobs. Alternatively, the child could forgo a school trip and the money could be used to pay for the damage. Making a mess in the classroom could result in staying back and cleaning up. Fighting or hurting others in the playground should result in losing the right to spend break at the same time as the rest of the school. In very serious cases the school may suspend the pupil.

You may wish to obtain their account in writing (Figure 5.4, page 88) so you can help them see where they went wrong. Letters of apology are also a good way of making the point. The letter could be sent home for the parent to sign before it is given back to the teacher.

Do my consequences need to be harsh?

The most effective consequences are not necessarily the most severe. The children need to see the consequences happen every time, so you need ones that are easy to apply. Remember that if you give a detention, it is your own time you are giving up, so make sure you are prepared to do that. Once you have gone beyond warnings, the consequences should happen and they need to be uncomfortable but not necessarily harsh. Most of the class will behave well once you begin your plan, so do not set things up that target the few poorly behaved children, because the consequences will apply to everyone.

A consequence should be uncomfortable enough to remind the child that they made the wrong choice. In less serious cases, such as failing to follow directions, use warnings first. Once a child has had all their warnings, the consequence should be administered within the room. For example, they may have to move to a different desk or work away from the rest of the group for five or ten minutes. Continual disruption after this consequence could lead to a deferred consequence after the lesson or at the end of school. When possible, holding the child back for one minute can be a very powerful consequence. It does not cause any disruption to your own routine and makes the child feel isolated because everybody else has left and the new class is waiting to come in. It is quick and effective. This consequence will generally work for 90% of the daily disruptions within the room. There may be some harder cases to deal with. Children who continue to behave in an unacceptable way will move on to the next set of consequences within your staged response. These consequences will be progressively more severe and need to involve more people such as the head teacher, the deputy, the special educational needs coordinator (SENCO) or parents.

STRATEGIES WITHIN THE CLASS

Let's see how this staged response works in practice (Case Study 5.9). The class is a Year 5 literacy set. The teacher has just taken them on mid-year and is beginning to coach the children in how she wants them to behave. She has a number of quite difficult kids. The class are predominantly working-class, coming from an area with considerable unemployment, ethnic diversity and one-parent families. They could not be described as easy.

Case Study 5.9

Val was introducing electronics to her class. She started out by reminding them of how to behave while they were doing group tasks. She demonstrated how to make a simple circuit with the components, conductors and crocodile clips. Then she talked about how some materials could conduct electricity and some couldn't. She broke the circuit in front of the light bulb then used the crocodile clips to hold a knife. The children could see how the metal knife completed the circuit. When one of the crocodile clips was removed, the bulb went off. She explained that the task was to investigate which materials were conductors and then gave them a big box of things to test.

Val moved around the class monitoring the progress of each group and noticed one child messing about. He was trying to clip the wire onto another child's clothes. 'It's good to see that you are getting down to business, Tim,' she smiled, 'but you should be working together using the things I gave you, not your clothes.' She redirected him back to the task.

'I was just seeing if clothes conducted electricity, Miss.'

'Good, well quieten down and let's see you working as a group and testing some of these,' pointing to the box of objects.

Tim was a bit excitable and not easily calmed. Val turned away and moved to another group but within minutes Tim was at it again, so she had to come back and speak to him. 'I have just had to speak to this group and particularly to you, Tim! I told you to get back to work and you have chosen to ignore me, so I am giving you your first warning.' She had a clipboard with a behaviour record sheet. On it she wrote Tim's name and put a mark in the first response column.

Tim was obviously put out but turned and got on with the experiment. Val watched him from across the room and noticed that he was not settling despite getting his first warning. About five minutes went by and then he began again. This time he had clipped together a load of conductors and was trying to suspend them across several tables. Val went over and spoke to him.

'You're still not settling, Tim. I want you to move to the table by the window and finish the experiment on your own.'

Many children will stop at this point because they realise they have gone too far. Tim did not. Val would have really liked to discuss his behaviour with him but the pressure of managing the practical activity with thirty children made it impossible. All she could do was stick to her staged response and hope that he eventually calmed down once he was away from the others. However, this wasn't to be the case.

Tim was looking for attention and kept turning round and trying to annoy the children near him. He took a wire from one group and a pen from another group. Val intervened, 'Tim, you are disturbing the other groups rather than getting on with your own work. I am giving you a warning and recording it. If you continue to misbehave you will stay back after the lesson for two minutes.'

Tim ignored Val. He was in one of those moods that children get into and there is little you can do but stick to your procedures because the rest of the class need your attention as well. Many teachers find it hard and end up getting frustrated when it reaches this point. It looks like the situation is deteriorating. Actually things are not getting any worse but you get the feeling that you're failing. If you can just hold on to the idea that the child has a choice and that they do not always make the right one, you will get through. Remain calm and don't get drawn into responding to their secondary behaviour, otherwise you will enable the child to take control. The solution in this case is for Val to move to the next stage of her response plan and have the child removed from her class so he will not do any more harm to himself or the other pupils.

EXITING A CHILD FROM THE ROOM

A time will come when a pupil's behaviour is unacceptable. They can no longer engage with the work and need some time to cool off and calm down. A child who is failing to respond after a period of time is obstructing the rights of the rest of the class to learn and feel safe and should be exited from the room.

It is a common practice in some schools to make a child stand outside the room. Check that this is in line with school practice before you consider using it. The child should use the time to cool off and be expected to sit quietly. You should limit it to five to ten minutes and make it obvious that you expect them to return to work after that time. The drawbacks are that they may try to distract others or they may wander off and then you have a bigger problem to deal with. Other teachers passing by may ask the child a question that gives them attention they should not be getting. Instead they should ignore them or just say a quick hello and walk on.

When you have no choice but to exit a child from your room, do it as unobtrusively as possible. You should explain to the whole class when you first set up your behaviour plan that being sent out is a consequence you will use. Make sure you have agreed the procedure with the other teachers. Some schools may have a designated place where the child should be sent. If this is not the practice in your school but you feel you will need to exit children, it is worth ensuring that:

- You have an arrangement with another teacher so they can go and sit in their room
- You send work with a child that they can do without requiring help
- You keep a record of the incidents, reasons for exiting the child and the consequences given.

Excluding a child from class is a serious step and you may find it makes you feel considerably stressed. It is therefore important to plan how you will do it. Aim to warn the child in advance that it could be a consequence you will have to use. Remind them of the rule and ask if there is a problem then redirect them to the task and offer to talk about it as soon as you have time. Here are some basic guidelines to consider when exiting a child:

- *Keep calm*: use an assertive voice and do not shout. Try to control your anger and do not express your feelings at this point.
- *Keep your distance*: do not invade a child's personal space.
- *Avoid making threats*: do not make statements about what may happen; stick to the procedure for your school.
- *Focus on the behaviour*: focus on the rule that has been broken and the rights of the other children.

Children who are beginning to behave in a way that will cause them to be exited from the room should be warned they are reaching that point:

'Robert. If you continue to . . . I will have to ask you to leave our class.'

This will ensure the child knows that exit will be the next step and you will avoid getting emotionally entangled.

GAINING SUPPORT FROM COLLEAGUES

Make sure you have discussed exit procedures with your colleagues and everyone is aware of what will happen. Always keep notes for use once things have calmed down. Your behaviour log sheets and a short written account of what was said and done will be sufficient. The aim is to exit the child with the minimum disturbance and then rebuild the relationship once they have had the consequence. You should contact the SENCO, the head teacher and the parents because there may be something going on outside school that has a bearing on the child's reason for behaving in this way. Keeping parents informed from an early point fosters good relationships, ensures everyone is working together and if it gets to a fixed-term exclusion, everyone concerned will know why.

WHAT HAPPENS IF THE CHILD WON'T LEAVE THE ROOM?

Difficult children may refuse when directed and there needs to be a procedure to assist their removal. Generally, children will dig themselves into a situation that is hard to get out of. They become cornered and will react in the same way as a frightened animal. They will freeze, run and hide, spit and snarl, or belligerently cling to anchorages affording safety or protection. They will say and do things that will then make it difficult to apologise. Once a child has sworn at a teacher, lashed out or done something equally serious, they know they are in a crisis that is hard to redeem.

Children like to be part of the group so the best way is to ignore them. Take the rest of the children out of the room to the hall, library, IT room or playground to do a 10 minute fun activity. Tell them what they will be doing and make it sound like something not to be missed. Remind them of the directions for leaving the room and then go. Leave your Learning Support Assistant behind to keep an eye on the child from a distance. They should be able to talk the child round and get them to go with them before the class returns. One effective strategy is to allow the child an advocate. This is usually another member of staff and not necessarily someone more senior, because the child will see them as an authority figure representing the school and will lose face if they give in to them.

Your school may have a behaviour mentor. They are often drawn from the learning support assistants and have special responsibilities for children with behavioural and emotional difficulties. Their different status enables them to form relationships with children as advocates that can be useful during times of crisis. Leave the child alone and do not attempt any further contact with them until the advocate arrives. They should then call the child from the room. This is done calmly, quietly and assertively:

'Robert, come with me please.'

The child now has a way out with a neutral third party that prevents loss of face. The advocate should follow an agreed procedure that will help the child to calm down, consider their choices and begin the rebuilding process with the teacher.

CHECKLIST FOR A CLASSROOM EXIT PROCEDURE

- When will you use the exit procedure?
- Did you warn the child? (Not applicable for serious incidents.)
- What will you do if they refuse to leave?
- Have you organised the exit procedure with other staff and do you have advocates if you need them?
- Have you a recording process?
- How will you follow up later?

- Have you involved the parents, head teacher and SENCO?
- What will be the consequence for the child?
- How will you rebuild the relationship with the child?

SUMMARY

- Rewards and consequences are needed to motivate the children to choose the right behaviour.
- Refocus your attention and catch them being good rather than bad.
- Rewards can be given to individuals and to the whole class.
- Consequences should never be given to the whole class, only those who choose to break the rule.
- Consequences must be inevitable and where possible they should match the behaviour.
- Exiting a child from the room is serious and should only be used as a last resort or during a serious incident.
- Always warn the child when they are getting near to being exited from the room.
- Have an arrangement with other staff for sending children to them when they are being exited.
- Send work with a child when they go to another room.
- Organise an advocate for when you have a child who refuses to leave.
- Consequences do not need to be harsh, just dislikable.
- Always repair and rebuild the relationship after the consequence has been completed.
- Aim to replace extrinsic rewards with intrinsic rewards so the pupils know what is acceptable behaviour.

6 EMBEDDING THE BEHAVIOUR CODE IN YOUR TEACHING

Learning is a journey of discovery. It begins in the early stages of a child's life when he starts to make the connections between his actions and the effects. As self-awareness develops, the child starts to identify himself as an individual person with his own needs and desires. The world becomes a fascinating place with so many mysteries waiting to be explored. Anyone who has had children of their own or worked with young infants will know that they seem to be so full of questions about everything they experience.

Children come to school with this thirst for knowledge about the world. So what happens during those eleven years? Why do some children get switched off whereas others take off and pursue their chosen careers? As teachers, we have expectations to fulfil. We must teach the children what they need to know so they stand a chance of passing their teenage examinations. They do not come to school knowing everything already but some do have a greater disposition to learn than others. The same goes for their behaviour. Some children will be better equipped before they come to school than others and this is due to the nurturing and parental bonding they have received at home:

- Some will pick things up more quickly than others.
- Some will have difficulties learning and need alternative strategies.
- Some will regard you as a leader in their journey of discovery.
- Some will find it so difficult to learn certain things that even your attempts to help may not work.
- Some will need the support of their parents more than others.

Teachers who expect children to behave but do not make their expectations clear will find that the children try to guess and will not always get it right. This leads to misunderstandings as the teacher interprets their errors as poor behaviour. This can easily be avoided by teaching your new groups the behaviour code. The difficulty many primary teachers have is the pressure of time. They have to cover the content in all the National Curriculum subjects and prepare classes for Standard Assessment Tests (SATs). It can seem a hard decision to use precious time at the beginning of the school year on things outside the subject content. Many teachers would like to launch straight into the curriculum while the children are still keen and fresh. However, investing time getting the routines, rules and study methods right at the outset will ensure the whole class will know what you want. Furthermore, you will be reinforcing your position as the teacher and adult in the room. It is not just the younger groups that will need this. All children will benefit from reminders at the start of a new school year or term.

Streaming and setting can result in certain groups of pupils being together in the same class. Children with below-average ability may include those who are having difficulty with their behaviour. Most teachers will be aware of this and plan accordingly. The danger comes when a teacher who is less confident managing behaviour finds himself with an above-average ability group and assumes they will behave well. Children do not necessarily behave well because they are bright. There will always be some who will want to test the teacher, some who are not challenged intellectually and some who are good at school work but are less mature and act in silly ways.

Investing the time establishing the correct classroom climate is worthwhile. The more able children are likely to adapt more rapidly, so you may need less time to establish the system. The less able will need more time to process and practise the rules and routines. They will also need to revisit what they are learning to make absolutely sure they know what you are asking them to do. Therefore you need to build in time to teach the plan in the same way as you would include things like fire drills and health and safety procedures.

WHAT ANY LEARNING PROCESS SHOULD INCLUDE

- *Context*: give the pupils the big picture. Help them understand why good behaviour is necessary and how it will help them to learn.
- *Anchoring*: begin with the familiar and show how the new knowledge and skills stem from it. Help the children remember new things by anchoring them in their minds to memorable experiences.
- *Organisation and processing*: new things need to be filed in the brain in ways that will make sense when they are retrieved. Break down ideas into small chunks and show how they are connected by using mind maps, lists, groups and categories. This will help the children commit them to their short-term memory in a logical way. For example, you could attach rewards to the notion of choice. When going through sets of directions for different routines, group things like technology and art or PE and assemblies.
- *Consolidation*: get the children to explain to each other what they have learned. Telling someone else about what they have just learned will help them understand it themselves.
- *Long-term memory*: revisit what you have taught a few days later. Devise activities that enable the class to use what they have learned in a different way. Help them tackle different problems and find solutions, drawing on their new knowledge. Using it in a variety of ways creates a number of links to it in the brain. Making more links will increase the likelihood of remembering it. In this way, the children will be taking what they have learned and committing it to their long-term memory.
- *Practice*: practising and using new things will strengthen the links and pathways within the brain and make it easier to remember.

WHERE TO BEGIN

What

Teach the following:

- Rights and responsibilities of everyone in the class
- Reasons for having a behaviour code
- What could go into the code
- Your approach, which will be based on choices
- How you will recognise good behaviour
- The consequences of poor choices.

How

Design special lessons that will help your class to contribute to the behaviour code and to learn it. Use discussion and involve everyone. Brainstorm and mind-map ideas on the board. Then practise some of the routines with the whole class to test and refine them.

When

Do not feel you have to spend the whole of the lesson. Short bursts may suit your groups better. Revisit and remind the class of what they have learned at the start of each lesson. Five to ten minutes may be adequate for this.

A commonly held understanding

The basis of a behaviour code is a commonly held understanding of the rights and responsibilities of the individual. Primary school children may not be able to engage with this notion, so they will need to be taught it and then have it reinforced in other areas of the curriculum such as citizenship, religious education and history. Many children will have a strong sense of right and wrong and should be actively encouraged to join in and contribute to drawing up a class behaviour code with you. They will probably not be able to do it without your help. You may have to assist them in making the links between choices and negative consequences. This chapter includes some activities that will help your class engage with the ideas and guide them towards your own objectives.

The experience of drawing up the rules may not be a new one for your groups. Many children may have done it with other teachers. The difference will be in things like the hierarchy of responses, the rewards and consequences, and the subtleties between rules and directions. The beauty of having a plan is that it gives you an enormous confidence boost, so the next time a class gets difficult you will feel prepared. Here are two advantages of having a behaviour code:

- Your class will be aware of their choices and know what the consequences will be.
- You will become more consistent in the way you deal with the many different incidents that occur, and this will minimise any chance of shooting from the hip or overreacting.

SAMPLE SPECIAL LESSONS

Boxes 6.1 to 6.7 contain some activities that have proved successful. You may want to use them as they are or adapt them to suit your own purposes. Like any lesson, you will need to gather the resources and prepare the delivery. The suggested sessions that follow can be as long or as short as you choose. Sometimes it is better to keep everything as short and direct as possible, because the children need the system in place to help them immediately. This will probably be the case for teachers taking new groups mid-year or supply teachers who are filling short-term absences. When you have new groups at the start of the year, there will be more time to spend teaching the behaviour code, so these ideas could be used. Times are not specified for individual activities, so you can decide how long to make them for yourself. As a guide, most of the activities should be between five and twenty minutes long.

Box 6.1: What makes a good teacher?

Objective: To identify the qualities of a good teacher.

Resources: Whiteboard or flip chart, marker pens, Figure 6.1.

Activity: As a whole class, brainstorm what the children feel makes a good teacher. Write up all the ideas no matter how outrageous they seem. Impress on the children the contractual obligations that teachers have then review the list to remove any suggestions that would be impossible. Show the class how to connect their chain of thought. For example, the suggestion that the teacher 'helps us if we make a mistake' can lead to 'not taking the mickey if we get something wrong'.

Keywords: Respect, sense of humour, interested, flexible, mistakes, protects, fair, consistent, approachable, believes, fun, firm, friendly, knowledgeable, helpful, kind.

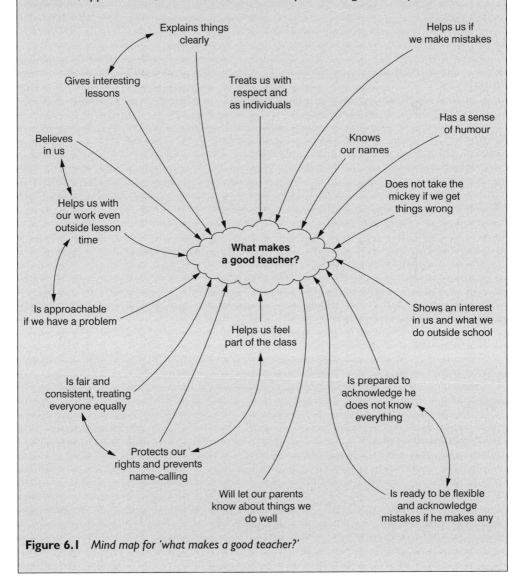

Figure 6.1 *Mind map for 'what makes a good teacher?'*

Box 6.2: What makes a good pupil?

Objective: To identify the qualities of a good pupil.

Resources: Whiteboard or flip chart, marker pens, Figure 6.2.

Activity: Begin in pairs and spend two minutes thinking of things that would make a good pupil. Then each pair share their ideas with the whole class and record them as a mind map. Links could be made with the ideas from Box 6.1. For example, 'listening when someone is speaking' can link back to 'being aware of the feelings of others'.

Keywords: Listens, speaks kindly, mistakes, support, preferred learning styles, boundaries, example, deadlines, homework, helpful, organised, prepared, asks questions, tidy, neat, legible, clever, determined.

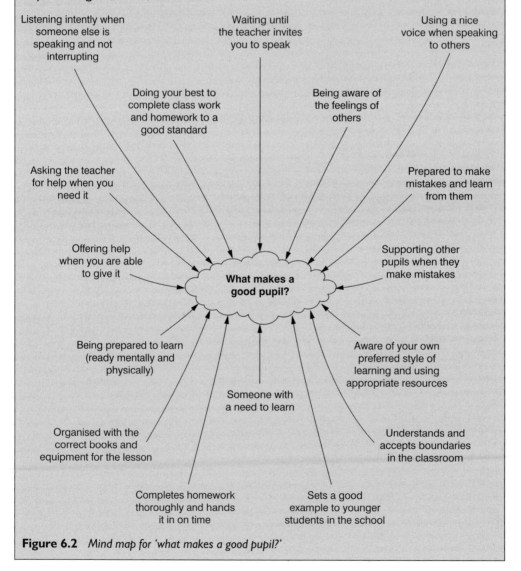

Figure 6.2 *Mind map for 'what makes a good pupil?'*

Box 6.3: Linking rights and responsibilities _____

Objective: To identify and list some rights and responsibilities of children.
Resources: Whiteboard or flip chart, marker pens, Figures 6.1 and 6.2.
Activity 1: Discuss the rights of the individual in our society. Talk through the links between rights and responsibilities and how everyone in the community has a responsibility to uphold the rights of the individual. List the rights and responsibilities of pupils and teachers.
Activity 2: Working in pairs or small groups, talk about one right from the list and try to find the role of the teacher and the pupils in protecting it. What do they each have to do to uphold it?
Keywords: Right, responsibility, uphold, support, protect, safe, secure, laws, opportunities, individual, community, opinions, boundaries, freedom, fair.

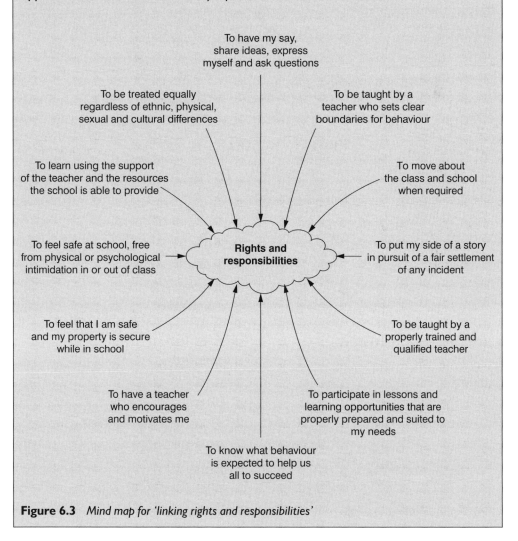

Figure 6.3 *Mind map for 'linking rights and responsibilities'*

Box 6.4: Protecting rights and responsibilities

Objective: To produce some rules for the class.

Resources: Whiteboard or flip chart, marker pens, A1 sheets of paper, Figure 6.3.

Activity 1: Introduce the notion of rules then, working in pairs or as a whole class, think of one rule we have in our country and discuss why we have it. What happens when it is broken?

Think of one rule you have at home. Explain why you have it and what happens when it is broken. Think of one rule we should have in the school or our class. Why should we have it? Share the outcomes of the discussions as a whole class and list the rules on separate, large sheets of paper together with the consequences. This will enable the class to contribute their ideas about the rules that could be used in the school.

Activity 2: Help the class to distinguish rules, which should be in force at all times, from directions, which apply to specific routines and circumstances.

Keywords: Rules, community, home, school, directions, consequences, rights, responsibilities, stability, laws, codes, conduct, behaviour, crime.

Laws and Rules in Our Society

LAW	CONSEQUENCE
30 mph speed limit	Three points on your licence and a fine
Travellers must purchase a valid ticket before travelling on the train	£100 penalty fine
No smoking	Asked to leave
Dog owners must not allow their pets to foul the pavement	Fine

SAMPLE RULES AT HOME	CONSEQUENCE
In bed by nine o'clock	No television in the morning
No jumping on the beds	Make own bed
Put your dirty clothes in the linen basket	Wash own clothes

SAMPLE RULES AT SCHOOL	CONSEQUENCE
No toys in class	Toy confiscated
No fighting	Internal isolation
Everyone should wear a tie	Lent a tie by the office for the day
Wear correct PE kit	Lent kit by teacher and a note home
Don't drop litter	Litter patrol at break

SAMPLE RULES IN CLASS	CONSEQUENCE
No swearing	Detention and write an apology
No running in the classroom	Go back and walk

Figure 6.4 *A finished chart for 'rules and laws'*

Box 6.5: Rules and laws need to be kept

Objective: To link actions to consequences.
Resources: Figures 6.3 and 6.4, whiteboard or flip chart, marker pens.
Activity 1: Using some of the rules from the last activity, work as a whole class to decide the consequence for breaking each rule. Stress the difference between a punishment and a consequence.
Activity 2: As a whole class, decide which rules apply to the classroom. Agree some basic rules including 'follow directions'.
Keywords: Rule, law, direction, consequence, dislikable, uncomfortable, illegal, crime, punishment.

Box 6.6: Rewards

Objective: List the rewards that the class would value and want to work towards.
Resources: Whiteboard or flip chart and marker pens.
Activity: Brainstorm with the class what rewards they would value. Begin by reminding them that their suggestions need to be realistic. Asking for things like a day off school would not be possible. During the activity you could begin to separate the rewards into those the individual children would get and those the whole class could work for.
Keywords: Reward, earn, motivate, value.

Box 6.7: Consequences

Objective: To make a list of consequences that could be used in the lessons.
Resources: Whiteboard or flip chart and marker pens.
Activity: Remind the class of the connection between their actions and the consequences. Explain that consequences need not be harsh, just dislikable and that they should be linked to the action wherever possible. The whole class then work together on thinking up consequences for their rules.
Keywords: Rule, direction, poor choice, consequence.

Once you have constructed your behaviour code it needs to be circulated to everyone concerned together with an explanatory letter. The children should get a copy of the code to put in the front of their home/school diary. You will also want to send copies to the parents to gain their support. Figure 6.5 is a sample letter to help you structure your own. You may want to give copies of your code to some of your colleagues. The code itself should be simple and short. The contents should include the rules, rewards and consequences (Chapters 4 and 5). Put a copy in a prominent position on the classroom wall.

12 October 200X

Dear Mr and Mrs ...

I am writing to introduce myself as <pupil name>'s new teacher. I will be setting high standards and working with <pupil name> to ensure s/he makes good progress and gets as much out of the course as possible. To achieve this, s/he will need to do two things:

- Always come to the lesson with the correct textbook, exercise book, writing equipment, ... (make your own list as appropriate).

- Complete homework by the deadlines and to the required standard. I will use exemplars so that the pupils are aware of what this entails.

I also have high expectations for behaviour. To achieve this, I have a behaviour code that is in line with the school policy. I enclose a copy with this letter for your information. The pupils have contributed to the code over the previous weeks and have agreed to use it in the lessons.

Our approach is based on the positive reinforcement of appropriate behaviour. We encourage the children to make choices and reward them when they choose to behave well. When they make a poor choice and behave inappropriately, they are sanctioned. In this way, children learn that there are consequences to their actions.

Please talk to your son/daughter about the behaviour code and if you have any questions related to it, feel free to contact me and I will try to help.

Yours sincerely

Class teacher

Figure 6.5 *Letter introducing the behaviour code*

REINFORCE THE BEHAVIOUR CODE AT EVERY OPPORTUNITY

Introducing a new code (Table 6.1) will not be a simple process. The children probably won't adopt everything and adhere to the rules exactly. They may have seemed very enthusiastic about it while they were drawing it up, but when it becomes a reality it may cause difficulties for some of them. Anything that requires a change in routine obviously needs to be learned. Not everyone learns at the same rate so, undoubtedly, some children will forget or make a mistake and get caught out by the new system. The question teachers often ask when introducing a new code is, 'Should concessions be made?' Concessions can be made but they might confuse the child. They will see you are making a concession that may conflict with what they believe should actually happen. It is better to adhere to your system.

Table 6.1   *A behaviour code containing staged consequences*

Incident	Consequence	Behaviour log
First incident in the lesson	Warning given	Enter a tick
Second incident in the lesson	Five minutes of time-out given	Enter a tick
Third incident in the lesson	Stay back after class for two minutes	Enter a tick
Fourth incident in the lesson	Lunchtime detention	Enter a tick

Adhering to the system without waiving the consequence will demonstrate that it is consistent. You will be giving the rewards to those who make responsible choices, so it would seem reasonable to give the consequences to those who do not. It may seem hard at first but with persistence your efforts will pay off (Case Study 6.1).

Case Study 6.1 *Molly*

Molly was finding it exhausting. She tried her best and always made sure the children were progressing with work that stretched everyone but their behaviour was getting her down. The children seemed to test everything she said, not in a bad way but they would not get straight down to work when they were given something to do. The class were not making the sort of progress that Molly thought they should be, because of the time being wasted. She had a clear understanding of what worked well and last year her class really did well. However, this year the story was quite different. Perhaps it was because the group was made up of a much wider ability range and quite a few of the children seemed to get distracted easily.

Molly began to feel that she was not doing a very good job. By half-term they seemed to be lagging behind and she realised that the work they had covered was nowhere near what she would have expected. If only she could find a way of controlling the class so they would get down to work more quickly and see the tasks through instead of leaving so many things unfinished.

She went on her half-term break determined to come up with a solution. A friend had recommended a couple of books on behaviour management and so she set herself the goal of reading them and coming up with a plan while she toured the Greek islands. By the end of her odyssey she had worked out what she was going to do and returned to school with an optimism that things were going to change.

After registration and countless comments about her suntan, she quietened them down and explained the changes and her new seating plan. When all the children had moved to their new places, she explained the behaviour code she had designed. Many of the children took to it straightaway because they liked the orderliness and security it provided. The rest of the day went well for Molly and she felt reassured as she drove home that night.

The next day she stood at the door, greeted each child and reminded them of the new rules before entering the room. Many of the children did not heed her directions and failed to follow them. The result was that she gave out lots of warnings and some children even received consequences. However, she kept resolute and stood firm throughout the morning. Things improved in the afternoon. By the end of the week only a few children were getting warnings and they responded well by turning their behaviour around. The majority of the class adhered to the directions and worked hard to earn the rewards.

Looking back, Molly could see how she had changed the culture in her room. She could also see the difference in the work they did. The whole class, including the children with special needs, had made up most of the lost ground and her room felt like a haven of calm and learning.

CONSOLIDATE THE CODE BY REVISITING IT

Introducing the plan is the first step but it does not stop there. The class will need reminding until they have accepted it and made it part of their working method. This is done by briefly running through the rules, rewards and consequences at the beginning of each lesson during the first few weeks. The children will see that you are taking it seriously, not simply introducing something and letting it run on its own until it gets forgotten.

In the establishment phase, rewards should be given more generously as incentives to take on the new routines. The class can then be gradually weaned off the rewards. The best time to use the extra rewards is when you need specific children to follow directions that they may not be used to. For example, lining up outside and entering a room can be noisy and disorderly, so giving a lot of rewards will help the children recognise when they are doing things right for you.

One way of making the start of the lesson a positive, educational experience is by giving the children a task as they enter the room. It should take them about five minutes to complete and can be done individually or in pairs. Boxes 6.8 to 6.12 contain some activities you could try. Reward the children if they come in quietly, follow directions and get on with the task without making a fuss.

Box 6.8: *Memory game*

Use: This activity is used once the children have begun a unit of study. It challenges them to think quickly and gets their brains in gear at the start of the lesson.
Aims: To enable children to recollect and summarise the two most significant things they can remember from the previous lesson. To produce a mind map of the key points that will then remain on display during the week of study.
Resource: Post-it notes.
Time: 3–5 minutes.
Procedure: When the children arrive they are given two Post-it notes each. They are asked to think about the last lesson. Their task is to think of the two most significant things they learned in the previous lesson and write them on the Post-it notes. They can work alone or discuss things with another person. Then they come out and stick their notes on the whiteboard, return to their seats, take out their books and wait for you to start the lesson. The result is a board covered in key points that the children remembered. This can be very useful as a starting point for the lesson, a revision aid and a very good way of checking the effects of your teaching.

Box 6.9: *Spaghetti words*

Use: This activity is used to help the children remember the keywords from the last lesson.
Aim: To enable the children to link the keywords to their meanings or uses.
Resource: Activity sheet.
Time: 3–5 minutes.
Procedure: The children are given a sheet with five to ten keywords that have been jumbled up. They work in pairs to solve the anagrams. Then they have to decide where they go on a diagram that is also on the sheet. Once they have completed the task, they should agree between themselves what is going on at each stage. This is a very good activity involving a process or life cycle.

Box 6.10: Science

Solve these jumbled words. Use them to label the pictures (Figure 6.6). Be ready to describe what is happening at each stage and what will happen next.

- Valra
- Dtual
- Geg
- Uapp.

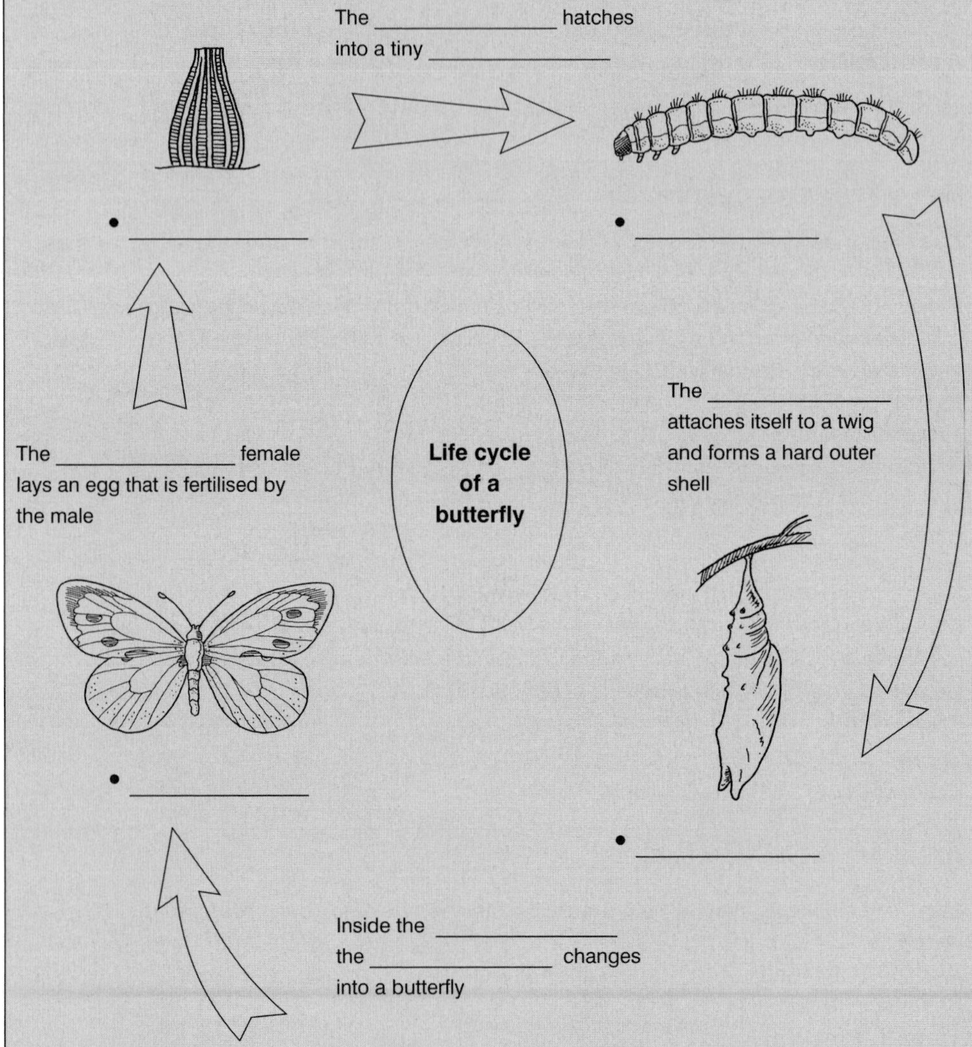

The _____ hatches into a tiny _____

• _____

The _____ attaches itself to a twig and forms a hard outer shell

The _____ female lays an egg that is fertilised by the male

Life cycle of a butterfly

• _____

• _____

• _____

Inside the _____ the _____ changes into a butterfly

Figure 6.6 *The life cycle of a butterfly*

Box 6.11: Mind-map game

Use: This is used near the end of a topic or unit and will help the children link the ideas together.

Aim: To enable the children to work together in building a list of keywords and know their relationships.

Resource: A4 paper.

Time: 3–5 minutes.

Procedure: Each child is given a keyword from the topic. Their job is to make the links with other parts of the topic and be able to describe them. For example, the words may be connected with the life cycle of a plant (Figure 6.7): roots, leaves, flowers, pollen, seeds. A child could be given any one of these words and has to draw a mind map to connect them up. They then have to be able to speak about the process involved.

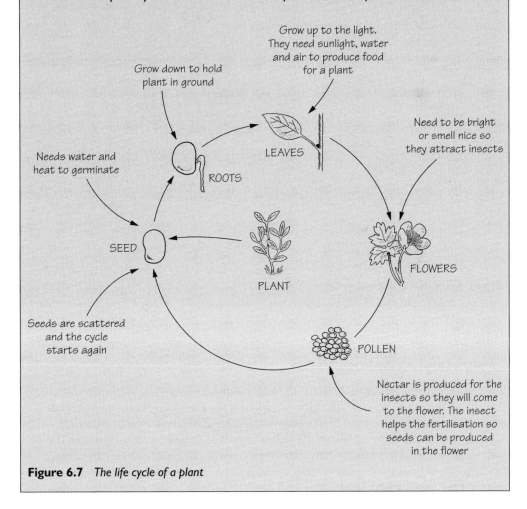

Figure 6.7   *The life cycle of a plant*

Box 6.12: Cross challenge ————————————————————————————

Use: This activity is an ideal one to bring together knowledge gained in a mathematics or science topic. The puzzle is a cross where all the numbers are obtained by finding the solutions to clues.

Aim: To use the knowledge gained during a topic to solve a related puzzle.

Resource: Activity sheet.

Time: 3–5 minutes.

Procedure: The clues are given on the same sheet and the challenge is to build up the algorithm using the solutions. There is a missing number in the middle that also needs to be solved once the students have worked out the other clues (Figure 6.8). They need to add the signs to make the puzzle work.

a. The number of centimetres in a metre

b. ?

c. The number of degrees in a right angle

d. The number of sides in a hexagon

e. The number of minutes in an hour.

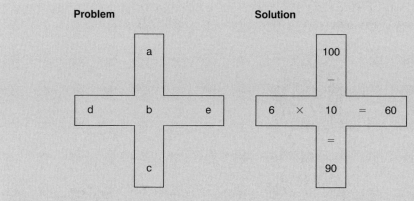

Figure 6.8   *Cross challenge: problem and solution*

CONSISTENT CONSEQUENCES

The purpose of the behaviour code is to help the children make sensible choices about their behaviour so they will eventually be able to take their places as well-adjusted members of the community. The cooperation of the children is secured by an agreement that depends on fairness. The majority will accept the consequences if they feel the judgements are fair. You must demonstrate this by tackling every incident where a rule is broken or a direction is not followed. There will be children who will be watching to see whether you deal with everyone in the same way. If they feel that you have let a child off or treated them in a different way, they will react. They may complain that it does not seem fair. You will have to deal with their grievances, which can be time-consuming and pull you away from your teaching. During this time another incident may occur that will also need your attention. The result will be a very stressful situation for you that could have been avoided with forethought. In extreme cases the child may take his grievance away with him and it could surface later, causing quite serious and perhaps unexpected repercussions (Case Study 6.2).

Case Study 6.2

Billy was a very active boy and some would even say he showed many signs of being hyperactive. The school called in an educational psychologist who agreed and recommended that he see a doctor. The parents had refused; they believed it was just due to his age and all boys were like that when they hit their teens. They did not take the school's advice, so Billy just carried on disrupting lessons when he felt like it and getting up and moving around when things did not go right for him.

Part-way into the lesson, Billy decided to get up and wash his brush but failed to ask for permission. Tania noticed this and called him back, but he ignored her and carried on going to the sink. Just before he reached the sink, he caught his foot on a bag and jogged another boy, who then knocked a jar of water over the desk. It splashed over the pictures the children were painting. Peter was very upset because he had been working on his painting for a while and was very pleased with it. Now that stupid Billy had ruined it.

Tania intervened and finally got Billy to sit down. The support assistant helped Peter to clean up the mess on his table and sponged his clothes. He was very cross and scowling at Billy. Billy smirked and leaned back in his chair, obviously pleased with the disruption he had caused. From Peter's point of view, nothing had happened to Billy. Tania was reluctant to do any more than get him seated. She was worried about the scene he might cause if she started telling him off for getting up and walking about. She was feeling thankful that she had got him back in his place, because he could be very defiant and difficult if he was challenged.

The playground was buzzing when Tania came in the next morning. As she walked down the corridor she sensed something was up. The head called by her room as she was preparing the resources for her first lesson. Apparently, Peter had got into some kind of fight. He had been playing in the park when Billy turned up on his bike. Peter had gone for him in a big way and really laid into him. It started with Peter jumping on Billy's bike wheels and buckling them. Billy was on the other side of the brook and came rushing over. By the time he reached Peter, his bike was wrecked. Peter had pushed it over the side of the concrete drain and it had landed five feet below in the rubbish and mud. A fight broke out and ended with Billy and Peter being separated by two men on their way to play tennis. Peter had explained later that he was fed up with Billy always annoying people. He had also ruined his painting and nothing had been done. He felt this was wrong and he was not going to let Billy get away with it this time.

Tania hadn't realised how angry Peter was and did not know that he was going to take things into his own hands like this. She reflected on what had happened and although Peter should not have done what he did, she could see how she might have prevented it. In future she would challenge pupils when they didn't do as she asked.

Rule reminders

Before any action, consider what reminders could be given. It will enable you and the child to refocus on the direction that was given. Prefacing a warning with a rule reminder enables the child to see where they went wrong, which will prevent disputes that accompany secondary behaviour. The behaviour code will only be successful if you keep up the reminders and continue to coach the children for as long as needed. After long holidays, you will probably find that refresher sessions are needed to prevent the children making poor choices because they have forgotten what to do.

Summary

- Involve the parents in formulating the behaviour code so they will feel they have some ownership of it and will support you in implementing it.
- Create special lessons to teach the class the behaviour code in the same way you would teach a subject.
- Underpin your behaviour code by discussing the rights and responsibilities of everyone in the class.

- Put up visual displays that summarise the rules, rewards and consequences.
- Circulate the behaviour code to parents and staff in the school.
- Give the children a copy of the code to put in the front of their exercise book or folder.
- Revisit the behaviour code to refresh it with the class when necessary.

7 Developing a positive atmosphere

Behaviour and learning are inextricably linked. Children who find the lessons interesting and engage with the work are less likely to misbehave. The challenge for any teacher is in planning lessons and designing activities that suit the needs and interests of all the pupils in the class. This is a tall order when you consider the widely differing intellects, interests, backgrounds and experiences that each child brings to the lessons. Classes can no longer be considered as homogeneous groups and given the same things to do. Each child is an individual with their own needs and expectations, and the teacher is charged with meeting them. Unacceptable behaviour can occur when children find the work too easy, too hard, uninteresting or irrelevant.

Where to start

The aim throughout this book is to describe a method of managing behaviour that places the choice with the child. The goal is to use the behaviour code to aid the learning and teaching processes, not to control the children. For this reason, it is worth spending time examining how people learn and what we know about the learning process.

The primary needs of the body must be satisfied before a person can begin to learn effectively (see Maslow's hierarchy of needs on page 2). We all need nourishment, shelter, warmth and a feeling of security. Without these, our mind becomes distracted trying to find them. Consider trying to learn how a timber-framed house was built during Tudor times in a classroom that is so cold you are shivering and trying to get warm. Or imagine studying the effects of light on plants when you are hungry because you missed breakfast. Perhaps you have had a traumatic event in your life. What might it be like for a child going through something similar? For example, a child whose parents are splitting up will be feeling vulnerable, possibly erratic and ill-tempered during this period of uncertainty and will find it hard to give the required attention to their school work.

The human body consists of complex hydrocarbons. The body's life processes are chemical reactions. The brain controls these processes and also relies on the same kinds of chemical reactions, many of which take place in liquid environments. Water is a vital requirement of the body and provides the medium where reactions can occur. It is very easy to underestimate this and ignore the need to maintain a healthy intake of water. There has been a growing awareness of this among the educational community and many schools have begun providing their children with bottles so they can have their own supplies of fresh water to drink whenever they need to, in or out of lessons. When the children are first given their bottles they seem to drink all the time and have to go to the toilet, which can become an issue during lessons, but they settle down after a few weeks.

Fresh air is another basic requirement. Hot, stuffy, poorly ventilated rooms result in lethargic, brain-numbed pupils. A steady flow of fresh air can do wonders for the levels of participation and work output. In the summer term some classrooms can become unbearably hot from the sun shining through the windows, as many schools in the UK do not have air conditioning. There are several solutions to this problem. Sheets of darker-coloured sugar paper or newspaper can be put over the windows to reduce glare, and a portable fan can get the air circulating to make the room more comfortable.

The appearance of the room can make a tremendous difference. You can set the tone by making sure everyone who comes into your room respects the rights of others. Putting positive affirmation signs around the room can help. Slogans like 'You are now entering a no put-down zone' can be useful because they give all the children the same message that verbal abuse and negative comments are not tolerated in your room. The appendices contain examples for you to photocopy.

GETTING THE LESSON RIGHT

Good lessons have structure, challenge, interest and opportunities to practise what has been learned. Lessons should include the following features.

The big picture

Children will switch off for many different reasons but a common reason is for lack of knowing why something needs to be learned. They need to know how it fits into the big picture. The lesson is part of the learning journey. The big picture is an overview of that journey. It is like the picture on a jigsaw-puzzle box. The whole thing becomes clearer and makes more sense when the children can see where the piece, the lesson, fits into the whole jigsaw of a subject. Here are three ways to draw the big picture:

- A new topic or unit should be introduced together with a brief description of the steps the class will take to reach the end.
- At the start of each lesson, the children should be reminded of what they did previously.
- Describe what the children need to do next and set the objectives and learning outcomes for the activities they will engage in.

In this way, the children will have a good idea of where they have come from, where they are now and where they are going. It is like giving a road map with directions and it will minimise the chance of children getting lost.

Whole-class teaching

Whole-class teaching is the time when you introduce the class to new ideas, concepts and material. The children can ask questions and you move forward together in the search for answers, acquiring new knowledge and skills. The teaching takes place during this part of the lesson. It is where you will use your own particular strategies to introduce and explain to the children what they need to know to complete the activities that come next. Words alone will not be enough, because not every child will learn by linguistic methods. The challenge for the teacher is to find alternative ways of getting over what they want the class to learn. At the end of the lesson, the children are reminded of how the work they have been doing fits into the whole unit and what they will be doing in the next lesson.

Small group and individual work

Once the whole class have been introduced to the new material and the teacher feels they are ready to venture forth, they can get started on the tasks and apply it to a range of problems. Activities need adapting so they are differentiated or open-ended to enable children of all abilities to try them and be challenged by them. This is often the hardest part of planning lessons. You need to know the abilities of your pupils then you can devise the tasks so they will gain success.

The plenary

A fundamental part of the lesson is the ending – bringing the children back together as a group and getting them to discuss what they have learned. It enables individuals to test their own learning and you can assess whether your teaching has been effective. This part of the lesson also allows you to recap the main points, put them back into the context of the big picture and tell the children where they will be going next. Good lessons will contain many of these features and address the needs of the class as a whole as well as the individual pupils. Getting the interest level, pace and challenge of a lesson right will minimise problems with behaviour that arise through the boredom and difficulty of the work.

ENCOURAGE AND PRAISE

Imagine you are the coach of a football team and your pupils are the players. You will give them the tactics to succeed in the form of the behaviour code plus the new subject knowledge and skills. When they go out and play, they will try to give you their best but sometimes things will not go as well as everyone would like. In sport the support of the fans plus the extra push from the coach can lift the team and raise their game to new heights. There is nothing like the buzz you get when you know someone is rooting for you and willing you on. The best kind of support a teacher can give is encouragement, especially when things are going wrong. Knowing you are there will prevent them from giving up.

A team that starts to lose will grow despondent. Individual players will have their own views on the value of the game and their chances of turning it around. Some will continue to persevere whereas others will feel there is no way back. Any attempt to win seems futile to them. They will begin to feel that they might as well give up, except that would be embarrassing. Footballers do not walk off the pitch in the last ten minutes when they are obviously not going to win. Something keeps them playing but only just. They will have lost the fire they had at the start and may feel there is nothing worth playing for. The team with its loyal fans will be spurred on by their support and keep trying even when there seems no chance of winning. Strange things do happen and surprises can occur. Teams get lucky breaks and score goals in the dying minutes. When this happens their supporters suddenly explode into life, supplying a barrage of sound to raise their team's morale.

Children go through similar trials. They may keep making the same mistakes and just cannot seem to see why. They will look like giving up and they will give up, unless someone can show they believe in them. We need to be alert and spot the changes in mood that occur with children when failure looms. Stepping in with a few well-placed words of encouragement or praise and some advice can be all that's needed. However, some children are very needy and will require considerable support to get them out of the failure zone. It is then that their behaviour can break down. The child who is struggling and feeling success is nowhere in sight may give up and vent their feelings as aggression, abuse or distracting behaviour. They may slam doors, kick over chairs, throw books and bags, tear down displays, and spew out a tirade of foul language at the teacher or other pupils. This can be avoided with the right response.

MOTIVATE

Lift morale by noticing the good things children do. It may be their work or their behaviour. The knack is to identify something they have been working on and praise them promptly. Make the praise specific. Avoid non-specific comments like these:

'You are doing well.'

'You are working hard.'

Praise like this will probably be well received but it will not be as effective as praise for a specific effort made by the child. This shows you have noticed an improvement the child has made. Here are some examples:

'I can see a real improvement in your playing now you are thinking about the dynamics of the piece.'

'I noticed you double-checking your calculation and it's paid off because you've got it right.'

'Your diagrams are really neat and clear since you started using a fine pen.'

'You have made big efforts to take turns in your group recently. Well done!'

'You have really been trying to ignore Hassan when he makes personal comments.'

Praise should be made personal so the recipient knows you are addressing them. General comments to the whole class have some use but the individual pupils will not feel the same sense of pride as if they had been addressed by name. It is not always possible to give praise to every child in a lesson, because there is simply not enough time. The solution is to use personal and collective praise. In that way, a positive atmosphere will start to pervade your lessons. Personalise the praise by saying the child's name first:

'Jessica, that was very well read with such expression.'

When there seems to be nothing worth praising in a child's work, look for aspects of their behaviour to comment on.

SHY CHILDREN

Not everyone wants to be singled out from the crowd, even for something they have done well. There will be children who are shy or modest and prefer to remain anonymous. They will still need to be encouraged and motivated but a different approach is required. Use private signs or comments made when the rest of the group are busy on the task. Alternatively, well-composed comments at the end of written work or on reports will ensure that only that pupil can read them. Telephone calls and letters home may also be an option but it is worth checking with the child first. They may not want you talking to their parents and they may prefer written comments.

STREET CREDIBILITY

Some children view praise coming from a teacher as damaging to their personal image. In a culture of independence where young people strive to define themselves apart from adults, any public praise or comment that appears to condone their behaviour or make them acceptable will harm their status among their peers. The irony is that they may like the praise but do not want to be seen to like it when they are with their friends.

When praising these apparently 'anti-adult' individuals, care must be taken to do it in a way that will not harm their social status. For example, giving out test results is best done quietly and privately so the child does not have to reveal their score unless they want to. Those who decide to tell others will often use a variety of interesting tactics to preserve their image. For example, the boy who does well in a test may tell his friends his mark but play down his effort. He will make a big deal about not having done any revision because he had a new Play Station game he wanted to finish or he was out on his bike with his friends and did not get time.

USE 'DO' INSTEAD OF 'DON'T'

When a child gets it wrong, we can either turn it around in a positive way or tell them off in the hope that they will learn from the experience. Here is a 'don't' comment:

'Don't use a ruler like that, Jason!'

This comment does very little except tell the child what not to do. It does not direct them back to the right behaviour and does not put the responsibility for action with them. Changing it into a 'do' comment makes it more positive and useful:

'Jason. Hold the ruler with your left hand and lean your pen on it as you draw the line. Would you like me to show you?'

This statement gives the child something to do and corrects in a positive way.

TURN ASSESSMENT INTO A TOOL FOR LEARNING

Assessment begins in the lesson immediately a new piece of knowledge or skill is learned. Showing your class that you are actively involved in the learning will help to build a relationship and a partnership with them. Offering constructive comments instead of critical ones will motivate and encourage the children to search for their own answers and improve on their performance. When you do use questions, make them open questions to help them explore an idea. Open questions usually begin like these:

'Can you explain . . .?'

'What kind of . . .?'

'How could you . . .?'

'Describe . . .'

The responses you can expect from the children will draw on their experiences and opinions and be more detailed than if you had asked closed questions:

'When did Columbus discover America?'

'What is the area of a rectangle?'

'Do you think Northern Ireland should be part of the British Isles?'

Questions like these reveal which children know the answer but not whether they understand the circumstances or processes that led to it.

There are several useful ways of finding out how much children understand about a subject without resorting to a series of questions. Here are some examples:

- *Talk partners*: one child explains the concept or idea to another.
- *Key points*: children summarise a piece of work.
- *Hot seating*: children construct questions and the teacher or another pupil takes on the role of a character so the class can ask them questions.

Self-assessment

Checking for learning on a regular basis is a good way of gauging the effect of your teaching and empowering the children to judge for themselves how well they are doing. A good practice is to set objectives, targets or learning outcomes that are specific, distinct and achievable within five to ten minutes. This is done by breaking down the objectives even further. When the child completes the task, they should be able to tell whether they have been successful and decide if they:

- Understand the work
- Grasp most of it but need a bit more help
- Are having a great deal of difficulty and really need significant support, further explanations and practice.

The children will need some way of indicating how they feel at the end of each lesson. Younger children can be quite happy with smileys (Figure 7.1, overleaf). Older children will not want to put smileys on their work, so a numerical score could be used (Figure 7.2, overleaf).

Critical signposts

Many teachers write brief qualitative comments like 'excellent', 'good' or 'more effort required'. Some teachers prefer to write more copious notes about a point or idea

Figure 7.1 *Younger children like smileys*

| 10 – 8 | 7 – 5 | 4 – 1 |
| Got it | Nearly | Help needed |

Figure 7.2 *Older children like scores in a circle*

together with ways to improve it. Do children read anything teachers write or are they satisfied with the grades? Marking a piece of work and giving it a grade may just encourage the children to compare themselves with others, whereas questions like this will invite a response:

'You have made some good points but several technical words are spelled wrongly. Can you find and correct them?'

Then, when you give back the books, you can allow five minutes for them to read your comments and do the corrections. In this way, they will engage with your comments and learn by making the changes.

GIVE YOUR PUPILS THE RESPONSIBILITY FOR BEHAVING

Use the language of discipline (Rogers, 1994) to help children learn. Place the responsibility with them and use words and phrases such as you, yours, choice, choose, your action, you decide. Emphasise the choice and then show them how it can lead to a reward or a consequence. Stress that if they choose unwisely, they will end up with the consequence because they are responsible for their own actions. You do not need to get involved with their choice. They have the freedom to decide that for themselves. But advise them when necessary.

SELF-ESTEEM: THE ROUTE TO GOOD BEHAVIOUR

Children who feel good about themselves will have less difficulty learning how to behave. Children who have issues in their life that affect their self-esteem will communicate their feelings through excessive or undesirable behaviour. This can be addressed by treating them as individuals. Learn their names and get to know more about them such as their birthdays, their likes and dislikes, and what makes them tick.

When a child does something well or achieves something in or out of school, note it down so you can use the information to boost their confidence at appropriate times.

Greet the children at the door. Show them you value their presence. Share your own experiences with them and show you regard them as worthy of attention. Try to avoid demeaning experiences that will have a negative effect on their view of you and the school. Be wary of using draconian methods by setting up routines in the rooms to avoid problems arising.

Young people with low self-esteem will often avoid taking risks because they fear failure. They may make up quite elaborate and creative reasons why they should not do something. Alternatively, they will simply say they can't do it. Reinforcing a 'can do' culture requires you to reply positively. Scenarios 7.1, 7.2 and 7.3 show how this can be achieved.

Scenario 7.1

'Now, Susan, we are going to start designing a pair of slippers.'

'I can't do it!'

'Susan, you mean you can't do it *yet*, but by the time we finish this activity I have here, you will be able to design the slippers.'

Scenario 7.2

'We are going to learn how to bounce the ball while we are moving towards the basket.'

'I can't do that, I'm no good at basketball.'

'You can't do it *yet*, Luke, because I haven't shown you how to. But once I have and you've practised it a few times, you will be able to do it.'

Scenario 7.3

'The next activity involves finding the area of the room so we can calculate how much lino we will need.'

'I don't know how to do that, so I'm not bothering.'

'Of course you don't know how to do it *yet*, because I haven't shown you, but I bet that in five minutes, after I've taught you how to work it out, you will be able to do it.'

The emphasis is on being able to do something eventually. Nurture the 'can do' culture in your class. It depends on putting down the right foundation. Children in your class must feel safe if they are to start taking risks. They must trust you and feel that they will not be ridiculed when they make a mistake. You need to help them see mistakes as learning opportunities not failures.

One way of doing this is to teach them something that usually begins with making lots of mistakes such as learning to juggle or playing a game where they have to throw something into a bucket. Make it difficult to begin with but possible to do once they have practised and made judgements that lead to success. At the end of the game you can discuss it and show them how their errors were necessary so they could adjust their aim or improve their coordination.

Keep the lesson moving

Lessons with the wrong pace will become nurturing grounds for poor behaviour. Go too quickly and you will leave some children behind; they will give up, go off task and cause trouble. Go too slowly and some children will not be challenged; they will get bored and eventually misbehave. They become lethal because they are quicker-witted than those who get left behind. They end up using their intelligence to wind up other children and bait the teacher.

Gauging the pace correctly comes with experience but a new teacher can minimise the risk by finding out about their pupils. Knowing their strengths and weaknesses and pinpointing any barriers to learning will help you judge how they will engage with the work and complete the tasks. Once you have matched your normal ability group against the task and feel you are addressing the needs of the majority, you can start to consider how the work can be made more or less challenging to cater for needs outside this norm.

How positive is the classroom?

A positive classroom is a happy place where interesting things happen and individual success is celebrated. It is useful to review your own classroom from time to time to check how positive the atmosphere is and how the physical environment supports this aim. The following questions will help you do this. Not all questions will apply but they will help in striving for a well-organised, positive environment that is conducive to learning.

- Do you know the first names of the children?
- Do you welcome the children individually?
- Is the room easy to move around in when it is full of children?
- Do you adjust the heating and ventilation when necessary?
- Do you use the walls for notices and displaying the children's work?
- How do you plan activities to cater for the different learning styles of the children?
- Do you praise and encourage more than you criticise and reprimand?
- Do you link criticisms and praise to specific things the children have done?
- Do you phrase your directions using 'do' or 'don't'?
- Do you use open questions that help the children to explore a concept?
- Do you praise and acknowledge effort?
- How do you offer choices?
- How do you encourage the pupils to try to resolve conflicts?
- Do you tactically ignore low-level disruptions when they first occur?
- Do you defer consequences to prevent the lesson from being interrupted?

- Do you try to treat all the children in the same way, even the children you consider disruptive, uninterested or showing characteristics you don't like?
- Do you model the behaviour you want?
- How do you challenge a child who is abusive to others?
- Do you tolerate negative peer pressure?
- How do you deal with bullying?
- How do you deal with a child who attempts to wind up another child?
- Do you challenge racist or sexist comments?
- How do you broaden the horizons of your pupils?
- How do you promote equal opportunities in your room, your lessons and your resources?

WORKING WITH PARENTS

The most effective approaches to behaviour management are based on good partnerships between the school and the home. These partnerships need to be developed; they do not exist at the start and do not happen by chance. It is worth writing a letter of introduction to the parents when you take a new class at the start of the year. Introduce yourself by name, briefly outline your personal ethos, and signpost important events coming up during the forthcoming term. This letter should be sent home in a sealed envelope with the child. Figure 7.3 is a model letter.

Dear parent/carer

My name is .... and I will be teaching <pupil name> this year. I believe that learning is a journey. When children set out, they need a great deal of help by teaching, explaining and coaching. As they get older, they become more confident and can take on more responsibility for their own learning.

I believe that the best way to support your child is for us to work together in partnership. I will keep you informed of your child's progress via reports, parents' evenings and a home/school diary. Please do not hesitate to contact me if you feel it is necessary.

Behaviour is an important foundation for effective learning. Every child will have a copy of our behaviour code. Please take the time to read and discuss it with them.

Here are some important dates for your diary: <important dates>.

I look forward to meeting you in person in the future and I'm sure that together we will be able to support your child on the next step of his/her educational journey.

Yours sincerely

Class teacher

Figure 7.3 *Letter introducing yourself to a parent or carer*

EMERGING PROBLEMS WITH BEHAVIOUR

The first signs of inappropriate behaviour do not necessarily warrant seeking SENCO support for the child. You need to try out your own strategies for a reasonable period before you call on other professionals for help. In the interim, things may become quite difficult for you in the lessons if the child is causing low-level disruption and not responding to your attempts to manage him. It sometimes feels like there is no one to help because the incidents are not that serious, just sufficiently time-consuming that you feel drained by the end of the lesson. Seeking the assistance of colleagues is the most obvious course of action but if you want to avoid feeling a failure and a victim, you need to take control. One way is to begin your own research project on the child. Observe and make notes of:

- When they misbehave
- What the common features are between the incidents
- The frequency and scale of the behaviour
- Where it occurs most in the school.

Consider the behaviour in the context of what you know about the child. You are searching for possible triggers, so try to connect behaviours to events. The child's home environment and family dynamic may be contributing, so they are also worth investigating. You may decide to arrange a meeting with the parents or carers to discuss the downward trend in the child's behaviour. This is also an ideal opportunity to get more background information. The questions in the home profile (see appendices) may be useful in helping to structure the meeting. They will also help you in recording the parents' comments. The questions are designed to get at the parental experience and parental perceptions of the child's behaviour. The meeting will enable you to discover more about the family routines such as mealtimes, leisure activities and their attempts to manage behaviour. The appendices also contain a set of questions to ask the child. These questions will help you find out more about what the child does at home and how they feel about their family.

Digesting, analysing and evaluating this information together with your own observations of the child will help lead to a clearer understanding of why they have started to behave differently. Embarking on this will give you a positive feeling of empowerment because you will be doing something that will eventually lead to a solution. It will also alert the parents at an early stage that their child is in difficulty and the meeting will begin the process of sharing experiences and searching for solutions. The next step is to call a meeting of colleagues and consider which other professionals could provide support or guidance in helping the child. Cracking hard cases usually requires more than a behaviour code. Different solutions will be needed. The next chapter describes the characteristics of children who exhibit extreme behaviour and uses case studies to illustrate how they might be addressed.

SUMMARY

- Classes are not homogeneous groups. Pupils have very different needs and learn in different ways at different rates. Teachers need to consider the varying needs of the children when planning lessons.

- The brain is a site of chemical reactions and to function properly it needs water, the correct temperature and other requirements. People learn best when their brain's requirements are satisfied.
- Good lessons have structure, pace, challenge, interest and opportunities.
- People respond positively to praise and encouragement. The most effective praise is specific and directed at things the child has done well.
- Some pupils will not want to be praised publicly. This may be because they are shy or because they do not want their peers to see them being acknowledged by the teacher. Praise should be given sensitively with these reasons in mind.
- Positive directions and corrections should be framed as 'dos' rather than 'don'ts'.
- Assessment is a powerful tool for learning. Children should be given the opportunity to talk in depth about a subject to help them refine and develop their own ideas.
- Focus your comments on the work to help the pupils understand what they have done well and what they could do to improve.
- Children who are confident and feel good about themselves will be less likely to have behavioural problems. Boosting the confidence of children with low self-esteem is vital to ensure they become better learners.
- Building partnerships with parents is important in ensuring that the children get the best support available.

8 THE CHALLENGING CHILDREN

The most wearing children are the challenging children. Every school has them from time to time. Some schools seem to get more than their fair share. They are demanding, time-consuming and sometimes frightening. Their behaviour will go beyond the limits of your behaviour plan as they stretch the boundaries and test the rules. Dealing with a tough child requires a great deal more than the teacher can be expected to give. The most effective way is through a team effort, drawing from the experience and knowledge of a wider group that may include members of the leadership team, the special educational needs coordinator (SENCO), parents, educational psychologists, social workers, police, young offenders case workers, access and attendance officers, and medical representatives such as mental health specialists and doctors. These children first become noticeable by their continual flouting of the rules with low-level disruptions.

GATHERING INFORMATION

The first thing to do when you realise you have a difficult pupil in your class is to find out more. You will want to know whether other teachers have had problems with them and if so, what they did about it. You will also want to know whether the SENCO has any knowledge of the child and whether there has been any action. The child may have a history of incidents unknown to anyone in the school, so you should also read through the file.

The SENCO will make the decision to involve other professionals. An educational psychologist could be asked to observe the child and carry out an assessment. Their report is essential if the SENCO is considering applying for a statement. The social services may already be involved. They will work with the child and the family and can provide valuable insight into the domestic situation. The family doctor and other related practitioners, including mental health practitioners, will work closely with a school when the child is at risk of exclusion. Their knowledge of the child's medical history can be illuminating. The police youth offending teams will have information about the child if they have been involved in any incidents outside school.

A meeting of these professionals provides a unique forum to share information in a quick and efficient way. Much of what is known about a child does not always get written down, so it will not get passed on. The meeting enables everyone concerned to get access to that information and to discuss strategies and support that have worked in the past. Parents and carers are a vital part of the jigsaw but sometimes they may be unwilling to engage. Their support will be needed to help their child address their behaviour and to redefine boundaries in school and at home so conditions will be right for learning.

THE CRITICAL INCIDENT

Behaviour is context based and children learn how to behave from the others around them. Behaviour can also be a means of communicating emotion. When a child has a traumatic experience the damage can be deep and the effects can surface in ways that seem unconnected to what has happened. If you believe that undesirable behaviour has its triggers then it is possible to move away from a culture of blame to one of understanding. To illustrate this point, you may have gone to work one day with a splitting headache and felt you didn't have the strength to be as patient as usual. When a pupil misbehaved, you snapped at them. Normally you are calm and rational but on that occasion your head was banging and you just couldn't be bothered. Your change in behaviour was due to how you felt that day.

Challenging children will invariably have a range of common factors that contribute directly or indirectly to their behaviour. One of the factors will be some kind of critical incident that has occurred in their past. Here are some examples:

- Parents divorcing
- Witnessing parents arguing or fighting
- A parent addicted to alcohol or drugs
- Parental depression
- Disowned or neglected by a parent
- Redundancy or long-term unemployment of a parent
- Witnessing abuse or being abused
- A family member going through a serious illness
- Bullied at home or in school
- Involvement in crime or drugs
- A family member convicted of a crime or in prison
- Refugee from a war zone.

The Framework for the Assessment of Children in Need and Their Families (Department of Health, 2000) provides a useful starting point for considering triggers of challenging behaviour. Figure 8.1 (overleaf) shows the assessment framework.

LOOKING FOR THE FIRST SIGNS

How can you tell from the first signs whether a child is going to be really challenging or just having a bad day? With difficulty, because both may fail to respond to your behaviour management methods during the lesson but challenging pupils will persist and continue to behave inappropriately over time. They will fail to respond to controls used by teachers and the result will be a referral to a more senior member of staff. Here are some signs that point towards specific problems:

- Arguing with others in the class, especially between children who you would have regarded as friends.
- Work will suffer. The presentation will become untidy and the condition of books will deteriorate. The quality and quantity of what is produced will go down below your expectations for the pupil as they begin to underperform.
- Things will be forgotten. The pupil will miss homework deadlines they used not to miss and books and equipment will not be brought to lessons.

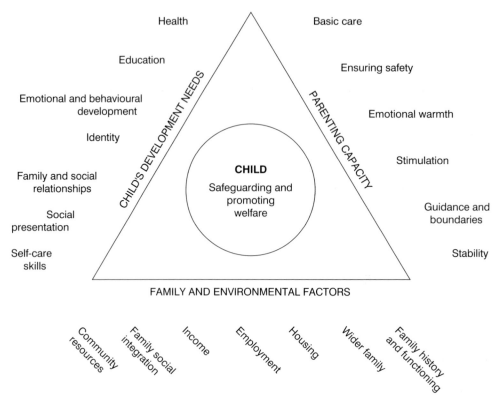

Figure 8.1 *Assessment framework (Department of Health, 2000) The Framework for the Assessment of Children in Need and Their Families*

- Irrational outbursts and a lack of patience and tolerance in coping with daily life.
- Physical appearance may change. This may happen in several ways. Weight loss may be due to worry, forced dieting and undernourishment, all with their associated causes. These could include relationship problems, poor self-image, illness or lack of parental care. Bruises and injuries may arise from accidents, sports injuries or deliberate violence. Vacant expressions coupled with glazed or heavy-lidded eyes can be attributed to a lack of sleep, illness or substance abuse. Take care over reaching a conclusion about the cause but any of these changes combined with a sudden swing in temperament could be early indicators of something going wrong.

Persistent inability to conform to class directions may be another indicator:

- Calling out
- Queue jumping
- Being frequently off task
- Leaving their seat and wandering around
- Continual chattering
- Winding up other children
- Continually interrupting
- Overly fidgety

- Easily distracted
- Poor attention when instructions are being given
- Noisy play
- Dangerous activity.

There may also be repeated incidents of unsocial behaviour outside the lessons:

- Theft
- Bullying
- Fighting
- Being alone for long periods of time.

Note that the signs described are not always direct indicators of a critical incident but when viewed alongside other information they may help to construct a picture of what is going on in a child's life at that moment.

DEVELOPING THE STRATEGY

The aim is to identify potentially challenging children and help them before a serious incident occurs. When this is possible, the strategy will have several strands:

- Analysing any incidents that have occurred so far
- Working with the child to identify areas of behaviour that can be improved
- Providing ways for the child to manage their behaviour when similar incidents occur
- Putting together a personal support plan (PSP).

There are numerous tools for profiling a child's emotional and behavioural development. Primary teachers may use the Boxall profile (Bennathan and Boxall, 1984). Two members of staff who know the child well, such as the class teacher and the learning support assistant, usually complete it. A development wheel could also be used and yields a visual picture of aspects of the child's emotional and social profile, which could then be used to plan where support should be given and how.

Many incidents in primary schools can be efficiently dealt with through the normal methods used by teachers on a daily basis. The serious incidents require more attention and time to be spent on them to make sure that everyone concerned receives fair treatment. The standard procedure in many schools is to separate those involved and get them to write their accounts of what happened. These are then compared to ascertain who was the perpetrator and who was the victim. Separating the children prevents them from discussing what they will write. The accounts can also be used in subsequent meetings with parents, who sometimes find it hard to come to terms with the fact that their child has done something wrong.

A useful tool to use alongside the written account is a behaviour sheet (Ayers *et al.*, 1993); Figure 8.2 (overleaf) shows an example. The interview should be carried out quickly while the details of the incident are still fresh in the child's mind. It requires a member of staff to work with the children because they sometimes conveniently leave things out and need reminding. This could be the teacher but if the child's anger is directed at the teacher, it may be difficult getting the child to cooperate.

Date/time	Antecedents	Behaviour	Consequences
	The trigger	The child's response	The outcome to the child

Figure 8.2 *A behaviour sheet*

There are three steps in the process. The first step is about the triggers that prompted the behaviour. The interviewer aims to engage the child in when the incident happened, where it happened, who was involved and what they did. The second step is concerned with the child's own response to the triggers. The child is asked to imagine that a camera is filming them as they respond to the trigger and then to describe what it would see. Wherever possible, the child should reflect on the action and say what the consequence might be for what they did. In the third step, the child lists all the consequences of their actions. Some may be positive pay-offs and some negative. The interviewer places a plus or minus sign against each one. Ideally, there should not be any pay-offs. The third section is then used as a prompt for discussion and development to help the child track each consequence back to its trigger.

HELPING CHILDREN ACQUIRE SKILLS TO MANAGE THEIR BEHAVIOUR

The child will need help to enable them to control their response when provoked. Schools can have very varied approaches:

- *Whole class meetings* to discuss areas of difficulty that are common to several pupils.
- *Small group coaching* led by behaviour mentors whose role is to help children redirect anger, control outbursts, ignore distractions and seek support during stressful times. Successful approaches include role-playing to practise how to respond, empathy to enable children to appreciate how a 'victim' feels, and simulations to test out strategies they have learned.
- *One-to-one counselling* to help the child work through their own feelings. Various therapeutic methods can be used by staff trained in them or by professionals from outside the school.

The emphasis should be on teaching the child new ways to behave. Dreikurs *et al.* (1982) devised a method to use when there are no obvious reasons behind the child's behaviour such as a critical incident, difficulties at home or in school. The child is helped to examine his own behaviour and suggest reasons for it. This requires a great deal of skill from the adult working with the child, because the child will probably be very reluctant to talk and visual cues will need to be used:

'I can see you are angry . . .'

'It is clear you are not happy at the moment . . .'

This enables a dialogue to open between you. You can then start to discuss his behaviour and make an offer of help:

'. . . and I would like to help you out. You know you keep interrupting me at the start of the lesson.'

The child will probably not seem as though he is paying attention. He may turn away or preoccupy himself by fiddling with something, but you ignore his silence and carry on:

'Do you know why you do it?'

This directs the child to the problem but do not expect an answer. A response such as '**** off!' or getting up and walking away will be a prompt to suspending this approach until another time. You will know you are getting somewhere if the child remains silent. Tell him what you think the reason is:

'Shall I tell you what I reckon?'

Do not wait for an answer:

'Is it that you want me to notice you?'

'Could you be trying to get me talking about something because you do not want to do the work?'

'Are you trying to show everyone what you know about the subject?'

The aim is not to embarrass the child. You are trying to show that you know what the child is doing. You may get a response, so watch the child very closely for any slight changes in behaviour. He may change position, fidget, look down, turn away, relax his shoulders, etc. Any of these may be an acknowledgement that you have guessed the reason. Alternatively, he may adamantly object, so you will need to reply:

'Well, I thought that was the reason for your interruptions. Tell me what the real reason is then.'

Then he can be encouraged to explain his reasons and you should listen and show you understand:

'You succeeded in what you tried to do and I can't stop you interrupting me but I need you to help me put together a plan that we can use together.'

PUTTING THE PLAN TOGETHER

A personal support plan in a primary school will require the support of all the staff that teach the child, the parents and outside agencies that are involved. The plan will provide a means of reorganising the child's experience. Here is what it contains:

- Expectations placed on the child
- Targets for behaviour that are realistic and broken down into steps
- Rewards and how they can be earned
- Consequences
- Exit procedures
- An individual timetable (which may be less than the full timetable)
- Arrangements for before school, breaks, lunchtimes and home time
- Review dates.

Some staff may express concern about having the child in their class and need training, such as training in positive assertive methods, restraint procedures, devising non-age-related teaching materials and baseline assessment methods. Everyone involved, including the child, should agree the contents of the plan and the first review date to ensure it is properly supported and stands a good chance of yielding success. Figure 8.3 shows how to establish a personal support plan.

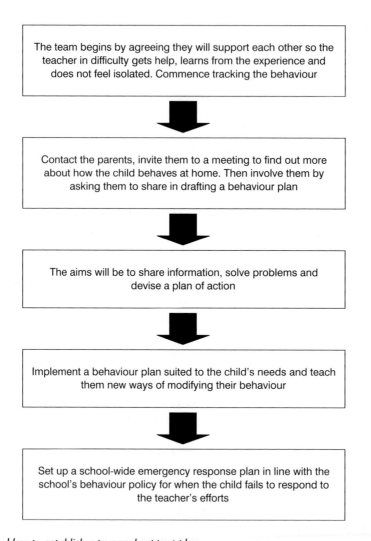

Figure 8.3 *How to establish a personal support plan*

Types of challenging children

Challenging children will exhibit particular kinds of behaviour, described in this chapter's case studies. Individual children will not fit a category exactly as they have complex needs that manifest in many ways. For example, a child fitting the controlling type may also be hyperactive and even end up being diagnosed with attention deficit hyperactivity disorder (ADHD). Finding strategies for dealing with tough children will not be easy and the pragmatic approach is to identify the type that has the best fit then use it as a starting point. The other facets of the child's behaviour can be dealt with as discrete issues alongside the main strategy.

THE CONTROLLER

In any group there will be some individuals who emerge as leaders but the controller is someone who needs to dominate. Their needs extend beyond the classroom and into the home. They will rule the roost and the parents will be impotent. In the classroom they will attempt to monopolise your time by asking countless questions, trying to engage you in conversation and wanting to do the activity first. They will question everything and try to undermine your decisions whenever an opportunity arises such as an ambiguity around an incident. They will point out things that seem unfair to them and tell you if another child is doing something wrong.

At home they will dominate virtually anything and everything they can, including mealtimes and menus, what is watched on the television, where and when they go out and for how long. They will make life very difficult for their parents and eventually provoke sibling rivalry as others in the household start to resent their selfishness.

The reasons behind their behaviour will vary but it stems from a need in the child. Perhaps the child needs attention that was lacking in their past, so they try to secure it for themselves. They may have been deserted by one of their parents and feel they need to fill that space; the other parent may have allowed them the power to do so. Alternatively, it may be poor parenting over a long period, giving them so much freedom that they have lost the boundaries associated with normal adult–child relationships. The result will be a very difficult home life where the parent feels powerless and ultimately bullied by the child. The child in this position will get into difficulties at school because their behaviour will be unacceptable and ultimately create incidents that could lead to exclusion. Outside school, they will have so much freedom that they may eventually get involved in crime or antisocial behaviour because the parent has no control and the child will come and go at will.

Identifying the behaviour is the key and the child will often also exhibit other behavioural traits such as ADHD or poor self-esteem. The strategies for dealing with controlling children are often complex. The child will need to have boundaries redefined and when the boundaries are tested they must be adhered to rigidly. The main aim is for the child to learn that the adult is in charge and has the responsibility for making decisions until they reach the recognised age of adulthood. They also have to learn that things need to be shared and that they cannot always go first. The noticeable sign that your strategies are working will be that the child will appear more relaxed, less prone to outbreaks of temper and easier to be with in general (Case Study 8.1, overleaf).

Case Study 8.1 *Ben*

Ben was a victim of a very sad experience that began at his birth. His mother was unable to cope with his brother, who was several years older than him. His grandmother took care of him after his mother hurt him on several occasions. While she was pregnant with Ben she contacted the social services and told them she was having problems coping, so they accepted her into the mother and baby home, where she was cared for until he was born.

Ben's mum had moderate learning difficulties and trouble controlling her anger. The staff felt she was a good mother but could not be relied on to keep Ben safe when she was going through her depressions. Eventually she could not cope and left Ben on the doorstep of his birth father's flat because she was angry that he was not helping her.

Social services got Ben back with his mother and placed him on the child protection register but things did not improve and finally it came to a head when she lost her temper and punched Ben in the eye. An interim court order was granted that meant she shared parental responsibility with the local authority, which could then make decisions to ensure Ben was safe. After the court order was made, Ben was fostered and allowed to see his birth mother once a week.

Ben's development was slow and his speech was behind, but perhaps more seriously, he didn't seem to know how to play with things. He found it very difficult to play with other children and adults. This has remained the case and Ben hates any competitive games or losing at anything.

After a succession of foster carers, Ben finally found some stability with long-term foster parents. He loved to play with their daughters but would sometimes get very angry if he couldn't get his own way and he ended up having a temper tantrum. They tried to help him cope with his tantrums by showing him how to let them know in other ways what he wanted. His speech developed and he started to make some progress but he got very frightened at nights and used to hide under the quilt. This may have been caused by some recollection of the very early incidents when he was a baby watching his father beat his mother. As time went by, these memories faded and he got more confident. He started doing the things normal children did, like going to playgroups and being with his new family.

The social services decided to look for parents to adopt Ben. He was three years old and they felt he was ready to settle somewhere permanently and start a new life. A couple were found who were looking for a brother for their other adopted son. They took him home and in time legally adopted him. But the story doesn't stop there.

By the time Ben was in Year 6 he was really having difficulties. His teacher was at her wits' end. His behaviour was so bad and she could get very little work out of him. He spent most of his time with his head in his hands slumped on the desk or wandering around the room annoying the others. The teacher coped with him by putting him outside with a support assistant. He would be allowed to do a bit of art or whatever else he felt like. They felt it was a good day if he did something. Sometimes he would not do as the teacher wanted at all and in the end the head was called. She would usually get him to move but that was as far as her authority stretched. He could be very annoying and poke and pinch other children until they got fed up and told the teacher. He had gone too far on several occasions and been excluded. The staff at the school had tried everything they could think of and involved all the agencies to try to get him some help. He was finally awarded a statement that specified he should get thirteen hours of one-to-one support but that did nothing to help. The support worker could not manage him and he just carried on what he had been doing before.

Anyone who provoked him and tried to get him to do something he did not want to do would get a response of either angry yelling or whining and whingeing. He didn't seem to have any fear. He would push certain children to their limits and not realise the risk he was taking. Occasionally one of them would retaliate and give him a thump. This would push him completely over the edge. He would rush around swearing and slamming doors with such force that the building shook and the hinges came loose.

On one occasion he ran out of a classroom into a nearby room, grabbed a boy's book and tore it up. The boy was quite volatile himself and went for Ben. The teacher just managed to step between them in time and then Ben was removed. The boy did not leave it there. Later, at lunch, he managed to get near enough to Ben to give him a kick. A support worker took Ben off and was instructed to keep him in the dining room during lunch play. However, he managed to get free and found his way outside. The other boy was playing football and Ben went up to him and called him a name. The boy turned and lunged at him, catching him square in the chest. This set Ben off and he went away yelling and swearing. What was completely mystifying was that ten minutes later they were both playing together over by the bushes and seemed to have forgotten the incidents.

Eventually the head contacted the pupil referral unit (PRU) because she believed that perhaps he would benefit by being in a new environment with a more structured regime and smaller classes. At the PRU things went from bad to worse. The staff recognised some of the signs in Ben's behaviour and believed him to be a controller. He wanted everything his way and the other children had to be his friends. He tried to gain their attention but found that they could not give him what he wanted. To get more attention he started annoying them. He found that it worked but not in the way he intended. He grew more unhappy and frustrated and the downward spiral continued where he had left off at the school.

Annie had seen children like Ben before, so when he came to her class he was not going to have the control he had become used to getting. She used a number of strategies that had been developed from situations in nature. Herds and packs have very strict hierarchies and that was what she needed in her class so that Ben would know his place. When he joined the class, Annie explained that everyone had a specific place in an order and he was last because he was the newest member. This applied to anything he wanted to say or do. To reinforce this pecking order, the staff would always go first. The hierarchy that was being established placed the most important adult at the top then the other adults, all the way down through the pupils to Ben. Whenever he made a challenge or complained and said something was not fair, the standard reply was always, 'I am the adult here, Ben, and it's my job to decide what happens.'

Ben spent the first few days fitting in then he started to challenge the new boundaries. The staff stood their ground and he buffeted it. Then he began his campaign of almost total resistance. He started running out of the class and the building. He slammed the doors more forcefully and threw things around the room. He also got more annoying and aggressive towards the other pupils.

At home he was also resistant but his parents started working closely with the staff at the PRU. When Ben left the class and wasted time, he was given the work to make up at home. His parents would not let him have his tea or use the Play Station until the work was done. He resisted like mad but they held firm. He would protest for a considerable time but eventually resigned himself to the fact that he wasn't going to win.

Ben was not getting his way and was also not able to control others, so he tried something different. He dug his heels in and refused to get ready for school. His parents were gaining strength from the staff at the PRU and decided he was not going to dictate terms to them. They gave him the choice of getting ready or going in his pyjamas. He refused so his dad said he would have to go as he was. He told them that he wasn't going to move, so his dad replied, 'Either you bring yourself out to the car or I will bring you!' Ben huffed, folded his arms and sat down, then to his dismay, his dad brought him out. As they neared the school, Ben hurriedly changed into his school clothes so that when he arrived he would be ready to go in.

The daily grind of making him do the work he missed and giving him the red cards after the two warnings when he did not comply, eventually moved Ben on. He realised he was not winning and had to change. He may have felt that the incidents in his early life had made him helpless and so he needed to hang on to things he could control. Perhaps his mum's lack of control and her anger had deeply affected him and so he needed to feel he was the only one making the decisions. His parents, who had hurt or disowned him, had made all the decisions about his life until then. His foster carers and social workers were never around for long, and anyway they always passed him on to someone else. His teachers didn't do as he wanted and the new parents seemed weak and were unable to say no until recently.

The turning point was when the PRU head allocated him a personal tutor. The tutor was able to build a relationship with him and talk about his tantrums without him going into one. Working away from other children prevented him from getting into trouble and gave him time to relax. Special play sessions were set up between Ben and one of the other boys he called his friend. This allowed him to learn to play with other children. He could just play and not have to worry whether he won or lost, because he trusted his friend. Ben started to make a real improvement and some steps in the right direction.

At the time of writing, there was no happy ending for Ben, just the feeling that his rages were getting less frequent and that some solutions were being found. He had come a long way. He could rarely stay in the classroom for long but he would do some work every day with his tutor. He had not done any work in the mainstream school but now he was doing the National Curriculum and the work was challenging him. When the work he did was lacking in quality or quantity, he was required to take it home and improve it. He would often have two hours of work to do each night but he seemed to be all right with the arrangement. He had also started to enjoy playing games and did not get so worried about losing.

In Case Study 8.1 Annie realised that there might be problems and initiated a professionals' meeting to establish what the difficulties might be. Once it becomes obvious that your normal behaviour-management methods might not work, it is time to plan an individualised approach. Early identification of the triggers will enable you to think creatively and plan some strategies for the year team to try. Adopting a multi-agency approach will provide the resources to work with the family. The strategies Annie used were successful because the team were well informed and there was a consistency in approach that prevented the child from getting confused or finding a crack to exploit. Sometimes the child will not respond immediately and the team need to review and be prepared to modify their approach if it is not working. Individuals learn at different rates, so be patient and persistent.

THE MANIPULATOR

Manipulators have many similarities with controllers. The differences are in the frequency and subtlety of the things they are trying to manipulate. For example, a child who is happy with a particular teacher will not try to change anything. They will participate in the lesson and appear to be fine. The problem will occur when they get a teacher they do not like for some reason.

The things that a child tries to manipulate will vary. They may try to change their timetable, the people they work with or how something is done because it may clash with their personal agenda. The reasons for their need to manipulate can vary. They may be seeking attention and have learned that by imposing their will they have got their way and the attention they crave. It may be that they do not like people of a certain gender. This may stem from the treatment they have had, which may include abuse. It may be that the parent perceives the child as weak and despises them for it. They may dislike someone because of their position, such as a teacher, or someone who has no power and is therefore an easy target.

Strategies for helping manipulators are very similar to strategies for helping controllers. Identifying the cause will enable you to tailor your response most effectively. Children should not be allowed to dominate, otherwise they will continue to feel that their manipulative approach is working. The teacher should set up an alternative plan for the child that provides them with a choice of either working in a satisfactory way with the person or working away from everyone and losing the benefits they may have had, such as equipment, computers and the company of others. Sometimes it may be possible to get the child to work one-to-one with the member of staff over a period of time so they have to come to terms with their dislikes (Case Study 8.2).

Case Study 8.2 *Phillip*

Phillip was in Year 4 when it all started. His family had just split up, leaving his mum to look after him, his younger sister and one of his older brothers who was 12. He had six other brothers, well half-brothers really. Nearly all of them had different dads. The brother he lived with had a different dad too and resented Phillip. He didn't think he should be living with him and wanted him out. They shared a room and he was always down on Phillip. They had a very uneasy relationship. Phillip liked his younger sister though. She was 4 and they enjoyed playing with her toys.

Phillip loved his dad. He was a proud man from Jamaica but he came from a culture where certain kinds of behaviour were considered acceptable. The break-up of Phillip's parents was a messy business and ended in a domestic row with the police being called because the neighbours heard screams coming from the house. They feared for the safety of the mother. Eventually his dad was escorted from the house and his mum was taken in by a neighbour to recover from the shock. They forgot about the children until the next day, when his mum finally came out of her shock and asked where they were. When they went back to the house they found Phillip cooking beans on toast for his sister. He seemed very organised but later revealed that they had spent the rest of the night hiding away under the bed together.

Phillip did continue to see his dad. He usually went to stay with him at weekends, once a month. He had one of those relationships based on fear. He enjoyed his time with him but was scared of what his dad would do to him if he did anything wrong. His dad openly admitted that on one occasion he had hit him with his belt, the buckle end, because that was what parents did where he came from. These experiences must have affected Phillip and changed the way he viewed other people. He seemed to be all right with women teachers and caused few problems. When there was a problem, the trigger could usually be traced back to something that had started at home, some incident with his brother or a visit from his dad.

Nick Wells became the head of the pupil referral unit (PRU) in April, a few months earlier than Phillip. It was his first job in this kind of provision. He had previously spent three years in a special school working mainly with children who had learning difficulties. Before that he had worked in secondary schools and had gained a lot of experience managing difficult children. He found the work very interesting because it enabled him to work with individual children on their specific problems.

Nick got the usual comments from the children that he was not very nice and didn't let them do things they had been allowed to do before his arrival. As the head, he expected this because changes needed to happen. The unit needed a shake-up because it had been ignored by the overall head of the service, who had been more interested and involved with the secondary provision and developments at the local education authority (LEA). Nick ignored their comments and got on with the job, so when Phillip arrived the new practices were already in place.

Phillip sized up Nick, realised there were few opportunities to get his own way and he didn't like it. He did not like Nick and he was certainly not going to let him boss him around. One day near Christmas he had been having a bad time at home and had planned to do nothing at school. He began the numeracy lesson with that aim and offered nothing during the whole class activity. When it came to getting on with the individual tasks, he was all right going on the computer and doing RM Maths, because he liked that, but that was all. He was definitely not going to do the work the others were doing.

Nick could see him starting to go and went over to him. Phillip didn't like Nick much and certainly did not want to talk to him about what he thought he should and should not do. As Nick talked, Phillip stared down at the desk. Nick tried to get him to make eye contact but he would only do it reluctantly. Phillip eventually gave in and started to do the work, to get Nick off his back, but he stopped once Nick was busy with another group of pupils. Nick returned to him later in the lesson and discovered he had done nothing. He decided to leave him and would get him to do the work in his own time. The children nearby could see Phillip was getting away with it and some of them asked why. Nick decided that, in the interests of fairness, he needed to apply the sanctions and he explained to Phillip that if he didn't get on with the work, he would move him to the time-out table and anything that was not finished would be done at break.

Phillip was getting cross with all the hassle. He pushed his books onto the floor and threw his pencil at the window. He swore at Nick and then got up and tried to leave the room. Nick stood in his way and then directed him to return to his seat. 'Get out of my way!' he shouted. Then he kicked some chairs over and made for the fire door. Within seconds he was out of the door and walking towards the gate. He got halfway there then stopped. He loitered for a short while then wandered around the flowerbeds and trees along the perimeter fence. He was obviously angry but did not look like he was going to run out of school.

Eventually he returned, with some help from one of the support assistants he liked working with. They discussed Phillip's behaviour and he told her he did not like Mr Wells, and he was not going to do as he said. The staff met at the end of the day and talked about Phillip. After considerable thought, Nick drew up a plan. He felt that Phillip should work with whoever he was given. Children cannot pick and choose their teachers and he thought it was better to help Phillip come to terms with that. He decided to go into the classroom as Phillip's support assistant for a couple of days and literally swamp him so he had no option but to do as Nick said if he wanted to have the freedom to go to playtimes.

Nick began by discussing his expectations for behaviour. Then he went on to explain that Phillip could earn some rewards if he worked well and Nick was satisfied with his efforts. He would have to earn his breaks but Nick offered him some extra time at the end of the morning and afternoon sessions where he could choose something he liked. Phillip really enjoyed using the computer. He had a program with virtual dogs and cats that allowed the user to look after them as pets. Nick agreed that this could be one of his special rewards. Then Nick outlined the consequences and showed Phillip a special chart he would use to monitor him. He had divided the whole day into fifteen-minute sections. He could get a point every fifteen minutes if Nick decided he had made a good effort to behave and work well. He had to get all the points to earn a full session on the computer. Reduced sessions would be awarded down to 85% of the points. If he got below 85% of the points, he would get no session.

They returned to the classroom and Nick told Phillip where he wanted him to sit and what he was to do. He sat next to Phillip and gave him the work from the lesson he had walked out of previously. Phillip was not happy about this but resigned himself to doing what he was told. You could see by his body language he did not like having to work with Nick. Nick reminded him of the rule about following directions and redirected him. The day progressed with Phillip losing a number of points for trying to resist Nick. Nick controlled everything around Phillip. He opened the windows and kept possession of all the resources so that Phillip had to ask to use them. Whenever they had to go anywhere outside the classroom, Phillip had to walk beside Nick. He would have to wait to enter the room until Nick gave him permission. At lunch he had to collect his meal and sit at the table until Nick had joined him before he could start eating.

Phillip didn't do very well at first and did not earn his break because of his resistance. He just missed getting the full computer period at lunchtime, but he did earn five minutes. By the afternoon he had tested all the boundaries Nick had given him and found they wouldn't budge. During the afternoon there was a noticeable difference in his behaviour. By the end of the first day, Phillip was fed up with having to spend all his time with Nick but was very pleased to have earned a full computer session.

The next day was an improvement on the previous one. Phillip must have gone home and thought about things because he made an excellent start and seemed happy to work with Nick. Unfortunately, it didn't last and he didn't earn his break. Nick could see Phillip was having some problems and coached him through them. He explained that Phillip made his own choices and if he did not want to miss out on the rewards, he had to do the right things. The talk seemed to help him and by lunchtime he had turned things round. The day improved as he got used to having Nick about, but he blew it again just before the end of school, so he did not earn the last computer session. Phillip was obviously put out and disappointed but took it well.

During the two days, Nick realised it was not male teachers Phillip disliked, but certain kinds of men. If you could help him believe that you would not be a threat, he would warm to you. Nick had found this out and from then on he was able to work with Phillip. He needed to be assertive to ensure that Phillip knew who was the boss. When Phillip eventually returned to his mainstream school, he was able to work much better with any male teachers once they knew how to work with him.

THE TOTAL SHUTDOWNER

The total shutdowner is particularly difficult to manage as they do not do things that are really bad. They do not throw things around, hit or shout at other pupils or teachers, destroy school property or truant. They use silence and non-compliance as a means of demonstrating their feelings and desires. The more you try to provoke them into doing what you ask, the more resilient they appear to be. It is as if they are using the teacher's emotional energy to fuel their wall of silence. Unlike children with low self-esteem, they do not feel the need to go into a corner, cover their face or run away and hide. They have enough strength to remain where they are and literally shut down.

Their stubbornness has probably been learned as a result of being made to do things that they do not know how to do. They become frozen and cannot take the next step, and the adult has either been unable or unwilling to help them. They may have experienced anger from the adult, who perceives their inactivity as insolence. They try to ignore the adult in the hope they will be left alone. They channel their energy into ignoring the adult. They will not seethe then suddenly explode. They will remain rooted to the spot and fixed on something they can see near them until they feel the threat has gone.

Dealing with the shutdowner involves restating the direction, followed by a rule reminder. Assume he has heard you and then give him some take-up time. Return to him at the end of that time and remind him of his choices and the consequences of not following directions. When he fails to respond, inform him that you are giving him his first warning. Restate the direction, offer help and then leave him to it. Repeat the directions, going through your behaviour code, pointing out there will be consequences but do not over-service his behaviour. The rest of the class will know you have been fair and dealt with him in the same way as everyone else. Do not make any emotional investment. Wait until another time to tell him the consequences of his actions (Case Study 8.3).

Case Study 8.3 *Andy*

Andy had been at the centre of a lot of problems at school for quite some time. He gave the impression of a child with little confidence. He was a slow learner and had been making very little progress for the past eighteen months. The staff at the school had identified him as one of the children at most risk in his academic progress. They had applied for a statement but it had been held up due to his absence. He would often be away from school for several weeks. When investigations were initiated he would suddenly start attending again. Some of the teachers who knew him and his family felt that his absence was due to his mother's inability to manage her own life, which resulted in him being left to his own devices.

Andy's mother was a single parent and had a young baby aged nearly 2. Her partner had left her during the pregnancy. Andy's real dad had been involved in petty crime and got himself into bad debt then disappeared off the scene when Andy was 4. Some men had come to their home one day and taken their television, the video, some furniture and jewellery. Andy was just a toddler but had vague memories of their visit and of his mum being pushed aside when she tried to stop them taking the stuff. They hadn't seen his dad after that but the rumours were that he had gone up north and started his life again under a new name. Andy didn't know or understand, but when he got older he discovered his dad had fled his life of debt with his girlfriend and had been living in Manchester ever since. He hadn't tried to contact them and that made Andy hate him.

Anyway, his mum had eventually found a new partner called Gary, who she liked very much. Andy liked him as well, and then they told him that he would have a baby sister. Things seemed great for a couple of months but then it started to go wrong. Gary seemed to change. He used to stop out late and come back in a foul mood. Andy watched as Gary knocked his mum about. Then one night he didn't come back at all. His mum was relieved because she was weary of being hit and shouted at. She was getting worried about the baby and wanted some peace. When his sister was born she had some things wrong with her. Andy loved her and felt very protective towards her whenever anyone made a remark about the strange mark on her face and the odd expression in her eyes.

Andy had just returned to school after a period of absence. He was very moody and did not want to join in with the rest of the class. At break time he wandered around on his own and skulked by the fence. Whenever another child came over to him, he would turn away and ignore them until they left him. Emily, his teacher, was used to this. She felt he was a very unhappy child but couldn't work out why. She did her best to involve him and be positive but it was hard work. She had qualified as a teacher nearly three years ago. She knew she still had a lot to learn but felt much more confident now. Of course the workload was an issue but things had improved since the government brought in the workforce reforms. The free periods were certainly a great help. She also felt that she could have a bit of a social life outside school and had even found a boyfriend.

Most of her class were lovely and a real joy to teach but she had several who were different, Andy included. He was capable of real belligerence. This morning turned out to be one of those times, and when he did get stubborn he was very challenging in his own way. The lesson was English and the work was based on writing styles. The children were producing a set of instructions on how to make a sandwich. Once the class had been briefed, resources given out and questions answered, Emily began walking around to offer help and encouragement. When she came to Andy and found he hadn't started, she asked him why.

'This is boring,' he replied and turned away from her. His work was differentiated. He had to take some pictures of the sandwich-making process and arrange them in order. Once he was happy with the order, he had to write short sentences or phrases under each picture.

'Come on, Andy,' she said encouragingly, 'Do you want some help?' He stared at her with a vacant look in his eyes. He was clearly not going to make any effort to do the work at that point. Emily decided to leave him for a few minutes and then try again. She watched him from the other side of the room. Five minutes went past and he hadn't moved. He just slouched in his chair and fiddled with the edge of the table. She didn't really know what to do. Here was a child in her class who was making no effort to do the work and she had no idea how to deal with him. She knew he was challenging her and the anxiety gradually changed into panic. She needed to do something but what? She went back to him and could see he had done nothing.

'Andy, you can't sit and do nothing. If you don't get on with your work, you will have to do it at lunchtime.' He cast his eyes sideways at her, folded his arms and then stared back at the table in front of him. By now the other children in the class were beginning to notice. They hadn't seen Andy go this far before. He normally sulked a bit but eventually did what he was told. Emily knew she couldn't leave it there. Andy was completely blanking her. 'Okay, well if you are not going to start work, you will have to stay in later and I will be calling your mother.' If anything would shift him into action, she thought it was that. But he didn't flinch. He didn't look at her or make out that he had heard what she said. What was going through his mind? What was he thinking? Was he thinking, 'Look at me, I have got you going, I am winding you up well here. You can try to make me but you know you can't touch me.' Emily was getting very frustrated and the rest of the class were beginning to enjoy the show.

'Start work now or you will be in trouble and have to stay in tomorrow as well!' Emily was beginning to shake as she blurted out the threat but got no reaction from him. He had gone into a kind of trance as if he could neither hear nor see her. He was transfixed and unreachable. To Emily, the tension seemed to be growing unbearable. The only relief came with the bell for lunchtime. The rest of the children tidied their things and got ready to go. Andy just sat still for most of the lesson. Now she had to follow through with the lunchtime consequence but he was still acting very belligerently.

No teacher looks forward to this kind of experience, but Emily's response was ineffective and she showed her loss of personal control. The net effect for her was a feeling of frustration and failure. She had used the consequence but now had to face a further period of the same treatment unless he came out of his current 'trance'. Andy was trying to cope with own feelings of stress caused by what was happening at home in the only way he knew how. That was to shut out everyone and everything. He sent out a signal to Emily that he was not playing ball. He was not going to do the work whatever she said or did to him, so it was pointless going down that route. Sometimes it is difficult to discover the cause. In Andy's case it could have had something to do with the work but he also had some more serious difficulties because he seemed unable to resolve problems without resorting to extreme actions.

Emily's response did not reinforce her position as the adult in charge. Andy undermined her position and he was allowed to dictate. The end result was that Andy did not do any work and remained unreachable. With a different approach, Emily could have demonstrated to the class that she had procedures to deal with incidents like this and that consequences would always follow. It is important to stay composed and not invest any emotional energy in the child's power-broking. Either they do what you ask or have the consequences that will be deferred. The choice is with the child. This approach will help you avoid a sense of failure and feeling deskilled. You will also be helping the child to take responsibility for their own actions even if they do end up making poor choices.

Emily discussed Andy's behaviour with other staff and together they worked out what she could try. She braced herself at the start of the next day but she felt confident. Andy probably thought he was in control because he had got away without any punishment for his behaviour. When it came to doing the individual work in the first lesson of the day, he folded his arms and switched off. He was going into the same pattern of behaviour and this time Emily could see it coming. She approached him once she had settled the class.

'I can see that you haven't started work yet, Andy. Would you like some help?' There was no response. He was transfixed, staring at the chair. 'I'll come back in a few minutes to give you some time to consider my offer.' Outwardly, Emily tried to appear calm but inside her heart was beating like thunder. She moved from one table to the next, helping the other children, then she returned to Andy. He was still sitting at the table. 'You haven't made a start yet, Andy. I can give some help to get you going but if you don't do the work in the lesson, we will have to discuss it later in your time.'

Andy didn't acknowledge her but that didn't matter, because she hadn't waited to see. She had turned away and was giving help to another pupil, allowing Andy some take-up time. The rest of the class carried on working until Emily told them to finish up and put their books away ready for the plenary. She didn't go back to Andy anymore. She had told him what to do and given him a chance to choose. When she dismissed the class at break, he started to get up and she moved across to him. 'You have lost your break, Andy. You did not follow my directions and I gave you that choice. You will stay here while the others go out.' Andy looked taken aback. He thought he was going to get it all his own way like yesterday. 'You haven't done the work. If you do some now, you may get the rest finished before the end of lunch play. Then you can go out for the remaining time.' He looked at her then begrudgingly started to do his work. Emily saw him make a start and felt she had made some progress. He did not want to spend his whole lunchtime stuck inside.

There were no more problems for the rest of the day and Emily felt good about her intervention. The next day came but Andy did not show any long-term improvement. The moment he had to do any work on his own, the same thing happened. Emily decided to respond in the same way but she also had another powerful consequence she could use. Her year group was first for lunch, so they got the best choice and the longest playtime. When he refused and went into his trance, she offered him the choice as if he could hear. She told him he would be last for lunch if he refused to do the work. He ignored her again and spent the entire morning challenging her in silence. When it came to lunchtime the class went off to the dining room but Emily stopped Andy. 'You will stay here and only go to the dining room when I say. Then you will wait until everyone else has been served before you get your dinner.' He turned away and stared back at the table but Emily stood her ground. The whole experience was difficult for Andy but she made sure he was last.

In the afternoon she noticed a slight change in Andy. He did not seem to be so out of it. In the music lesson he did the things he was told to do. During the circle time he even spoke up when they were talking about various people in the community who are useful. He briefly mentioned the lollipop ladies at the crossing.

Emily was worried that her approach seemed negative but at least it was consistent now. When she gave him the choice, the consequence was actually carried through. She needed to try to reach him in a positive way and see if she could find a way of helping him instead of ending up in these conflicts. It happened quite by accident. She had an up-and-down week with some days that were better than others. Her tough stand against his belligerent stubbornness usually resulted in him having to do the consequence. On one occasion he changed his response. Instead of shutting down he got up, pushed the chairs over and ran out of the room. He was eventually found in the Year 1 room. The teacher sent a message to the office informing them he was there, sitting watching the hamster.

Emily wondered whether this might be her way in, so she picked an opportune moment later in the week when he appeared to be listening and put the idea of a class pet to the

children. She noticed Andy engage and even get involved in the discussion about what they would call it. She also noted that he had a book with him the next morning. This was unusual because he never brought anything into school. She asked him about it and he came over to her desk and showed her the cover. He was behaving in a shy way and did not speak, so she took the initiative. 'That looks interesting, Andy, is it a library book?' He nodded then turned to put it in his tray. 'When we get our hamster, would you like to be in the team who will look after it this term?' Suddenly his eyes lit up. Bingo! She had found something and made a connection. 'Of course anyone who is involved will have to make sure they have done all their work first.' He nodded and you could see he knew what she meant.

Emily got the hamster and Andy was made one of its keepers. He started to make more effort in class. He did have one or two episodes, but Emily was able to help him turn it around using the hamster as the consequence. She was also able to connect with him via the books about hamsters that he brought in. She used them to explain various things about how to look after the pet. Sometimes they did the shared reading from a hamster book. It is never easy finding some way into a child's trust. Emily was lucky with Andy. She moved away from her emotional response that was not working to one that put the responsibility on Andy. Her consequences were tough and consistent but her rewards balanced them once she had found some that he valued.

THE ATTENTION SEEKER

Attention deficit hyperactivity disorder (ADHD) is one of the most common psychiatric disorders that appear in childhood. It is generally first diagnosed during the primary years. Symptoms are present before age 7 and can continue well into the teenage years. It is most commonly found in boys and if left untreated could have a significant effect on the well-being of the child and family. Research shows that ADHD tends to run in families, so there are likely to be genetic influences. Children who have ADHD usually have at least one close relative who also has ADHD. Furthermore, at least one-third of all fathers who had ADHD in their youth have children with the disorder.

ADHD is not a learning disability but will affect the child's performance in school. This is because one of the symptoms is acting before thinking, which leads to problems with teachers and other children. Children with ADHD tend to show hyperactive and impulsive behaviour and will have problems paying attention and concentrating on things. They are aware of their condition but have difficulty staying still. As a teacher, you should notice when a child exhibits some of the signs of hyperactive behaviour:

- Excessively fidgets or squirms
- Has difficulty remaining seated
- Is easily distracted
- Has difficulty taking turns in games
- Blurts out answers to questions
- Has difficulty following instructions
- Has difficulty sustaining attention
- Shifts from one activity to another
- Has difficulty playing quietly

- Often talks excessively
- Often interrupts
- Often doesn't listen to what is said
- Often loses things
- Often engages in dangerous activities.

Children with ADHD have higher than average rates of injury. ADHD often occurs alongside problems such as depressive and anxiety disorders, drug abuse, and antisocial behaviour.

The ideal diagnosis will be carried out by a medical practitioner and involves input from the parents. Medication is available and is best used in conjunction with behavioural therapy to help the children control their activity level and impulsiveness. Stimulants are commonly prescribed and include methylphenidate (Ritalin), dextroamphetamine (Dexedrine) and amphetamine (Adderall). The medication is normally prescribed to help the child at school and is not taken in the home unless the need is great. Once a correct diagnosis has been made and the medication and therapy have begun, significant changes will be noticed. The child will be more settled, more able to participate and more able to learn in the classroom environment, and their behaviour can be improved using the same methods you would use with the rest of the class (Case Study 8.4).

Case Study 8.4 *Cam*

When Nikki read Cam's file before he arrived at her school, it made her very worried. It was what the education authority called a 'managed move'. He was close to permanent exclusion from his school and was in Year 6. It would be very difficult for him if he were excluded at this late point in his primary schooling. He would miss out on the Standard Assessment Tests (SATs) and the transition activities that the secondary schools organised.

He lived down on the estate overlooking the river near the docks. His dad was a bit of a character and kept some exotic pet snakes. His mum was one of those slightly older, salt-of-the-earth women. She had five children and Cam was the second youngest. A number of his older brothers who had left school had police records. His older sister went to the new secondary school with state-of-the-art facilities but she was often in trouble. Cam had been involved in a number of well-documented incidents where he had supposedly hit a member of staff and run out of school. Apparently he was unmanageable and could not be contained in the classroom. The deputy had to have him working outside her office.

There were a number of school reports and trial SATs papers in his file as well. Each time they had tried to test him, he had caused a disturbance and the test had to be abandoned. Their assessment of his ability was that he had a reading age of six years and one month and was working at just level I in maths and English. A statement had been issued for his learning difficulties just over a year ago but it made no mention of his behavioural difficulties.

The day came for his visit to the school, and when Nikki saw him she was quite taken aback. He seemed really friendly and chatty. He had a nice open face and good manners. She did notice that he didn't like to remain seated and kept looking round at the things in the classroom. She let him go and explore while she talked to his mum, who told her he was like that at home. He would watch television for no longer than ten or fifteen minutes then he would be up and looking for something else to do. She found him very difficult to manage at home and she was feeling extremely tired. He went to bed late and could not get to sleep very easily. He would wake up in the early hours and start playing with things in his room. This would wake her up and her husband too. They couldn't get back to sleep and in the morning they were both exhausted.

He had been wetting his bed every night for several years. The doctors had given all sorts of advice and a few pharmaceutical remedies but none of them had worked. The net effect was that Cam and the rest of the family were having night after night of broken sleep. On good days he would be very nice to his mum and younger sister. He would play with the little girl and invent all sorts of imaginary games. The play was noisy because he was always talking, telling her about the characters and the things that were happening. On bad days his mood would swing and he could become quite abusive, especially to his mum. He could swear and cuss her and he made her feel small and insignificant. He would also charge around and behave in a reckless and dangerous way. She would fear for his safety as she watched him swing from a rope in the garden, or jump from a dangerous roof he had climbed on.

In a way, Nikki's fears were allayed when she met Cam. She was expecting someone quite different. Here was a normal-looking boy who was very endearing. His reading was clearly delayed and this had affected the rest of his learning. She decided to carry out her own tests in the first few weeks. The special educational needs coordinator (SENCO) helped her with this and Cam was allocated some hours of support that Nikki used to improve his literacy and make sure he had a good programme of homework activities that could reinforce his class work. He was a handful in the lessons at first but she explained her classroom code to him and the points system, which he took to with enthusiasm. She also decided that she was going to teach him some of his tables that only involved spending five to ten minutes each day. This time would allow her to get to know him better.

Cam responded well to her efforts. He had a good memory and within the first few days he had learned his six times table and could answer any question about multiplying or dividing by six. Her computer-based numeracy assessment revealed that he was actually capable of doing work much nearer his age range than the reports in his file stated. The assessment software used a multimedia approach and did not rely on the pupil having to read the problems. This could be the reason why he was unable to show what he knew. His frustration with not being able to read probably explained why he walked out of the tests in a mood. Her reading programme for him was a sound one based on learning the main blends and word sounds. The support assistant commented that Cam had no knowledge of these but after a few weeks of working on them he was making very good progress.

The main problem everyone had with Cam was his inability to concentrate. The educational psychologist who came to observe him once he started in the new school thought he might be hyperactive but was not sure whether it was a clinical problem or something to do with his diet. Cam had a statement and the local education authority (LEA) was keen to make his move a success because of its sensitive political nature, so it fast-tracked a request for a medical diagnosis. The doctor who saw him decided to try him on Ritalin (methylphenidate) to see whether it would calm him down at school. The effect was very satisfying. It lengthened Cam's attention span and reduced his movements around the room during lessons. His mood swings grew less frequent but were still evident. He did go off his food but the doctor adjusted his dosage and the times he took his medication to alleviate that.

At the parents meeting four weeks later, there were significant improvements to report. His reading was progressing extremely well, which was having an impact on the work he did in the other lessons. There had been a few incidents involving his behaviour but nothing serious. And his parents had something really interesting to report. They said that he really liked school now and looked forward to going every day. He was much more helpful at home and stopped treating his mum badly. He seemed so positive about school work and read his books with his dad, which was something he had never done before. His sleeping habits were better. Most nights he slept well but there were still one or two bad ones where he would get up, go downstairs and watch television but eventually he would return to bed. The most remarkable change was the bedwetting. It had completely stopped about a week ago and he had been dry ever since.

Cam remained on medication for the rest of Year 6 and managed to complete his primary schooling. He was still quite a way behind the other children in his year group but was making good progress. He loved history and would look for books about the Tudors and the Egyptians whenever they visited the school library. He started to get into sport, especially football. He could contain his temper better, so he was able to last the whole game. Nikki was very pleased with Cam's change and was sorry to see him leave the school, but he often came back to visit as his younger sister had joined the infants.

THE CHILD WITH AUTISM

Children with autism will exhibit a range of behavioural traits. The most common form you will come across is Asperger's syndrome. A person with Asperger's syndrome will have some of the features of autism but not the actual disorder. Some people who have Asperger's syndrome can go through their entire lives without realising they have it. It is hard to diagnose because it varies in severity from person to person.

Many people who have Asperger's syndrome have problems maintaining eye contact with the person they are talking to. You may think they are talking to someone else not you. This is called gaze avoidance. Socially, they may not grasp what is going on and react in a way that is out of keeping with the situation. They may also find it hard to join in with physical activities because they tend to be weak and have poor coordination, often described as clumsiness.

Young people with the syndrome have a tendency to become angry at a change of routine and anxious about doing things they do not normally do. They will cling to routines and outwardly exhibit the signs of being obsessive, although the root cause will be different. They have a tendency to become preoccupied and engulf themselves in one subject which, when turned to positive ends, could result in their making a career of it and becoming very successful.

They do not experience a delay in the development of language but may speak in a different manner or in language that appears odd. They do this because it gratifies them and they feel more comfortable doing it. Some children may be able to read well but are not sure what they are reading. Some also have a problem dealing with facts. A child may have an extensive vocabulary but poor reading or comprehension skills (Case Study 8.5).

Case Study 8.5 *Mitch*

Mitch had been having serious difficulties with his behaviour for a long time. His parents were convinced they were not emotional difficulties because their internet research had led them to believe that he may have some form of autism. They fought against the doctors who had tried to tell them that it was his age, or that he was hyperactive or even just naughty. They pushed for a specialist diagnosis. Finally they found a consultant who specialised in autism and she diagnosed him as having Asperger's syndrome. This meant that he found change of any kind difficult. He had learned ways of dealing with changes in his life but was still extremely anxious and needed considerable time coming to terms with them. His parents had fought hard to get him the support he needed so that he could stay in mainstream education. There had been a lot of pressure to move him to the special school in the area.

The primary teachers said they had not got much experience of autism and didn't know how to help him. The educational psychologist had advised that the teachers in the special school who were skilled in teaching children on the autistic spectrum would best serve his needs. He would be with other children like himself. The special educational needs adviser had supported this view and pointed out that it would be better to go to the special school while he was still at the age for Key Stage 2, because he would be able to continue there until he left school at 16. However, his parents felt that he would become institutionalised and find it difficult to manage once he left school for good.

Mitch's parents visited the special school and found it to be a good place. The teachers were friendly, dedicated and genuinely interested in their pupils. The children seemed happy and the progress they made was incredible. Ofsted had highlighted this in its recent inspection report of the school. But in the end, they decided that what they really wanted for Mitch was a mainstream experience because he was slightly above average academically and would possibly do better being taught by teachers in the mainstream and might benefit socially as well. They researched Asperger's syndrome and pushed the local education authority (LEA) until he was given a statement and the support he needed.

In the end, the primary school took their wishes on board and got support from several specialists. One of the teachers got so interested in Mitch's condition that she signed up for TEACCH. TEACCH stands for the treatment and education of autistic and related communication-handicapped children, a special programme specifically for teachers of children with autism. She set up the support for Mitch, trained the staff in the methods designed to help him in the class and also produced an impressive bank of resources so he could get the best out of the curriculum. The problem was that there were few, if any, other children like Mitch in his chosen secondary school, so the expertise they developed would need to be shared, and quickly.

The teachers met and developed a joint strategy for the transition. Then the special educational needs coordinator (SENCO) in the secondary school arranged some in-service education and training (INSET) meetings as well as some planning meetings for the Year 7 staff, and by September everyone felt confident they knew what to do for Mitch. Over the summer break his parents helped him with the changes and new routines he would need to face. By September he was really looking forward to his new school. The first few weeks went well under the circumstances. He needed to use his exit cards for some of the lessons and there were one or two incidents in the playground at break. Most of the students had been briefed about Asperger's syndrome and how it affected Mitch, so they knew what to expect.

Then a calamity occurred. His form teacher and English teacher – English was one of Mitch's favourite subjects – went off sick and a supply teacher had to be brought in. There was very little time to prepare him or Mitch for the change. From Mitch's point of view, things were going well then suddenly everything was wrong. When he walked into the room, someone different was waiting to take the register and yesterday's visual timetable was still on the noticeboard. Mitch had a set routine for doing things when he came in. The teacher had given him the job of switching on the computers, cleaning the board and then he could have five minutes on the computer doing his football project while the rest of the students were coming in. Mitch stood just inside the door and stared down at the nearest chair leg to his side. His expression was fixed and he clutched his bag to his chest. The supply teacher didn't notice him at first because he was looking through the register. After several minutes he became aware of someone standing by the door, so he looked up.

'Come on in and sit down, I will do the register when the rest of the class get here. What is your name?' Mitch didn't reply, just remained as still as a statue. Dennis Luckock had been a supply teacher for nearly nine months. He had come over from New Zealand soon after he had qualified. He was hoping to get some money together so he could go off and tour Europe. He had worked in a number of schools in and around London but never encountered a student like this. The boy didn't seem to hear what he said so he tried again. 'I said, sit down while we wait for the others,' but Mitch didn't move. He couldn't, it felt like his whole body was locked up. 'You can't stand there, now do as I say and go to your place. You will be in the way and the others are coming now.'

Mitch suddenly felt his body unlock and he shrieked. 'Noooo!' Then he spoke in a very strange way as though through his nose. 'Where is Miss Thompson?' he snapped.

'She is off sick and won't be in for a couple of weeks,' replied Dennis, trying to be friendly.

'She can't be, she should be here, she is my teacher.'

So Dennis explained that he was going to fill in for her, but Mitch had turned his back and was fiddling with one of the posters. Tears had welled up in his eyes. Dennis wasn't sure what happened but the next thing he knew was that a large poster was ripped off the wall. 'What did you do that for?' asked Dennis getting quite angry.

'I'm sorry,' said Mitch quickly. 'It was an accident, it fell down.'

Dennis could see that wasn't the case. 'Posters don't just fall down, you pulled it off and tore it. Now look at it.' He knew he had to discipline the boy but didn't quite know how. 'Right, you're in detention.'

'I didn't do it, you ****er! I'm going to kill you and chop up your body!' Dennis couldn't believe what he'd heard. The boy was seriously out of control. He went towards the door to get another teacher to come and assist but as he did so, Mitch turned towards him, threw his bag hard in his direction and turned and ran. As he ran down the corridor, he grabbed at pieces of art and ripped them off the wall.

'Leave me alone, leave me alone,' he screamed. The SENCO was called and knew where to find him. He was skulking in the computer annexe next to the learning support base. He was quite distraught and could not be persuaded to leave for over an hour. She explained that his teacher had had an accident and was likely to be off for several weeks and they had been lucky to get Mr Luckock at short notice. She also told him that she was sorry they had not managed to speak to Mr Luckock about him. She would make a point of meeting him at lunchtime to tell him all about Mitch and in the meantime he would probably be better off staying in the learning support base until the afternoon. Gradually Mitch calmed down. He knew he had done wrong and with some careful talking the school helped him understand that he had wilfully damaged school property and been very rude to a member of staff. There would have to be consequences even though Mitch had done them because he was upset. He accepted it and agreed to apologise to Mr Luckock after lunch.

The SENCO met the teacher and explained that Mitch had been diagnosed as having Asperger's syndrome. She briefly outlined the characteristics that were applicable to Mitch. These included fear of change, need for routines, odd eating habits and an interest in detail. She also explained that he had a very good memory for detail and a love of words and reading but only non-fiction. She outlined the things already put in place to help him. Mitch had a timetable made up of Makaton signs that he had been using for many years. The teacher had signs for all the lessons, breaks, etc., and would put them on a Velcro strip on the noticeboard by the door so he could see what his day included. He also had a folder he carried around with him that contained the same signs. He would copy the timetable using his signs so he always knew where he was and what he would be doing.

All the teachers were aware of Mitch's dislike of change. Someone would see him in advance if something was going to change and explain what it was, why it was necessary and when it would happen. Mitch felt secure with this and was able to deal with his own feelings during the change. Mitch's teachers would always try to go through what would happen during the lessons, step by step, which is good practice anyway. They would explain how each step related to the big picture, what they had been doing and what they eventually hoped to achieve. Then, during an activity, the teacher would announce to the class that they would soon be finishing what they were on and tell them what they would do next. This clear signposting of events helped Mitch enormously and allowed him to function at his best. During break and lunchtime one of his classmates would have the responsibility of reminding him in advance that the bell would go soon. What he disliked was the high-pitched sound as loud noises frightened him.

Lunchtimes were a problem. Sometimes he would eat only a dry roll. He had very finicky eating habits and never ate anything sweet. Outside in the playground he would get into arguments because he would try to tell other students how to play a game or correct them if they did anything wrong. He was a stickler for getting things right and would go into a very heavy mood if someone appeared to be cheating. In the end it became easier to let him stay in and use a computer than to let him out and deal with the disputes. However, the SENCO insisted that he went out at least once a day, so she used the exit card system to provide him with an escape route if things got too difficult. She also began using social stories. This is a treatment strategy developed by Carol Gray to improve social behaviour. It involves giving the child short stories to teach socially appropriate behaviours. The stories are used to help the child get a better understanding of their behaviour and other people's.

The other students in Mitch's class were very understanding about his condition and were extremely helpful but sometimes he tried their patience and conflicts would occur. The teachers didn't let Mitch get away with clear breaches of school rules or classroom codes but they would be understanding and not put consequences in place immediately. They would wait until he had control, because it was senseless trying to reason with him while he felt anxious or angry. Dennis felt much better about Mitch being in his class once he knew all about his condition. He quickly got organised and it was really rewarding to see the change in

Mitch once everything was in place to help him cope. By the time Miss Thompson returned, Dennis had learned a lot about working with students on the autistic spectrum and decided that he would like to specialise in special education once he returned to New Zealand.

THE CHILD WITH LOW SELF-ESTEEM

The way we view ourselves in relation to others is vital but can vary according to who we are with and how others treat us. Teachers have a great impact in this area and can help children perceive themselves positively or negatively in the things they say and the expectations they have of each child. Self-esteem is the value we have of ourselves as individuals and is the sum total of the interactions we have with other people. However, young people create their self-image from the images others have of them as well as their own perceptions. For example, a child may believe they are very good at drawing because their parents and family members have praised their pictures. This perception can be completely shattered by a few misplaced comments made by a teacher in front of peers. The teacher's authority will work against the opinions of the parents, and comments from their peers will cut deeply into their view of their artistic ability.

When a child's self-esteem is dented in this way, they will become anxious about their ability to do other things and less motivated to try in case a similar negative experience occurs. If the same child moves to a class with a teacher who can motivate and praise effectively to produce a positive climate, the child's perception of their ability may change. They will believe they can do something well and feel secure enough to try to do better. Their feeling of belonging will be strengthened along with their feeling of being secure.

The child with low self-esteem will probably have had negative experiences in the home, community, school or a combination of these. They may have been verbally, physically or sexually abused. The child may have experienced an imbalance between success and failure that has scarred them. They may have actually been successful like the boy who swam in galas at a national level but was constantly criticised by his father because he was not swimming fast enough.

A sense of failure is a common factor, and a key variable is the way a teacher, parent or trainer works with the child. The child will experience failure when he cannot live up to his parents' expectations or is told that he is no good at something. The signs of low self-esteem and a poor self-image are visible but need to be interpreted with care. Just because a child presents with one or more of them does not mean they have a poor self-image. There may be more to it. However, it is useful to list them so you can be alerted when you spot them in an individual. Any of the following may be present:

- Destroying work that has been praised
- Destroying personal possessions
- Running away from things
- Standing right in a corner facing the wall
- Pulling a jacket or jumper over their head to hide inside
- Covering their face or lying face down on a desk
- Going under a table or desk

- Attempting to bully or be aggressive to others
- Using diversionary tactics to avoid failure, e.g. work avoidance, complaining about illness, needing the toilet, being the class clown, changing the subject by being chatty
- Saying they are useless at things
- Failing to show enjoyment in relaxed, free, unstructured activities
- Possibly even self-harming, although this will probably be associated with relationship problems within the family.

Changing an individual's perception of themselves is the way forward. Being very positive towards the child can reverse milder cases, and so can developing a classroom climate where there are no limits to learning, everyone feels secure and achievement of all kinds is recognised.

Children with a very poor self-image will need multi-agency help so that experiences and knowledge can be shared and strategies developed in and out of the school. Engaging a learning mentor will provide a useful starting point to monitor the child's behaviour and intervene when they are under stress. Change will not happen quickly, so staff should try to identify any small changes or differences in behaviour that indicate progress. These can then be built on and strategies revised accordingly (Case Study 8.6).

Case Study 8.6 *Ray*

Ray was a good-looking boy in Year 6. He had film-star features and was a brilliant footballer. His footwork was mesmerising to watch. His control of the ball was faultless as he wove in and out of the opponents on his way to the goal. He loved the game and played it whenever he could. He was popular with his peers and the younger girls would go out of their way to try to say hello to him. You would think a child like Ray would be very comfortable and happy at school but he wasn't.

Ray's family background was a bit mixed up. He had a 14-year-old brother who was nearly deaf and attended a special school on the other side of London. His dad had gone through a very difficult time over the past three years. He had suffered from depression and had to give up work. He was on medication but it affected his sleep patterns. He would often stay in bed for long periods, which would prevent him from getting a full-time job. He could be extremely moody and Ray often found himself on the raw end of his dad's temper. This didn't stop him loving his dad, because he had a good idea of how tough it was for him. Ray's mum was the strong one. She held down a full-time job, looked after the two boys and supported her husband through his illness. She would come home at lunchtimes and check he was all right. She suffered quietly through all of this, so when things started to go wrong for Ray, it was very hard for her to keep going, but she did.

Ray was beginning to find things were not going well at school. Kath, his teacher, found him difficult. He would not follow instructions and on several occasions he hurled some furniture around then stormed out. She tried to talk to him when he was calm but could not get through. She didn't know what to do because she had never encountered a child who behaved like this before. Kath spoke to the SENCO about him and together they set up a meeting with the parents. Kath found them to be quite difficult and in denial about Ray's behaviour. They couldn't shed any light on why he should be behaving in this way but instead they seemed to be blaming the school.

They had a way of trying to get Kath to change things to suit Ray and themselves. For example, they suggested that Ray be allowed to opt out of certain lessons because he didn't like them and they would cause him stress that would aggravate his 'condition'. They were unable to describe what this condition was and said it was something that only happened at school. Kath felt that things were only fine at home because he was allowed to do exactly what he wanted. It was hard to find out if she was right, because Ray's parents always seemed to cover up and glaze over whenever something looked like it might be a criticism or explanation originating in their home life.

The real problems began during the application process for secondary schools. The parents were looking at a number of local schools and agonising over which one would be the best. They asked for a meeting about it, which was becoming one of their regular habits. Kath didn't feel they needed to discuss the school choice with her. That was something they could decide for themselves. She didn't know the secondary schools in the area very well and felt she hadn't got anything to contribute. They were becoming more dependent on the school and seemed to want to meet and discuss all sorts of things. Ray's mum told Kath that she couldn't see him being able to cope with secondary school, because his behaviour was becoming more complex and he didn't seem very happy.

In reality the problem of Ray's behaviour was a confusing one. For example, he wouldn't go to school one morning. His mum found it very hard to get him out of the house. After a long discussion he revealed that he felt self-conscious about the haircut he had just had. He said that everyone would be looking at him. Then there were all the times when he wouldn't take his coat off. He would come to school in a parka and keep it on in the classroom. Kath tried to get him to take it off but he resisted. She didn't know why he did it, just that he seemed very stubborn. Going in the room also became an issue. He would stay out for most of the morning and sometimes he wouldn't go in until halfway through the afternoon. He would misbehave or have a tantrum. His response was just to stand and look at the ground. When anyone tried to talk to him, he would mumble and they would have to ask him to repeat himself until they could understand what he was saying.

His mum was very concerned and told Kath that Ray tended to mirror his dad's moods. When he was particularly depressed, Ray would become more difficult. This seemed plausible, except that there were several occasions where Ray was positively happy and doing really well. When Kath talked to his mum it turned out that his dad had just suffered a relapse, so it was very hard to make the connection. In November Ray went into hospital for an operation. He had been having problems with his groin and was finally admitted. The operation was a routine one but left him very disturbed. Kath noticed that when Ray returned to school he held the left cuff of his coat over his groin. He wouldn't use his left hand for anything, which was a problem for him when he was playing football. She did not want to comment on this to him but realised it must have something to do with the operation.

The situation seemed ridiculous to Kath. She sought the help of the educational psychologist and the child and family psychiatrist but they were all overstretched and could not come for several months. Kath met again with the head and the SENCO to discuss the problems they were experiencing and perhaps come up with some solutions. The only ways forward they could see were through football and his fear of maths. They felt that he needed a special approach and some clear targets to help him overcome things like the coat and staying outside the room. Something deeper was behind the behaviour but they did not know what it was, so they just had to work on the things they could. Kath decided she was going to tighten up her behaviour code with the class to create a much clearer procedure that the children could see happening. She had heard about methods that used a stepped approach with warnings and fixed consequences. One of her friends working in another school told her about the timers she used, so Kath got hold of some. The children could watch the sand going through and decide what they would do.

Kath discussed her approach with Ray then moved on to football. Ray played in the school team and practised every week. She pointed out that if he was in the school team, he needed to show he was part of the school, which meant doing what the other players did, such as going into class and removing their coats. He said he would give it a try and Kath decided she was going to be far more assertive in future because she felt he was manipulating things to suit himself without compromising in any way. Then she went on to ask him about the subjects he liked and disliked. She discussed maths and told him about her little group at lunchtimes. It was a booster group for the most able. She described her special methods and the computer software she used to help the children. She offered to put the program on his computer at home so he could use it each evening. He seemed reluctant but was prepared to give it a try. They concluded by talking about secondary schools and he told her he wanted to go to a particular school but his parents were not sure if it would be a good choice. Kath offered to find out about it then talk to his parents.

Ray did not change that easily. He refused to take his coat off despite Kath's direct approaches. She reminded him he would have to prove he was like the other players if he wanted to be in the team. He ignored her. Then Wednesday came and he was expecting to go to the match. It was an away game and the team were leaving before the end of school. Ray was fidgeting to go but Kath put her foot down and reminded him that he had not met his target. The next day his mum rang up to speak with Kath. She argued that the football was good for him and was one of the few things that was going right at school. Kath was very assertive and reminded her that it was a school team and the players had to meet certain standards, which he was not doing. The call ended with Ray's mum stating that she was not happy. However, Kath's strategy seemed to have worked, because the following day Ray not only took his coat off but also came into class at registration.

Over the next week Ray made several other improvements. He attended the maths club and Kath began working on some of his maths difficulties. He was very cautious and reluctant to have a go, but with Kath's help and reassurance he suddenly found he could do the work. Not only could he do it, he could do it well. He seemed to grow in confidence from that point. Ray earned his football the following week but Kath really had to push him to follow her directions at times. There were things he definitely would not do. One was going into assembly with the class, so she let him stay out and he got a consequence each time. He seemed to feel this was fair. There were one or two days when he regressed completely and Kath couldn't do anything to change his mind; again he received consequences. She was not prepared to relent on her approach and she did not accept that he had a problem that ran much deeper. She had helped him change his behaviour for 80% of the time, and that convinced her he was in control.

She found out more about the school he liked. It was a good school and offered many of the things that parents valued. She discovered that only a few children from the school were going there and they were all in other classes. The reason that Ray wanted to go to the school on his own was to make a fresh start without any of the kids that knew him. They also had a good football skills club and a team with a reputation, one he hoped to join when he was old enough. She discussed all this with his parents and in the end they felt that it could be a good move for Ray.

The months passed and Ray improved quite noticeably. His shyness waned. His reluctance to do things changed and he put himself forward sometimes. His coat was no longer a problem and his maths improved enough for him to feel that he was no longer a dunce. He was still behind but he no longer felt he was useless and no longer frightened by it. Kath wanted the best for Ray and stood her ground in the classroom. She knew she was strong, consistent and single-minded. The telephone calls stopped and by Easter his parents' comments were all complimentary.

THE AGGRESSIVE CHILD

Some children will be aggressive. There are many ways this may manifest itself. A child may be verbally aggressive and swear and cuss other pupils and staff. The physically aggressive child will use violent force against other children and adults in a variety of ways. Their threats may be hollow but they should always be taken seriously. Aggressive children may use weapons to threaten or to cause harm, but they will generally try to harm someone by punching, kicking, pinching, biting and scratching.

The child is trying to communicate their feelings. The use of violence will be a learned response that the child has used and found successful in the past. Repeated use will reinforce the success and provide the child with a way of dominating the situation. Alternatively, they may have been subjected to violence in the home, witnessing it or actually being on the receiving end, which has resulted in violent tendencies.

There are many triggers for violent behaviour. A child may lash out for almost any reason if they have violent tendencies and cannot contain their anger. It is very difficult to prevent a violent child from getting involved in an incident by trying to remove the external causes. Identifying when the risk of violence is most likely and then containing the child could be an option but does not tackle the internal feelings that cause the child to be aggressive. Focus on the child's anger and lack of self-constraint.

There are many approaches to anger management. They may be based on the association of a pleasurable sensation with a physical object or action. When a stressful situation arises, the child tries to remember that pleasure by using the object or action. This sends pleasurable signals to the brain by releasing endorphins that swamp the negative thoughts. The other method is based on training the child to strengthen their internal self-control. This is done by conditioning. The child role-plays situations where problems occur and is given strategies to ignore the triggers that lead to their aggressive behaviour. They practise the strategies until they have internalised them so they become automatic responses in those situations.

An aggressive child can do harm to other children and staff, so their safety must be paramount when an incident occurs. A serious outburst leading to an assault on a member of staff can mean permanent exclusion from the school. A head teacher does not lightly take the decision to exclude a child but they must protect the safety of the other children and staff. When a head teacher cannot guarantee safety, action must be taken. It can be very stressful dealing with a child who is behaving violently. Staff can train in methods of physical restraint and this is advisable if the school has children who are known to be violent. Restraint must be performed by adults who know the proper procedures, as incorrect practice can lead to accidents and legal action (Case Study 8.7).

Case Study 8.7 *Claire*

You wouldn't think that a 5-year-old girl could be so challenging. Difficult to handle maybe but in a way like most infants. Claire was different. She lived with her mum in a busy cosmopolitan suburb. Her mum had seen some hard times during her life but had managed to come through them. She now had her own flat, a job and her parents living nearby. Her partner was off the scene but his departure had been traumatic. It was the culmination of repeated episodes of quite fierce domestic violence. Finally he had beaten Claire's mum badly until she fell unconscious. Her mum had hidden Claire behind the sofa just before he came home drunk. She watched the whole terrible scene and when she felt it was safe to come out, she went next door to get help for her mum. Things were different now. They were happy together but Claire didn't know about her mum's drinking. She had taken to the bottle when her partner had left and would sometimes end up sleeping it off in front of the television instead of going to bed.

Claire was good in school for most of the time but she was very headstrong. Sometimes she would flatly refuse to do what the teacher asked her. She would become so stubborn and belligerent that the staff couldn't shift her. As the weeks went by, the incidents grew more frequent. Then one day she turned to the teacher and said, 'No! I don't want to do this and you can't make me.' The support assistant tried to persuade her but she lashed out then scratched her on the face. The support staff who knew her were beginning to describe her as a 'little wildcat'. The frequency of her having to be sent home was increasing but her mother didn't think she was badly behaved. She had said on several occasions that the staff just did not know how to manage her.

Joan, the behaviour support adviser, observed Claire and saw her bite one member of staff and scratch another repeatedly. She was getting quite a reputation as more external agencies got involved. The irony of it was that she would be very violent to a member of staff then the next moment she would want to be very friendly and close to them. The other children in the class had become quite wary of her and kept their distance. She would insist they played with her, playing her games with her rules. She was obviously the controlling type as well as being aggressive. As long as she was in charge she was happy. Anyone who tried to remove that control would become a potential victim. She had a cousin in her class and she ordered him around. She dragged him into some of her naughty situations and they became the 'terrible twins'. He would not be violent but was easily led and did her bidding. The teacher was doing her best but did not really have much experience of children like Claire. She needed strategies and was very grateful to hear the behaviour support team were getting involved.

Claire's behaviour got worse and she even had to be excluded following one incident. The head met with Claire and her mum when she returned to school. They discussed her behaviour and the expectations. During the meeting the head watched Claire and concluded that she was not ready to go back into the classroom. She was fidgeting and being fairly uncooperative. She acted arrogantly when apologising to the teacher and showed no sign of remorse. The head asked if she thought she was ready to go into class but she just shrugged her shoulders. He asked her if she wanted to go back into class and she said she didn't mind whether she did or she didn't.

He concluded the meeting by explaining to her mother that there would be no point in her going into class if she was going to repeat the performance. Her mum agreed and revealed to the head that she did want to. She had been bored during the exclusion and had missed school. Claire was like most kids. No matter what they think or say about school, they do not really want to be excluded. They want to be like other children and they want to be included in things. Some children will tell you they want to be excluded so they do not have to come to school. But it is often just a front, covering up their fear of exclusion.

Claire had been looking forward to coming back. She had got up really early and got herself ready way ahead of their departure time. Her mum had talked to her that morning about her behaviour and she had promised to try really hard to be good. So Claire was shocked to hear her mum tell the head that she was taking her home because she hadn't shown that she was sorry. Claire pleaded with her but she refused. Her mum told the head that she would bring Claire back when Claire could show she was sorry.

When she came back again the next day, things were completely different. She was smiling and also very well mannered. She apologised to the head and her teacher. She said something that struck a chord with the teacher, who relayed it to Joan. She told her that she really didn't want to be naughty and tried hard but sometimes she just did it all wrong and didn't know why. Things improved for a few days then she reverted to her old ways. Joan came to work with her. She decided it was time to push her buttons and see how far she was prepared to go. When Claire didn't follow a direction, Joan redirected her. Claire retaliated by picking up a pencil. She went to stab Joan, but Joan stood her ground and did not look like she was afraid. She looked Claire in the eyes and said, 'Do not try that on me! Put the pencil down.'

Joan was very forceful. Claire stared at her for about thirty seconds then turned and started stabbing the table. This was a victory for Joan. The teacher was surprised that Claire had backed down and in the end she had taken her aggression out on the table. Claire followed all Joan's directions for the rest of the lesson. When it came to break, the teacher started giving out the children's fruit. She was just about to give it to Claire when Joan stepped forward and said, 'No banana for Claire, Miss Lomax. She doesn't deserve it at the moment!' The rest of the children were surprised but, more importantly, Claire looked dismayed. She really enjoyed her fruit. She would always choose it at lunch and loved the new scheme of having fruit at break. To be told she couldn't have her banana was a real shock but it worked. From then on she was really friendly to Joan. She loved working with her and would do anything to please. Claire didn't attack Joan anymore. She would manage to turn her behaviour around before it got too bad.

Joan planned a special programme to help the teacher manage Claire's behaviour. They explained it to her and then it began. The first day went fine. The next day was okay until Claire had to do something she didn't want to. She went into a strop just as Joan walked into the room. She picked up some books and threw them, then pushed over some chairs. Joan told the teacher to get the other children outside for their own safety. Then she worked with the support assistant to deal with Claire. Claire tried to attack the support assistant but Joan stepped in and held her arms so she could not move. She let her swear and call her names until eventually she broke down and cried. This was the signal that she was coming out of it. So Joan suggested she went to the toilet. They accompanied her and she went in and locked the door. She proceeded to pull all the toilet roll on to the floor but Joan ignored her and monitored her to make sure she was safe.

Half an hour later Claire crept out of the cubicle and asked for a tissue. Joan helped her dry her eyes and then they talked. Claire was really sorry and wanted to apologise to the teacher. She realised she had done wrong and knew she was going to have to face the consequences. She also accepted that she would have to find the money to pay for the toilet roll once her mum had been told. There was one more incident like this. It was not so prolonged and she came out of it much more quickly. Joan explained to the teacher that she probably needed to challenge her as well but once she knew she was not going to win, she would be all right.

Several months on and Claire is a changed girl for her teacher. She does not try to hurt anymore and actually enjoys coming to school. It is as if a burden had been lifted from her. She is really friendly and affectionate to the teacher and the rest of the staff say they can't believe it is the same girl. She continues to have a problem but the teacher and Joan have been working on it. She cannot make the change to another member of staff. She has to challenge each one. They have to go through a similar experience as the teacher and Joan, but there is no longer violence, just stubbornness. Obviously it is an important barrier to get over, because she will get a new teacher at least every year, perhaps more often if teachers leave or fall ill.

Ensuring the safety of the other children as well as your own personal well-being should be your primary concern. Remaining calm at all times is easier said than done but is also probably the most important thing you can do. Teachers who get emotionally involved and express anger fuel the situation as well as providing satisfaction for children seeking a response. Training in positive handling procedures will give you the confidence and the skills to deal with children who get physically aggressive. Well-kept records of incidents and the action taken are essential for other professionals who may eventually take up the case. They also provide you with useful memory joggers if a child decides to challenge decisions made about them. Most of all, be realistic. Try to remain consistent and fair. Look for small changes in behaviour, as progress will not be immediate. Do not take things personally. Most teachers find it difficult to deal with children who have challenging behaviour.

SUMMARY

- Pupils with very challenging behaviour will have special needs that may be based on clinical causes or emotional difficulties.
- Correctly interpreting the causes of undesirable behaviour is important for developing suitable responses.
- Find out whether a pupil has a record of poor behaviour in other classes.
- Investigate the pupil's family history and home life and ascertain whether there has been a critical incident that could explain their behaviour.
- When there is no apparent reason for the behaviour, you could try using Dreikur's goal disclosure method.
- Asking colleagues for help is not a failing.
- Use the knowledge and expertise of other professionals in seeking a solution.
- Stick to your behaviour plan even when the child does not seem to be responding. This will prevent you from becoming emotionally involved. Remember it is the child who is making the choice, not you.
- Reinforce the idea that it's the child's behaviour you do not like, not the child themselves.

9 THE TOUGH CLASS

Much of this book has been about how to manage individual children who behave in particular ways that disrupt the rest of the class. The point of having a behaviour code is to ensure that the pupils know the rules and the expectations placed on them and that you will have suitable responses worked out in advance to deal with incidents when they occur. Dealing with a tough class is different to dealing with a difficult child. The difficult child tries to disrupt the lesson for the majority, whereas the tough class prevents the minority from learning.

Certain classes develop a reputation for being difficult. This could happen at any time in any school. Some staff are more aware and are able to prevent the triggers that cause it by careful planning, grouping, timetabling and by supporting colleagues when things start to go wrong. A difficult class usually arises over time because of the context, the mix of individuals in the group, and the staff who teach it.

A tough class will evolve from a few individuals who draw the majority in and muster them as a force against the teacher and the school. The story is about who is in control. Normally it is the teacher but sometimes this changes and the pupils take power. They call the shots, decide what happens, make the decisions and dominate the time and the space. When this happens the teacher retreats and finds they are in a very awkward and demoralising position that is difficult to reverse without the support and help of colleagues.

Another position you may find yourself in is being given a group that already has a reputation for being tough. This will involve a different set of strategies. The pupils will not perceive you as someone who has been defeated. Instead they may see you as an adversary to try defeating. The difference is that the power and authority of the leader have not been surrendered to the class.

WHAT MAKES A CLASS TOUGH?

A class can be described as tough when the behaviour of the children is so disruptive in its frequency and intensity that the teacher begins to feel a sense of failure. The teachers will suffer professionally by questioning their own ability. They will suffer personally in their health. Typical symptoms will be related to stress:

- Inability to sleep well
- Loss of appetite
- Headaches
- Feeling tired
- Short temper
- Feeling demoralised.

After a while the teacher will look for ways of avoiding lessons with a tough group. They will feel they cannot face the group on some days and will ring in sick. On other days they will feel stronger and come in, only to be worn down by the class and then be off for several days afterwards. The teacher who does not get any support will only gain release when they give up and resign their post at the school. The teaching profession cannot afford this. Teachers commit four years of their lives training to do the job. When they qualify they are not experts. They are usually enthusiastic and have substantial theoretical knowledge of the work they will do. Their experience of the classroom and the pupils may be considerable and gained during several teaching placements but it may not prepare the graduate for tough groups. Therefore they need to be given a chance with proper support and guidance together with careful timetabling to reduce the risk of them coming up against a tough class. Suggesting that everyone finds it hard when they begin their careers is not a convincing argument.

NO BEHAVIOUR CODE

One of the common reasons for a class getting out of control is the absence of an explicit, detailed behaviour code. Taking over from a teacher who has not used a clear code can be a lottery. An aggressive teacher may have kept the class under control but the children would not have had the opportunity to take responsibility for their behaviour. Alternatively, the previous teacher may have had a lot of problems because they did not have a code. The absence of a code may be due to the school not having a coordinated approach. Teachers would have had to make their own arrangements, resulting in considerable variation between classes.

If you find you are taking over a poorly established class that has got used to working without clear boundaries, you will need to be resolute in putting measures in place. Most classes will respond positively because they will probably feel insecure. Young people need and want clear routines and rules. There will always be a minority who will exploit the absence of order but the majority will feel safe and want a teacher who can show they are in charge.

The implementation of a behaviour code can be very hard work with classes that have had a weak teacher. They will be used to ignoring, even despising the teacher and they will need a very clear, assertive approach from someone who is not prepared to accept any cheek, rudeness or deliberate non-compliance. That does not mean you become aggressive or dictatorial, just determined to achieve your goal.

NEGATIVE VIBES

Children are very adept at picking up the vibes. They can tell whether or not you are having a good day. This awareness can be very destructive at times. Teachers who send out negative messages will find that they are being picked up. The long-term effect can be disastrous for the children and the teacher.

Negative vibes are not always blatantly obvious. They may be hidden away in the things you say and do. For example, a throwaway comment like, 'How many times do

I have to tell you before it sinks in?' carries a message to the child that they are not able to remember something and so dense that even the most obvious point cannot penetrate:

Comments like this serve no purpose because they do not tell the child how they can improve. Be wary of making statements that sound final:

'I've had it with you lot.'

This implies that the teacher is not going to make any more effort or allowance and has given up on the class. They are also getting cross and frustrated, which reveals their own weakness. Describing the class as 'you lot' lumps them all together, which can be interpreted by some as unfair. The well-behaved pupils will feel they are being labelled and judged along with the less well-behaved. They will resent the punishment for something they haven't done and turn against the teacher. Making comparisons can be fatal:

'The other class in the year group have already started the next stage of this work.'

This can be very upsetting and demotivating for most children. The other class may be further on, but so what. This really says more about the teacher than the group. Teachers will find that they cannot help comparing classes in a year group. The groups would probably progress at approximately the same rate providing lessons are not missed. Groups with children who have special needs may make slower progress, so the role of the teacher will be to get the pace right and keep the whole group moving forward. Individuals within the group may feel they are doing their best, therefore a blanket criticism does not help anyone as it is unspecific. Blaming the group merely highlights the differences and some may perceive it as a fault of the teacher rather than the pupils.

It can be incredibly irritating for a child when a teacher compares them to an older brother or sister:

'You're always getting into trouble. Why can't you be like your brother? He always gets his homework in on time.'

Comments like this are guaranteed to get the hackles up. Teachers may have these thoughts from time to time but they should keep them for the privacy of the staffroom. Actually saying them to a child will not yield any benefits, only fuel resentment. And here is another negative comment:

'I just don't understand why children in this class feel they have the right to talk during assembly. You know the rule. All the other classes can manage it.'

Worse still is the treatment of the class as a homogeneous entity rather than a group of individuals. There will almost certainly be children in the group who will not like being addressed in this way. They will be aggrieved by the unfair treatment and may react badly.

The heartening thought is that if children can be so deeply affected by a teacher's negative and destructive comments, perhaps positive comments could have a very beneficial effect. Teachers who have high expectations, talk up their classes to other teachers and give the children plenty of support will find they achieve much more. It is certainly worth trying and you have nothing to lose.

THE NEW PUPIL

New pupils often join schools after the start of the year. In some schools this may be more common than others, so the staff become skilled in dealing with the changes. It can be a daunting prospect for a child. They have left their school and a local community that was familiar to them, where they were known and accepted. Joining a new school brings new challenges. The first one is entering the building and going into the classroom. No matter how great the preparation, there will still be barriers for the child to overcome. Many schools set up buddy systems and link the new child to someone with similar interests. This is a good practice but the child still needs to establish themselves with the peer group.

Peer group membership creates a range of problems in schools. There will be hierarchies in every class and the teacher needs to manage and perhaps control them. Children take their places in the pecking order by their ability to communicate status and leadership qualities. Status can be conferred or appropriated according to strength, achievement and persuasive influence. For example, a strong, well-built, powerful-looking boy will be feared and admired. A pupil who is attractive and good-looking will be more readily accepted in a group than someone with a physical anomaly.

A child may exhibit an air of confidence through their dress sense, posture, language and turn of phrase. Such street credibility may place them centrally in the group as an okay person. Some may even be elevated to positions of movers and shakers whereas others will become members of the peer group. The losers are the ones who fail to get accepted and find themselves ostracised and on the outside of all groups. They may eventually come together and be labelled by the others as misfits.

A new pupil trying to find their place will disturb the equilibrium within the group. They will be a novelty for a few days or even weeks as the rest of the class size them up. Some of the children may start to behave in ways that are out of character as they attempt to impress or dominate the new member of the class. Children who are not readily accepted will keep trying and cause further disruption. The incidents will become fewer as the child finds his place. There are many strategies to prevent some of the disruptions:

- Allocate a desk and a group for them.
- Find out their interests and achievements and put them in touch with friends who share the same interests.
- Set aside special sessions for discussing their interests. Plan these sessions so you know in advance what they are. Get the children to complete an interest audit of things they like doing, places they have visited and things they have done well. The appendices contain an audit form you can photocopy.
- This information can be used to help you organise groups and plan lessons. Children may have a specific interest that you can incorporate into an activity to bring it to life. Drawing on their own experiences will ensure you are anchoring the lesson in their culture as well as providing them with a useful starting point to explore new things.

A new pupil will threaten existing friendship groups by challenging the leadership and putting pressure on relationships between the boys and the girls. A new girl can cause a lot of friction with boys, especially if she is popular and good-looking. Other girls will become jealous as the attention shifts from them to her and then the reprisals and niggling behaviour begin. Friendships will become strained and the seeds of bullying may be sown.

The teacher needs to be on the lookout for these signs and should be prepared to intervene as early as possible. Reorganise the seating, regroup pupils and keep an eagle eye on them, especially when they think you are not looking; this will safeguard the vulnerable children who may become the target during the instability of the new pupil's arrival.

The sink class

A tough class can arise for various reasons. It may be a good group that has been poorly managed or the result of thoughtless grouping, setting and timetabling. When a class has more than 10% of the pupils with special needs there has been an error of judgement in deciding the groupings. Placing a large number of children with special needs in one class may seem like a good idea, because their needs can be better served if they are together. Children attracting support can be grouped to make better use of the support staff assigned to them. The lessons can be planned to address their specific learning needs and the pace of the teaching can be adjusted to ensure all the lower-ability pupils understand the work.

The disadvantage is that although the lessons seem to be well staffed, in practice there is not always enough support time to cover every lesson. The lessons without support then become extremely difficult to manage for the teacher, and the whole group starts to lose out, culminating in behaviour problems. The profile of the group gets skewed towards the lower abilities and you lose the benefits of having a mixed-ability group. The group as a whole will eventually perceive themselves as less able. They will realise they are the group that is least likely to do well. They will not have as many opportunities to engage with ideas as the more able groups. Their diet in the lesson could become simplified and even bland. The self-fulfilling prophecy of being the 'dunces', 'duffers', 'morons' or 'the thick class' will start to dawn on some of them and they may even use these labels themselves.

Self-belief blossoms in a positive class but will wither away and die when the teacher starts to label the children. Similar problems arise from setting and streaming. There are contrasting views on separating pupils by ability. Educationalists who argue for setting stress the need to focus on the ability range and present an argument based on common sense. The teacher who has pupils with a narrower range of abilities can plan tasks and activities that match their needs so that everyone is working on similar things. The hope is that it makes better use of time and resources. The most obvious disadvantage is that the children will make personal judgements about their own abilities based on the group in which they find themselves. This can be demotivating for those in the lower sets and also for the children in the top sets who cannot keep up. They start to see themselves as weak even though they may be in the top 20% of the year group of up to two hundred pupils.

Teachers of mixed-ability groups deal with the wide range of abilities by grouping or setting the children within the room. They differentiate the work for the groups. It does not take long before the children in the low-ability groups realise they are getting different work. This can become a source of conflict if it is left to fester.

TEACHERS WHO ARE AFRAID TO ASK FOR HELP

Some teachers believe that when the class behaves well it is a mark of their success. This is fine when things are stable and the children are learning and behaving well. The danger occurs when things start to go wrong. The confident teacher will ask colleagues for help and then the problem will be shared. The confidence comes from the knowledge that the behaviour is the responsibility of the pupils and that they do not always make good choices. Teachers who believe this will be more ready to ask for help, because they do not feel their skills in managing the class are being questioned. Even the most experienced teachers get very difficult children they cannot deal with on their own. Teachers who feel they should manage every incident without help put unnecessary pressure on themselves. They will probably try to manage their class using an authoritarian style, which will inevitably result in challenges they may not be able to win. When that happens they will start to feel threatened and the doubts will grow.

TEACHING

The best way to avoid poor behaviour is with good teaching. Get the activities right, pace the lesson well, engage the pupils with interesting activities and an upbeat delivery, add your own enthusiasm for the subject and you will have cracked it. It sounds easy, doesn't it? But there are so many variables. Conscientious teachers know it and plan their lessons to reach this goal. Occasionally a teacher will find it is too much of a challenge and give up. They resign themselves to what they know rather than seeking help. Perhaps they are too afraid or too proud to ask, or perhaps they do not even realise their lessons are dull. Whatever the reason, poor teaching eventually leads to switched-off pupils. When this happens the problems start, of course. There will always be some children who have their own personal difficulties and do not respond to even the best teacher. They will need very clear approaches to help them manage their behaviour.

Poor teaching causes all manner of problems. Individual pupils will become frustrated about the work for a variety of reasons. They may not be able to do it or the work may be too easy. It may be boring or made boring by a dull delivery. When this happens they will communicate their frustration by doing things that cause low-level disruptions. Some will do it in a way to test the teacher's response. They will try to find out whether the teacher can cope with their behaviour. An inadequate response will be the signal for them that the teacher is weak and ripe for systematic baiting designed to bring turmoil to the classroom. A ringleader may emerge at this point. He will orchestrate the disruptive activities and make comments outside the lessons that are designed to undermine the teacher.

Children can be merciless, so you need your wits about you when you are working with them. When they get a teacher in their sights they will go for the jugular. They will look for personal attributes they can exploit and these will form the basis of their comments. Protect yourself at the start by preventing them having information about you. Follow these guidelines:

- Do not reveal your first name or where you live.
- Do not express your own likes and dislikes until you are confident with the class and feel you have control.
- Refrain from using obviously outdated expressions or expressions the children use.
- Project an air of confidence.
- Do not get into any conversations during lessons. Children will try to take in a weak teacher by showing some interest in something they have found out about them.

The ringleaders will be clever and select their followers carefully. They will pick other pupils who are weak-willed and easily led or bold characters who share their view.

The process of undermining will spread quickly as impressionable young people, uncertain about themselves, gravitate towards a group to gain a sense of belonging. As more join the campaign, the low-level disruptions become more frequent. Here are some things they may try:

- Sitting in the teacher's chair
- Changing the computer settings and passwords
- Locking the teacher out of the room
- Going through the teacher's cupboards and drawers in search of personal possessions to abuse
- Calling the teacher by their first name
- Forgetting to address the teacher as Sir, Miss or Mr
- Deliberately ignoring the classroom code
- Making funny noises that are hard to trace
- Annoying pupils who do not join them in their disruptive activities
- Turning up for the lesson late or leaving early.

The teacher will become more aware of the incidents but find it hard to challenge the children because they will be very clever in concealing their activities. The rest of the class become the audience, spectators of a game that everyone enjoys except the teacher. When the teacher does try to challenge someone, they will deny any knowledge, seek the support of their peers and pass the blame to confuse and exhaust the teacher. Eventually the teacher will give up trying to challenge the children, because it is too hard to catch the perpetrator. They try to ignore the disruptions, but this merely gives the children licence to try harder.

Picture the scene; it is almost like something from *The Bash Street Kids* or *Please, Sir!* The teacher is desperately trying to teach but the class are not listening. Things fly across the room. Children get up and walk around and seem to be doing as they please. When the bell goes they get up and walk out, knocking books on the floor and overturning furniture for the poor teacher to tidy up before the next group comes in. Clearly the teacher has lost it at this point and the children do not want to know. They will become the teacher's nightmare class from hell. A victory will spur the children on and unless they are stopped, they will start looking for their next victim.

CHILDREN SEEKING POWER AS RINGLEADERS

Children seeking power as ringleaders will be very clever at rallying others around them to give them power and status. They will influence their peers to cause the problems or follow them in their challenge against the teacher. Their strategies will be quite covert (Case Study 9.1).

Case Study 9.1 *Martin*

Martin was a popular kid in Year 6. He held a lot of sway with the other boys in his class. He was good at football and athletics, he looked tough, he wore good clothes and he always had money in his pocket. He was able to walk with a swagger the other kids didn't have and it made him appear very confident. He liked being the leader and the others seemed to follow him willingly. In class he would sit as if he was holding court. His closest friends sat next to him and his admirers got as near as they could. He was one of those kids who effortlessly controls things around him.

For several weeks now, the teacher had been annoying him. She kept on at him to do this and do that. Things were bad enough, without the stupid teacher getting on his wick. Things came to a head when she had a go at him for rocking his chair. He was bored because he had

finished the work and was getting fed up just sitting around waiting for her to tell him what to do next. She wasn't even his proper teacher. *She* had left three months ago. The class now had this Australian woman and she was too strict and always grading them.

Martin had been doing fine up until a couple of months ago. It was then that his life started to fall apart. His parents decided to split up and get a divorce. His dad left home with one of his older brothers. He did not like the split and blamed his mum, so the relationship grew difficult. His mum found she was losing control and could not manage him. He stayed out late at night with boys much older than him. He got involved in activities that led to trouble with the police. At school he started getting grief from the teacher. All she kept doing was hassling him to do the 'stupid work'.

This was the turning point. His patience was running short. His life wasn't what it should have been and to top it all his mum didn't want him to go to the same secondary school as his friends. Why should he bother any more? In lessons his pattern of behaviour became a continual cycle of disruptions. He would do the work for a little while then stop and look for something else to get involved in, usually trouble of some sort. He pulled the weaker kids down with him. His influence was powerful enough for him to be able to take quite a few with him. Every day became a tortuous experience for the teacher. She didn't know what to do. She could not keep him on task and once he got going the others joined him. When she tried to intervene and use her authority, they just laughed at her. She felt this was something more sinister than the usual poor behaviour.

After several more weeks of it, she went to the head and poured out her story. The head was very experienced and went along to the class to observe. Martin wasn't stupid. He knew why she was there and he kept out of trouble. He got on with his work. It was a clever, polished performance but he just couldn't keep it up every time the head visited. The head knew he would make a mistake eventually and he did. He persuaded a couple of kids into messing about with the paint palettes. He forgot the head was sitting quietly at the back observing. This was his downfall. The head realised he was organising the whole thing and giving the class a bad reputation. Over the next few weeks she interviewed a number of the troublemakers in the class, who pointed the finger at Martin. A careful process involving warnings and targets eventually put a stop to the behaviour before the teacher gave up and resigned.

THE TOUGH CLASS ACROSS THE YEAR GROUP

Difficult classes manifest in several ways. They may be particular to one teacher because there are problems with the relationship. Alternatively, other teachers taking the class may also have experienced difficulties in the past. When this happens there needs to be a collective response to the problem. This is easier said than done, because a teacher may find it hard to admit they are having difficulties managing the class, as described earlier. Sometimes colleagues may suspect there is a problem and may be able to help. They may witness a teacher struggling or they may be called on a regular basis to help deal with children and begin to realise that something more is required.

Assuming there is the desire to help and support, the next step is to make enquiries among other staff who have taught the group. This will help you decide which way to go in resolving the problem. If all the other teachers have found the class difficult to manage, call a meeting to discuss what is hard about them. List the reasons with examples. During the discussions, staff will start to name specific troublemakers. Draw up a list and try to identify the ringleaders. Record anecdotal evidence to inform your decisions on tackling the problems. It is tempting to believe the child is at fault, but consider other factors such as the subject, the timetable and the collective approach of the teachers, who may be inadvertently treating a child negatively.

Move to solutions by ascertaining whether any of the teachers have done things that have worked. An action plan will be required and should include these strategies. The plan will ensure that everyone is clear about the interventions to be used. Work will probably be required to develop a suitable behaviour code that can be shared with the other teachers. When the action plan is in place, set up meetings to interview the ringleaders. These meetings should always be attended by two members of staff. Pay attention to teacher harassment. If there is evidence of pupils harassing a member of staff, follow the procedures on page 174. All action plans need to be reviewed. Figure 9.1 shows the steps for dealing with a tough class across a year group.

WHEN ONE TEACHER FINDS A CLASS TOUGH

A different response is needed when just one teacher in a year team finds a class difficult. Knowing they are having difficulties is the first hurdle. Some teachers are afraid to seek help but the signs will be there. Two tell-tale signs are excessive noises coming from the room and the teacher looking anxious and stressed. Immediate assistance should be provided to alleviate the stress while longer-term solutions are devised. The following ideas could be tried:

- Ask the teacher if it is okay to use one of the computers in the room because all of the others are in use, have crashed or have the wrong software. It could be a piece of equipment or a space in their room if there is no computer.
- Go in and relieve the teacher by telling them they have an urgent telephone call in the office.
- Send a message to the class with a list of children who you want to see in your room. These are the known troublemakers. It gets them out of the lesson and gives the teacher a chance to stabilise the rest of the class.
- Go in and ask the teacher if you can borrow some children from the class to help you do a job such as sorting out books, cleaning computer screens, resetting desktops on computers, tidying sports equipment or moving furniture. This will enable you to talk on a personal level to individual children about what is going on in the room and why they are behaving that way.

These suggestions provide immediate support as a lifeline but will not solve the problems. Real solutions need to be found in the longer term. The teacher needs help to set up and implement a new behaviour code. They need an experienced colleague to help them review their lesson plans to ensure they address the needs and abilities of the children. Teaching strategies that have been proven to work with the group should be considered and opportunities for the teacher to observe them in action should be given. Coaching the teacher in making successful interventions will also be very useful. The next step is to help the teacher practise the interventions with a different class.

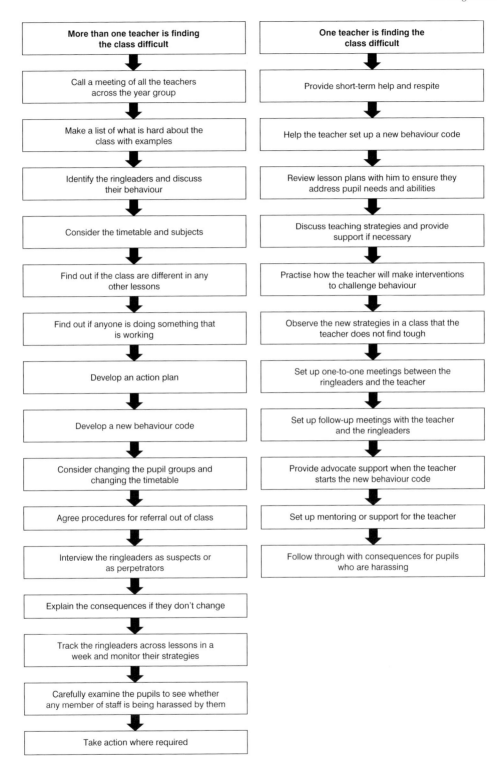

Figure 9.1 *Who is finding the class difficult?*

BULLYING AND HARASSMENT OF THE TEACHER

A group that becomes tough due to slippage of the teacher's behaviour management skills may eventually be perceived as bullying and harassing. Bullying is a learned response and can be stopped. Teachers who find themselves under pressure in this way will be distressed, have low self-esteem and be afraid to challenge children who are harassing them. Children who are not challenged will feed off their success, grow stronger and continue. It is vital that a teacher in this position confides in a colleague and shares the problem as early as possible instead of bottling it up.

A senior colleague should be included at this point and should organise a class meeting with the teacher to tackle general issues of bullying. Use the session to address the following issues:

- What is bullying?
- Why do people bully others?
- What do you think they get out of it?
- How do you think the victims feel?
- How do the bullies feel?
- Have you ever been bullied before?
- How do you think it affects the victim's life?
- How can we help the victims of bullying?
- What can we do to stop bullying?

Once the class start to talk openly, ask them whether they think it is a game. If they try to say it is just a bit of fun, point out that it is certainly not fun being on the receiving end. This is a suitable time to start to be more specific. Explain that adults can be bullied by other adults and even by children. Give some examples to illustrate what you mean. Introduce the word 'harassment' and emphasise that teachers are human beings and deserve to be treated decently. Tell them that their behaviour in the lesson is a form of harassment and has to stop. Most of the children will not have thought that what they were doing was very serious. By the end of the meeting they will realise it is serious and they will know the consequences if they continue.

The class meeting should be set up to allow the pupils and the staff time to talk. Avoid letting the children just moan and vent their feelings about marking, lessons, homework, school dinners, etc. Avoid having the teacher talk at the children. Help the children to consider how the victim feels by getting them to empathise. Suggest they imagine the victim to be someone they know; it could be a brother, sister, mum, dad or friend. Explain to them that the victim has feelings, a life and a right to be treated with respect. Teachers are the same and have these needs too.

Bullying exists in a climate of fear and secrecy. The bully threatens the victim with reprisals if they try to tell the authorities. They will gain status if their peer group become aware of their activities. Their peers will probably become too frightened to intervene or they will turn a blind eye to what is happening. Furthermore, a child who bullies an adult will gain greater kudos from their peer group. If you find they are slipping into this situation, keep records of exactly what happened, including dates, times, places, names and lists of witnesses. Then try to get some help. Do not leave it until it's too late. If you feel a colleague is being harassed, offer support. Do not legitimise bullying by ignoring it.

PICKING OFF THE RINGLEADERS

A tough class will have its ringleaders. Identifying and confronting them through the official channel of a face-to-face meeting organised by the senior colleague is the best way to put a stop to their activities (Case Study 9.2).

Case Study 9.2 *Kate*

Kate had become a teacher late in her life after her family were grown up. She had been working as a teaching assistant and had decided that she would like to try a new career as a teacher instead of returning to her original job in a travel agency. She embarked on one of the new teacher training schemes that could be done in school and got herself qualified. Then she took up a post in a primary school. Several years later she found herself with a Year 6 class teaching alongside two colleagues in a three-form-entry school. It was a large school in Greater London. The children came from a wide cross-section of the local population but the catchment area could not be described as well-off. The children were nice kids but, just like any school, there were the usual crop of difficult ones and an above average proportion in the current Year 6. The infant and junior schools had recently been amalgamated following an inspection. The infants had come out of it very well and the head had been given overall charge of the new school.

There is always friction in the first few years of an amalgamation and the infant staff were a challenge for the head because of their recent success with Ofsted. They felt they had been doing everything right and did not need to change. The head did not have the vision or the skills to move them on and a rift started to form between the two key stages. This is a common problem. The staff can become quite powerful and resist weak leadership. The result is a school that becomes complacent. New ideas pass them by. In this case it was not only ideas but also technology. The schools around them began getting equipped with the modern IT facilities such as interactive whiteboards in every class and software to turn lessons into new teaching experiences.

Eventually the head teacher realised that she was not moving the school on and decided to leave before Ofsted came again and her good reputation got damaged. A new head took up the post and was able to bring a fresh pair of eyes on how the school was run. He started to get to know his staff but it wasn't until the end of his first term that he became aware of Kate's problems.

Kate's class had been difficult since Year 3 because of the imbalance of children with special needs. She had eleven children with identified difficulties of one sort or another. This is a very high proportion for one class but the previous head had failed to address it. Luckily, the Year 5 teacher was very strong. She had kept good order and managed the children very effectively. There were few if any incidents during the year and she even managed to move them on considerably. They did not dare put a foot out of line for fear of losing out. The teacher had a good behaviour code and the kids kept within the rules to ensure they did not end up on her wrong side.

Kate took over the class in September and was very excited because she had not done the Standard Assessment Tests (SATs) before. She was a very confident person and usually had a lot to say about most things. However, that was one of her failings as a teacher. You felt that she was not really listening to you. She talked and talked, and when you contributed to the conversation she would either return to what she had just said or move to something new without heeding what you had said. Her lessons were a bit like this as well. She began them with lengthy explanations and when a child asked a question she would not give it sufficient attention. You could see the child was disappointed and frustrated that Kate had not given a satisfactory answer.

Kate was one of those teachers who assumed that the children would get on with the business of learning without the need of any direction about behaviour. This was obviously a misguided assumption that would eventually lead to her failure. The children had come out of their Year 5 experience to discover they had a new teacher in Year 6. They had been kept in check by a powerful personality but now their new teacher was an unknown quantity.

There was a small group of laddish boys in the class. As a group they stuck together. In the playground they were always engaged in games such as football or run-outs that involved a lot of noise. Their initial impression of Kate was that she was not as strict as their previous teacher. They saw opportunities for some freedom and a bit of fun at her expense and decided to find out what she would do. Things may have been different if she had acted in a less officious way. She snapped orders at them whenever they spoke to her. She never seemed interested in the things they tried to tell her. She would cut them short and order them to their seats: 'I am very busy, Tom, and haven't got time for this. Get to your seat before I give you a detention.'

When she called the register it was very dehumanising. She would run down the list calling out surnames and they had to reply with 'present'. She never looked up and it was as though she was doing an inventory of books in the library. She was very grumpy when she did break duty. Anyone who went over to chat was told to run along and play, because she needed her break away from them.

Kate felt very overworked, which is usual in the first year of teaching, but unlike new teachers she did not bother being nice. She was permanently tired and always behind with things other teachers were doing. She was supposed to have held elections for the school council but had forgotten. When the meetings came round, the class was not represented. Other teachers got their classes to do fun things for their assemblies but she didn't feel it warranted the time, so their assemblies always had readings by several of the well behaved, a lot of Kate talking and a bit of music at the end.

Kate was not lazy. She worked really hard and was dedicated to her job. The problem was that she did not get very much done. She always seemed to be putting in the hours but she was one of those people who did not work smartly. The result was that she put a lot of effort into things that were not very important. Her lessons were fairly mediocre and the children began to find them boring. She had not discovered how to motivate the children; in fact, her indifference had turned off many in her class.

The lads found that Kate was not stopping them from doing the little time-wasting things they had tried out. They realised that she was oblivious to them when she was working with other groups, so they downed tools and began messing about. From where she was it just looked like a few boys not on task, but she hadn't time to investigate because she was trying to help two pupils who were so far behind they could barely read, let alone do any writing. This became a pattern and the boys started to enjoy their new-found freedom after a year of a strict teacher. Kate finally intervened but she did not have much authority. They complied but on their terms. Five minutes later they were back doing what they wanted. She did not bother returning to them, because she thought it was their time they were wasting and they would have to make the work up later. This would have been fine if she had followed through, but she didn't.

On another occasion she arrived at the classroom late one morning to find a group of them playing with the glue sticks. They were hurling them up at the ceiling to see how many would stick and stay. She was furious and shouted at them to stop, which they did, but they were all in stitches because as soon as she had finished telling them off and they were back in their seats, it started raining glue sticks. Word got round and kids from other classes came to visit the room to see the glue stick 'stalactites'. Some children love to watch weak teachers struggle. They 'play' with them because they know they can get away with it. Inevitably, these incidents got home to the parents, who began quizzing their children about the unruly Year 6 class.

The concern soon spread among the parents of the children in her class. Parents of primary school children can get very wrapped up in their education. Some take it so seriously that it reaches fever pitch in Year 6, when the children move on to secondary school and parents compare the places they are offered. Kate knew one or two of her children were already being tutored and took it as a snub. It was as if they were saying that she was not able to teach them well enough, which was true really, because of the poor behaviour in the room most of the day.

Some of the parents wanted their children to take the common entrance examination for the local public school and some also wanted them to take the eleven-plus exam for the grammar schools. The public school seemed a very desirable choice because of its magnificent resources and the way it promoted itself. Kate was not sure it was as good as people thought, but when she tried to air this view, people responded that it would be a lot better than what they were getting at the moment. They had been impressed by the well-turned-out prefects, who always seemed so confident. The results were not brilliant considering the amount of money it charged, but the parents probably chose it because they believed they were doing the best for their children. It had to be better than the comprehensives. They may also have felt guilty that if they had the money, they should pay for the best education they could get.

The more the parents heard about happenings in Kate's class, the more concerned they became. The children tended to edit their feedback and remove the bits about their own actions. The message was that Kate was losing control. The angrier the parents got, the more they talked about her at home. This gave the children the freedom to join in, so they began to lose any respect for Kate, which in turn led to more mucking about in the classroom, and the cycle continued.

The term moved on and Christmas was rapidly approaching. The classroom became more and more difficult for Kate, exacerbated by her inability to get on the children's wavelength and show any interest in them. The poor behaviour became widespread in the class as more pupils joined in the games. Whenever she turned her back something happened. Things flew across the room, stuff fell off desks and silly noises broke the peace. Kate's response was to turn and yell in the general direction, which made the children who were not involved angry for being wrongly accused. The relationship was breaking down and Kate knew she would not be able to carry on this way.

The class next door had begun to wonder what was happening. By December they had got quite used to the outbreaks of laughter, shouting and loud noises. One day it all came to a head. There was the usual banging of desks and laughter followed by Kate yelling at someone. Then the adjoining door opened and she appeared in the doorway. She called across to the teacher and you could see quite clearly she had tears in her eyes. She was distressed and wanted help. The teacher went to the door and could see the mayhem. A number of chairs had been knocked over, there were books scattered around and most of the class were involved in throwing balls of screwed-up paper around the room. She turned to a responsible pupil in her own class and instructed her to go and fetch the head teacher. Then she went into the class and took over.

She had the authority in her voice that was needed and the children quickly stopped what they were doing and sat down. She tore one or two of them off for throwing things and then the head arrived. Kate went to the staff room and took a break. Eventually she was able to compose herself and return to the room, but she knew things had gone very badly. Her colleagues tried to help by doing the planning with her, but that wasn't really the problem; it was the behaviour and her own personal style that were the main issues. The head talked to her about it but he didn't have the experience or knowledge of how to deal with it; in his mind she had become a failing teacher. Kate hoped she could get to the end of the year, then she would have a new class and could start again. She also hoped she could take a different year group.

Just when she thought things couldn't get any worse, the news came that the school was going to be inspected. This was not good for her, because she knew she wouldn't be able to get through it. The head decided to employ another teacher, an ex-head, to work in the room with her during the inspection week. He also read the riot act to the class in the hope they would realise that the inspection week would not be a good time to misbehave. The weeks of preparation went by. Kate got her classroom looking really good. She removed the glue sticks from the ceiling and prepared her lessons meticulously. She went into school the weekend before the inspection to prepare the lessons for Monday and felt she was as ready as she could be.

The week did not go well. The kids were not as bad as they could have been, but there were some low-level disruptions. Furthermore, her music lesson was a disaster because she did not use any of the instruments. This did not match her plans but she thought it would be safer. She had visions of the class running out with the drums, which was usually the case in her music lessons. It was graded as unsatisfactory and started the inspectors on a trail that took them back to her for several other lesson observations. Even with the help of the ex-head, she could not keep the class in check. She scraped a satisfactory grade for one lesson but the other one failed. By the end of the week she was exhausted and ready to quit. Her heart was no longer in the job and she did not really know how she was going to make it to the summer holidays.

Case Study 9.2 describes a terrible state and one that no teacher should get into. The head teacher did try to help Kate but it was the wrong kind of help and also came too late. The whole messy business should have been dealt with much earlier. The problem was that no one knew what was going on in her room. They could only hear what was happening. Kate was slow in asking for help and then it would not have put things right for her. Imagine if it had gone like Case Study 9.3.

Case Study 9.3 *Monica*

Monica was having very similar problems. Fortunately for her, the head teacher had a lot of experience dealing with difficult classes like hers, so she was able to offer some very useful support. Monica began by going to a colleague, who advised her to make notes of the incidents and then go to the head and discuss what to do. The head was very supportive and set up a series of meetings between Monica and each of the pupils on the list. Monica then went away, worked out what she was going to say and practised with her colleague. On the day of the meeting, she started to feel nervous. She didn't know why, because at last something was being done and she was hopeful. She sat next to the head and the pupil sat opposite at the other end of the table.

The head opened by addressing the child in a very calm, serious and firm way. 'We called this meeting because I am very concerned about the kinds of behaviour in your class.' She went on to describe in detail the things the pupils had been doing. She made it specific, naming the particular pupils whenever necessary. Then it was Monica's turn. She explained to the pupil how his behaviour had affected her ability to carry out her job as the teacher. She looked the pupil straight in the eyes as she expressed her feelings in vivid detail. She could see he was feeling uncomfortable and ashamed. She described how harmful his actions had been and the disappointment she had felt. He found it hard to look her in the eye but she faced him and made him do it. He had nowhere else to look except down. She finished by telling him she wanted the behaviour to stop.

Monica felt her descriptions of the hurtful effects of the behaviour got through to him. She was not sure it worked for all the others, but certainly most of them seemed surprised. The head invited the pupil to speak and respond to what Monica had said. The pupil explained that he hadn't realised it would do this much harm. Looking back he could see that what they'd been doing was serious stuff but he just wanted to have a bit of fun. They thought Monica was someone they could do it to without getting into trouble. The head reminded him of her right to teach and do her job without being harassed. She pointed out that a campaign as systematic as theirs was bound to have harmful effects.

She reiterated the school rules, especially the one on bullying. One of the other pupils tried to deny that they had been bullying but the head was forceful and said that bullying would not be tolerated. This pupil got abusive and one of the other pupils remained silent and refused to acknowledge anything. The head handled them both very well by letting them know this was their opportunity to explain themselves and it was up to them to use it. Getting aggressive or refusing to speak did not help them in any way. She asked the pupil who had been abusive what he would do to ensure that Monica could teach the class and not have to endure any more of his disruptions and harassment. She then asked him how he was going to rebuild the relationship. It ended with him apologising to Monica. The head concluded by stating again that they would be expected to stop the bullying or face the consequences. She spelled them out in no uncertain terms and made a date for a review meeting with the pupil in two weeks' time. Then she signed and dated the notes, put them together and dismissed the pupil.

They had similar meetings with all of the pupils, and in all these meetings Monica felt confident and supported as she knew she had the backing of the head and the school. The reviews took place but the problems seemed to stop after the first meetings. She could see now where she went wrong. The whole experience was a powerful one and not a part of her career she looks on with pride. She learned a lot from it and appreciated how the school handled the whole messy business. She is a deputy herself now and has to deal with bullying between pupils. The situations aren't identical but the methods are the same. The meeting with the bully and the victim works very well providing there is a structure and someone in authority to chair it. They can then stress the consequences and the need for it to stop. Monica hasn't had to deal with a member of staff being bullied, because she can see how it starts and has set up a very clear behaviour code. She has channels for referring pupils when their behaviour starts to escalate.

CHALLENGING PUPILS YOU SUSPECT ARE BULLYING YOU

Sometimes it is very difficult to identify who is doing the bullying or whether it is in fact bullying. This needs a different approach to actual bullying. Keep notes of things that happen and once you have your evidence, go to a senior colleague and set up a meeting. The pattern of the meeting is very similar to the one for actual bullying; the difference is what is said. The senior colleague begins the meeting using a phrase like this:

'We are interviewing a number of pupils about what has been going on in the maths lessons.'

Replace 'maths' with the appropriate subject. This will inform the pupil that a systematic investigation is being carried out. Specific examples of behaviour should be presented:

'Mrs A has told me that some of the pupils, including you, have been deliberately ignoring her when she comes into the room. When she tries to call the class to attention they begin to hum and that lasts for about a minute. Then they stop and start laughing and jeering. Eventually Mrs A is allowed to begin but the same thing often happens again later in the lesson.'

The pupil is given an opportunity to comment:

'What do you know about this?'

This lets the pupil know you are on to him but gives him a chance to explain what has been happening, especially if he has not been directly involved. Then the teacher is invited to explain how she feels when the behaviour starts and how it is preventing her from doing her job. Empathy is used to get the pupil to think about how he would feel if he were the teacher. The senior colleague concludes this part of the meeting by stating:

'No one deserves this kind of behaviour. It doesn't matter who they are, a pupil or a teacher, it is wrong and it will not be tolerated!'

Sometimes children feel that a weak teacher is an easy target, or a teacher with characteristics that are funny or quirky. The senior colleague answers any suggestion of this with:

'If you feel you are not being treated fairly or have a legitimate complaint, you either speak directly to the teacher, the head or me and we will listen to you.'

The meeting is concluded by reminding the pupil of the behaviour code and detailing the rights of everyone, including the staff, and the responsibilities of all to uphold those rights. Make notes of everything that is said during the meeting and then make a date to review the pupil's behaviour in two weeks. Note that no one is blamed. Empathy is used instead. It is a more neutral way of getting the child to think about the implications of the situation. He will go back to his friends and talk about the meeting and they will know you are on to them.

BULLYING TEACHERS: A CONCLUSION

Serious bullying may need actual consequences and head teachers should not refrain from giving them when they are required. Here are three examples:

- Contact the pupil's parents
- Change the pupil's class
- Exclude the pupil.

These consequences should be used in the last resort and should only happen if the bullying recurs after the meetings. Prevention is best and there are several ways to do it. Figure 9.2 (overleaf) summarises them as a checklist. You could use it to see whether you are taking the right preventative measures.

<table>
<tr><td colspan="2" align="center">**Checklist to Prevent Bullying**</td></tr>
<tr><td>You plan and deliver lessons that are right for the pupil group</td><td>☐</td></tr>
<tr><td>You make the effort to get to know the children in and out of class in order to find out their interests and common ground</td><td>☐</td></tr>
<tr><td>Teaching is monitored to ensure the curriculum is delivered appropriately</td><td>☐</td></tr>
<tr><td>The school has safe confidential channels for disclosure where victims of bullying can seek support</td><td>☐</td></tr>
<tr><td>There is a school council that gives pupils the opportunity to air their views and contribute to the operations of the school community</td><td>☐</td></tr>
<tr><td>Regular class meetings are held to resolve difficulties and agree items to go to the school council</td><td>☐</td></tr>
<tr><td>Interventions are timely and follow an agreed procedure laid down in the behaviour policy</td><td>☐</td></tr>
<tr><td>Behaviour management is a whole-school procedure and individual members of staff are given guidance on how to carry it out</td><td>☐</td></tr>
</table>

Figure 9.2 *Checklist to prevent bullying*

TAKING OVER A TOUGH CLASS

Taking over a tough class can be a daunting prospect. Some might believe it is a rite of passage for the fledgling teacher, an initiation into a fraternity who have known the stresses and troubles caused by the occasional difficult class. When the staff in a school know there is a tough class, help should be on hand. It should not be an experience to be endured like running over hot coals. The tough class needs to be made normal again for everyone's good, but especially for the pupils. The solution is straightforward. It is what this book is all about, but it's not easy. It would be all right if you could just walk into a room and tell the class the rules, but getting their attention needs to come first. They will have become used to deciding when they will attend and when they will listen to the teacher. Cracking that will require help from colleagues, and so will getting enough time to show you are different from the other teachers they've had.

THE ADVOCATE TEACHER

An advocate teacher can help teachers who are being harassed as well as new teachers taking over a difficult class. It depends on the school recognising two things:

- New teachers will need support during the early weeks while they are establishing themselves with their classes.
- All schools have classes that could become difficult if they are not managed carefully.

Senior managers need to identify any potentially tricky classes that a new teacher has on their timetable before starting in the school. The subject team are then contacted and asked to meet with the new teacher to plan the first term. They will help the teacher plan the lessons for the first two weeks and help them with resourcing. This will ensure the teacher is prepared and supported for starting in the school. The advocate teacher should be a more senior member of the team who knows the class well and holds some authority in the school; they should introduce the new teacher to the class.

Introductions

The advocate teacher arrives at the lesson and makes sure the pupils line up and enter the room in an orderly fashion. He moves to the front of the class in the centre of the room and greets them. The new teacher takes his place at the side of the room and attends to what the advocate teacher is saying. He does not look at the class. His focus is on the front, like the children's. This maintains the advocate teacher's authority. The advocate teacher then says:

'Good morning. As you know, Mr Clark left us last term and Mr Smith has joined us to take his place.'

He maintains the children's attention and says nothing about the teacher's past experience or the poor behaviour of the class.

Handover

The advocate teacher then turns to the new teacher and signals him to move into the centre of the room at the front, where he introduces himself:

'Good morning. I am Mr Smith and I will be taking you this year.'

The advocate teacher moves to the side and maintains his attention on Mr Smith, listening intently to his introduction. He does not look round at the class. His body language is open and he shows interest in what the teacher is about to say. The handover is seamless and the movement of authority occurs without question. The advocate teacher needs to send out the right signals at this crucial time. He is there to introduce the new teacher, not to be his bodyguard. The children need to feel that both teachers are working together as equal partners and not detect any signs of seniority. They must see the new teacher in front of them as an experienced professional who knows what he is doing.

'I am pleased to have been asked to come and work at this school. I have taught in a number of other schools and am looking forward to working with you.'

A confident delivery will settle the children and ensure they do not try to test you on the first day.

Behaviour code

The advocate teacher should sit or stand in a relaxed way during this time. He should avoid surveying the room and fixing any potential troublemakers with a glare that says, 'I know what you are capable of and I am watching you.' Nor should he stand, arms folded, facing them like a bouncer outside a nightclub. The teacher briefly explains the behaviour code and takes any questions then begins the lesson. Any chatting, lateness or minor disturbance that occurred during the introduction should be dealt with assertively by the new teacher. Once the children are engaged in the tasks, both teachers use correction and praise when it is needed. This communicates the message that they are working together and team teaching.

Ending

The class comes back together at the end and the new teacher takes up his position at the front. The advocate teacher returns to the side of the room and gives him his full attention. His style remains relaxed and he appears interested in what conclusions the teacher will draw. His attention channels the attention of any children who are looking at him. They follow his eyeline towards the teacher at the front. The presence of an advocate has given the teacher a window of calm and order to begin establishing himself with the class. His presence has also given the teacher the confidence to concentrate on his teaching instead of worrying about the behaviour. This, together with a well-planned and resourced lesson, has led to a good experience for the teacher and the pupils, perhaps the first they've had for a while.

Next lesson

There are several ways to manage the subsequent lessons. The advocate teacher could stay with the teacher or go and come back after lunch or next morning. He observes the teacher's performance during the whole class and plenary parts of a lesson and makes notes in the same way as an inspector. During the tasks, he assumes the team-teaching role as before. This provides a presence in the room but allows the teacher to remain in charge.

The other way is to drop in and have a chat about something. The children will have begun their tasks, giving the teacher freedom to have a visitor. This way should only be used if the teacher and the advocate feel confident that things are going well. If the class is really tough, the first method is preferable, at least for several more lessons until the teacher has properly established himself and the children have settled into their new routines. The test is the number of disruptions and how they are handled. The new teacher should feel that disruptions are being handled well and the children are responding by accepting the consequences. The acid test will be when he has to give a consequence without the advocate in the room.

ADVANTAGES OF THE ADVOCATE APPROACH

- The new teacher feels supported by a team of colleagues from the first day and in the future he will not feel afraid to ask for help.
- The teacher will get a good start with the class and have a chance to establish himself knowing the advocate is there to help if things start to go wrong.
- The team will show the teacher how lessons are planned in the school and set the teacher on the right road with a couple of lessons planned collaboratively at the start.
- The children in the class will accept the teacher more easily if it is done through the advocacy of another teacher they already know.

- The new teacher will be directed to plan in detail the lessons and the behaviour code and the routines within the class such as lining up and entering the room. The advocate will be responsible for showing the teacher what is required rather than just assuming they know. Where the new teacher obviously knows what to do, the professional courtesy is to reach an appropriate agreement. The spirit is not one of patronising the new teacher but of ensuring they feel supported and free to ask for help.

INDUCTION PROGRAMMES

Schools without these systems would do well to consider them when planning their induction programmes. They should be incorporated into a whole-school approach for managing behaviour, the subject of the next chapter.

SUMMARY

- Tough classes come about for a variety of reasons, including a teacher's classroom management skills.
- A class may have been difficult for all the other teachers in the school or just one or two of them.
- Immediate interventions should be made. The ringleaders need to be identified and then meetings arranged between them, the teacher and a senior colleague.
- Empathy should be used to enable the perpetrators to get an idea of what the teacher feels.
- Children should be made aware of the consequences if they continue to disrupt the lesson.
- Class meetings can be used to try to resolve the problems between the pupils and the teacher.
- More experienced teachers should support the teacher in distress by helping them plan their lessons, acting as an advocate to give them a chance to change things in the room, and providing moral support.
- When taking over a tough class, the school should provide a programme of support that enables the new teacher to establish themselves with the class under the wing of an advocate teacher.
- The school needs to have channels of communication for the victims of bullying. These channels should include staff and pupils.

10 THE WHOLE-SCHOOL APPROACH

The whole-school approach is the most important factor in managing behaviour. Clear systems operated consistently and fairly by assertive staff will minimise problems and will lead to pupils taking responsibility for their own behaviour and making the most of their time at the school. The problems occur when there are no agreed procedures. Teachers start to interpret the rules in their own ways, set up their own behaviour codes and respond to inappropriate behaviour in different ways. This eventually leads to confusion. This book provides guidance on managing behaviour for individual teachers. However, it is best used as a resource by the whole staff when devising a unified school behaviour policy. Consequently, this final chapter is the most important.

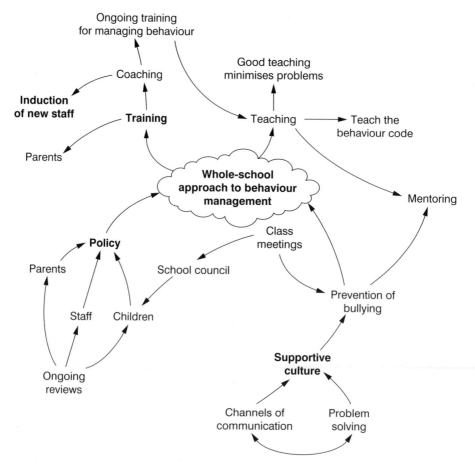

Figure 10.1   *A whole-school approach*

A whole-school approach has four key areas:

- Policy
- Training
- Induction
- Support.

They are interlinked and provide the cornerstones for building a management system that reaches into every aspect of school life. Figure 10.1 shows how each area contributes to the overall plan. This chapter looks at how to draft and implement a behaviour policy. It will take you through the steps to produce a document that will encapsulate the school ethos on behaviour management and outline the practices to use on a daily basis.

STEP 1: GETTING STARTED

The policy is a very important document. It communicates the ethos behind the school's approach and describes how it will be translated into practice. It can only be effective as a working document if everyone contributes. There are several ways to achieve this:

- Hold meetings to agree practices.
- Involve pupils in drawing up the behaviour code with rewards and consequences.
- Circulate drafts for comment.
- Provide special lessons for the children to learn the code.
- Train the staff in how to use the code.
- Invite parents to contribute to the annual review of the code.

STEP 2: ESTABLISHING THE RULES

The senior managers need to take a lead by producing a draft for discussion by the whole staff. At the end of the session, the staff should have reached an agreement so the actual practices can be formulated. A positive management ethos should include these three ideas.

Rights
The policy protects individual rights and makes that aim the responsibility of everyone.

Behaviour not the person
The underlying belief will be that everyone is capable of changing. A person who behaves inappropriately has the power to choose. It is the behaviour that is disliked not the person. They are in control and not perceived as a victim. This also prevents teachers labelling pupils as bad.

Responsibility
The use of choice places the responsibility with the child. It is up to them to make good choices. The aim is to help the children manage their own behaviour.

STEP 3: THE PRACTICE

It will take several sessions to bring together all the ideas and reach agreement on the practices the staff will use. The senior team need to agree the basic rules that will apply across the school. These rules are then discussed with the staff so they can see the difference between rules and directions. Individual teachers then work alone or in groups to write up the directions for the routines that operate in the school, but they do not form part of the policy. Teachers also take the plan to the children to gather their suggestions about rewards and consequences. The senior team should work out the hierarchy of responses, indicating when a child should be referred on to the next stage. They should also devise a means of recording incidents and a way of tracking them in the referral process. The following guidelines should help the staff clarify their practices.

Rules

Rules need to be fair and easily understood. They should be written as dos and don'ts wherever possible. The rules should stem from the list of basic rights.

Interventions

Teachers should consider how and when to make interventions. The policy should state clearly that all staff will be trained to be assertive and make interventions in a non-confrontational, detached and unemotional way.

Rewards

Pupils and staff should have discussions and agree on some realistic rewards; these rewards are then listed with an explanation of how they will be given.

Consequences

Consequences should be carefully considered by everyone concerned. Governors may also need to be consulted to ensure that everyone agrees on the consequences, how they will be given and who will make the decisions to give them. The use of more serious sanctions such as internal isolation and exclusion should be described with care; state clearly that government guidelines will be followed.

Stages of response

Where no guidelines exist, staff may refer pupils to senior colleagues for minor incidents. Alternatively, they will refer incidents straight to the head teacher and miss out the key stage manager. The policy should describe the stages, list the gatekeepers and outline the reasons for the referral. A report form should follow the pupil right through the referral process and be signed by each gatekeeper who has an input. Once the consequence has been completed, the form should be returned to the teacher so they are aware of the outcome. Then they put it in the pupil's file. Teachers who refer a child to a more senior colleague sometimes do not know what happens to them, so this system keeps everyone informed.

Records

Incidents that occur in the class should be recorded. Teachers should have a simple tick sheet to use during the lessons for recording verbal warnings, time-outs, one-minute detentions, etc. These record sheets should be kept and used when writing individual education plans and personal support plans.

Wider issues

The policy should show the links to other areas of school life. Make reference to other policies so that you demonstrate a unified management process.

PSHE

Personal, social and health education (PSHE) is one of the most obvious links. The PSHE curriculum is concerned with personal development in its broadest sense. It provides the teachers with opportunities to tackle behaviour alongside the other responsibilities needed to become a knowledgeable, well-adjusted citizen. It also offers space to engage with emotional intelligence (Goleman, 1996), arguably an important skill for success in adult life as it puts you in control of your own emotions and makes you sensitive to those of other people. Emotional intelligence provides a good foundation for managing undesirable behaviour that could stem from feelings of anger, frustration and aggression.

Teaching and learning

The teaching and learning policy will set out the school's ethos and make the link between interesting lessons and good behaviour.

Induction

The school's induction programme will prepare new staff for the work they will do. Give careful consideration to the ways the staff do things and outline training in the policy. Highlighting the provision of a mentor, the level of support given during the first lessons, etc., will communicate to everyone that proper support is available.

Pupil involvement

Describe the involvement of the pupils in behaviour management. It is a regular ongoing commitment of reviewing the code and the procedures. This gives the pupils a role in the school's management and ensures the leadership team remain informed on the day-to-day operation of the system. Regular class meetings and school council meetings are the forums for these discussions; any recommendations are forwarded to the relevant senior managers.

Parental involvement

Parental involvement is a vital part of any behaviour plan, and parents will be pleased to see they have been included in the policy. The methods of involvement should be described and could include their input to the annual review of the plan together with training sessions for those parents who want to improve how they manage behaviour at home.

Harassment and bullying

Refer to the anti-bullying policy. Briefly summarise the school's approach plus the main methods it will use, such as mentors and the buddy system. Stress the school's climate of openness and its supportive nature.

STEP 4: TRAINING

Training is at the heart of the policy. Good training will ensure that everyone concerned knows their role and the expectations placed on each individual. Staff who are trained will feel confident they can carry out their role in accordance with the policy guidelines. These will probably be the main areas of training:

- Induction for new staff
- Teaching the behaviour code to the pupils
- Helping parents improve their behaviour management skills
- Refresher sessions for all staff using problem solving.

Training in behaviour can be great fun as well as extremely productive. The school can organise its own training or bring in a specialist to facilitate the sessions. This largely depends on how individual schools like to go about it. The advantage of a specialist is that they know what works well and what doesn't. For schools wishing to do it themselves, the following model may be useful.

The case study model

The staff are given several scenarios like the ones featured in this book. They then work in small groups or pairs to discuss how they would deal with the incident. Their target is to suggest strategies that could be used. The facilitator should provide some generic guidelines before the groups begin. Here are some things to remember when considering interventions or responses:

- Offer choices.
- Either respond or tactically ignore.
- Use rule reminders.
- Redirect the pupils to the task.
- Do not respond to secondary behaviour.
- Do not provide a show for the rest of the class.
- Begin interventions at a low level and only move to a higher level if this does not work.
- Keep consequences and rewards in proportion and linked to the behaviour.
- Dislike the behaviour not the child.
- All behaviour is a communication.

The groups should write brief notes on their recommended responses to the case study. They could be asked to describe how *not* to respond to the incident. This allows them to focus on the potential pitfalls. The whole staff could be given the same case study, or each group could be given a different case study and the groups swap case studies at a convenient time. The facilitator's job is to gather up the notes and responses to each case study. These can be written up and gradually turned into a school manual on behaviour management. Wright (1988) is a rich source of case studies. This is a highly successful method for staff development. Staff enjoy the sessions because they can actively engage with the problems, devising new strategies and reviewing current practices at the same time. The end result is a very useful handbook for any teacher to use.

Input as well as output

Good training needs input from someone with experience for staff to feel they are gaining new skills and knowledge. It can be very frustrating to find you're on a 'do-it-yourself' staff training course. Senior staff planning training in behaviour management need to look at the school and judge where it has reached. It will be fruitless giving staff case studies to work on if they do not have enough experience to generate workable ideas. Schools that have developed behaviour codes along the lines of this book will gain a great deal from case study training. Schools that are just starting out on this road should consider bringing in a specialist to help staff think through their ethos and produce a policy. From this they can work on practices and test them using the case studies. Wherever your school has reached, I wish you good luck and I'm sure you'll enjoy the rest of the journey.

SUMMARY

- Consistency is vital so the pupils know what to expect.
- Every school should have a behaviour policy that clearly sets out its behaviour management methods and the ethos which underpins them.
- The methods should be clear, staged from low-level incidents dealt with by the teacher to high-level incidents that require action by the head teacher and the governors.
- The behaviour policy should be simple and practical so that the newest or most inexperienced adults can use it.
- Devising a whole-school approach should include all staff, pupils, parents and governors so the behaviour policy is owned by everybody.
- Special lessons should be timetabled so that pupils can be taught the behaviour policy at the start of the school year, and refresher sessions should be scheduled during the year when required.
- New pupils will need to be taught the behaviour policy.
- New staff should be trained in how to use the behaviour policy during their induction.
- The behaviour policy should be reviewed half-termly at the beginning and then annually in the policy review cycle.
- A serious breakdown in behaviour should prompt a review of how it was handled and the effectiveness of the behaviour policy; check for flaws or omissions that need addressing.
- Form partnerships with other schools, pupil referral units and external agencies such as behaviour support and the educational psychology service for support in creating and developing the behaviour policy.

CONCLUSION

While I was researching and planning this book it became obvious that there is far more to managing behaviour than just setting up a behaviour code. My questions led me to the work of Daniel Goleman (1996). He argues that there is more to intelligence than the academic intelligence quotient (IQ). The brain functions on several levels. The amygdala is a small area of the brain that controls our emotional responses and was a major force in helping our ancestors to survive in a dangerous world of predators, where food had to be hunted or gathered. The intuitive judgements made by the amygdala could have meant the difference between life and death for humans up to about a thousand years ago. Since then massive technological advancements have changed our world and our lifestyles. Those split-second decisions based on experiences gained in the early years of childhood and filed in a muddled way could now mean that we do something we may regret later. They are devoid of the rational thoughts of the cortex that could tell us to stop and consider what might happen if we went for other options.

Goleman describes one group of primary school boys with above average IQs. They were not doing very well in their academic work, so neuropsychological tests were carried out and revealed that the boys had impaired cortex functioning. They were impulsive, anxious and often got into trouble. It was believed they had faulty prefrontal control over their limbic urges. Their lack of control over their emotional life placed them at highest risk of failing academically and of getting involved in crime, alcoholism and drug abuse. I am sure you will recognise children who exhibit these tendencies in the classroom. The worry is that not enough is done to help children take control of their emotions and the results become obvious at school and in later life.

We teach the National Curriculum subjects but we need to go further to make sure every child is taught how to control anger and resolve conflicts positively. If we leave this to chance, we risk missing the opportunity given us by the slow maturation of the brain. Once a child reaches adolescence the pathways become harder to access and there is less chance of harnessing and controlling those urges. Catching children early and teaching them how to behave is the first step. However, we will be leaving the job unfinished if we do not try to teach them how to manage those times when they see red mist and how to control their emotions when their primitive amygdala kicks in.

As educationalists, we need to put pressure on the policy makers to consider more recent research into how the brain functions and to broaden their view of human intelligence. A different perspective needs to be adopted on what is required for an adult to function efficiently as an individual, a member of a community and a useful employee. If Goleman is right, we should be helping our young people to develop the qualities of self-awareness, impulse control, persistence, zeal and motivation, empathy and social deftness. Maybe this will bring a significant reduction in the problems teachers experience with children failing to behave appropriately. In the meantime they need strategies that are effective. I hope this book will help you develop them so that your classes will be well managed and you have no need to shout.

Glossary

assertive style
An assertive style is a teaching style that depends on a way of speaking and acting. Assertive teachers do not need to shout or use threats. They assert themselves in the way they say things.

attention seeking
Some children crave attention and will misbehave in order to get it.

choice
Offering choice is a means of placing the responsibility with the child. They have to decide.

consequence
All actions have consequences. Teaching children to understand this is one of the keys to successful behaviour management.

cooling off
Sometimes children need time to calm down and think about their actions. If they are given time, they may change their position and show you they have realised where they have gone wrong.

deferred consequence
A deferred consequence is a consequence that happens at a later time. The child will know they have got a consequence but will not receive it until later. Giving a red card is a signal that a deferred consequence has been issued and will need to be paid back later.

direction
The teacher gives a direction. A direction applies to specific activities whereas a rule applies all the time.

golden time
See motivational time

hierarchy of responses
A hierarchy of responses is a range of responses used by a teacher. The teacher begins by using low-level responses for minor disturbances, but the response level is increased if the child persists or the incident escalates. Ultimately the teacher will call for assistance from a senior member of staff if the child's behaviour becomes unacceptable.

intervention
An intervention is a teacher's response to a child's behaviour.

modelling behaviour
The teacher may model or show how they want the children to behave by doing it themselves. For example, a teacher may model good manners such as saying 'please' and 'thank you'.

motivational time
Motivational time is time that pupils can earn by behaving well. It may be earned by individuals or the class as a whole. It is also known as golden time.

off task
Children are off task if they are not following directions and not doing what the teacher has told them.

over-servicing
Teachers who respond or get involved in secondary behaviour (*q.v.*) will over-service the incident and possibly fuel it. When a child begins to misbehave, the teacher should redirect them with the minimum of fuss. Children who are looking for attention will try to draw in the teacher with their demands.

positive reinforcement
Praise positively reinforces the desired behaviour. Any form of reward will do this.

primary behaviour
Primary behaviour is the child's behaviour when they first respond to a situation. The teacher should deal with undesirable primary behaviour.

redirect
When a child goes off task, the teacher's response should usually be to get them back on task. This is done by redirecting the child to the work and offering help.

repair and rebuilding
After a teacher has given a child a consequence and they have served it, a period of repair and rebuilding is needed to help the child realise that everything is now okay in their relationship with the teacher. This will enable the child to see that inappropriate behaviour is unacceptable but that the teacher does not dislike them as a person.

responsibility
In a culture of rights, everyone is responsible for protecting the rights of others.

rewards
Extrinsic rewards such as stickers, certificates and motivational time are earned by doing things well. Intrinsic rewards are the feeling of doing something well or knowing you have won a race.

rights
A right is a basic entitlement of everyone within the group. Rights enable each member of the group to enjoy certain freedoms without hurting others or being hurt. Rights need to be agreed and defended by everyone.

rule
A rule is an absolute limit of behaviour within the group that applies at all times in the school.

rule reminder
A rule reminder brings the attention back to the rule that has been broken. If a child does not follow directions, the teacher will have to intervene. They will point out where the child did not follow the directions and remind them of the rule.

secondary behaviour
A child who has behaved inappropriately will often shift the emphasis away from their initial behaviour to secondary behaviour. For example, they may say that a teacher is being unfair and try to draw the teacher away from the initial behaviour on to the teacher's alleged unfairness, which is the secondary behaviour.

tactical ignoring
A teacher may deliberately ignore a child who is behaving inappropriately but they will highlight a child who is giving the behaviour they require. This will demonstrate to the other child what they need to do without having to reprimand them for not doing it.

take-up time
Some children require longer to process a direction than others. When a teacher challenges a child, they may allow some time for the child to think about their behaviour and decide how to put it right.

timed intervention
A timed intervention is a period of time that a child may take away from the school at a learning support unit. It is used to help the child work on their behaviour so they can return to the school and cope with working in a classroom.

time-out
A time-out is a period of time away from the class, either in the room or out. There may be a special desk in the room for this and the children go to it for a fixed period of time, usually one to five minutes. If they can behave, they are allowed to resume their place in the class.

warning
The teacher will give warnings before giving a consequence to allow the child an opportunity to put right their behaviour. The warning allows the child to think about what they are doing and make a choice. This places the responsibility with the child and removes the excuse of being a victim. Victims do not usually have choices.

REFERENCES

Ayers, H., Clarke, D., Ross, A. and Bonathon, M. (1993) *Assessing Individual Needs: A Practical Approach*. David Fulton, London.

Bennathan, M. and Boxall, M. (1993) *The Boxall Profile: Handbook for Teachers*. Association of Workers for Children with Emotional and Behavioural Difficulties, London.

Canter, L. and Canter, M. (1992) *Assertive Discipline: Positive Behaviour Management for Today's Classroom*. Lee Canter Associates, Santa Monica CA.

Department of Health (2000) *Framework for the Assessment of Children in Need and Their Families*. The Stationery Office, London.

Dreikurs, R., Grunwald, D. and Pepper, F. (1982) *Maintaining Sanity in the Classroom*, 2nd edn. Harper & Row, New York.

Goleman, D. (1996) *Emotional Intelligence: Why It Can Matter More than IQ*. Bloomsbury, London.

Maslow, A. H. *et al.* (1998) *Toward a Psychology of Being*. Wiley, Chichester, W. Sussex.

Rogers, B. (1994) *The Language of Discipline: A Practical Approach to Effective Classroom Management*. Northcote House, Plymouth.

Smith, A. (1996) *Accelerated Learning in the Classroom*. Network Educational Press, Stafford, Staffs.

Willis, P. (1977) *Learning to Labour: How Working Class Kids Get Working Class Jobs*. Gower, Aldershot, Hants.

Wright, D. (1998) *Managing Behaviour in the Classroom: Practical Solutions for Everyday Problems*. Heinemann, Oxford.

BEHAVIOUR LOG

Class ....   Date ....

Name	Verbal warning	Yellow card	Red card	Consequence given

CHILD PROFILE:
QUESTIONS TO ASK THE CHILD

Name ....   Date of birth ....

What is your name?	
Do you have a nickname? Who is allowed to call you it?	
How old are you? (Leave blank if s/he won't answer)	
When is your birthday? (Leave blank if s/he won't answer)	
Where do you live? (Leave blank if s/he won't answer)	
What is your phone number? (Leave blank if no answer)	
What school did you used to go to? (Leave blank if no answer)	
What do you do at home?	
What do you most like to do?	
What time do you have to get up in the morning?	
What do you have for breakfast?	
What time do you go to bed at night?	
What is your favourite food?	
What is your favourite TV programme?	
Do you support a football team? Which one?	
Do you play any sports, e.g. football, cricket, basketball?	
What other sports do you like to play?	
Do you go to watch a film or football with your mum or dad?	
What do you most like doing with your mum?	
What do you least like doing with your mum?	
What do you most like doing with your dad?	
What do you least like doing with your dad?	
What are your favourite items of clothing?	
What clothes do you hate wearing, if any?	
If you were shipwrecked on a desert island, what would you like to have as a:	
Food	
Game	
TV programme	
Film/DVD	
Possession	
Which person would you most like to be with you on your island if you were shipwrecked?	
Which person would you never want on your island with you? It can be anyone you know.	

Name ....
Day ....
Date ....

Morning	No warning	Notes
8.45–9.00		
9.00–9.15		
9.15–9.30		
9.30–9.45		
9.45–10.00		
10.00–10.15		
10.15–10.30		
10.30–10.45		
10.45–11.00		
11.00–11.15		
11.15–11.30		
11.30–11.45		
Total (12 possible)		
Afternoon		
11.45–12.00		
12.00–12.15		
12.15–12.30		
12.30–12.45		
12.45–1.00		
1.00–1.15		
1.15–1.30		
1.30–1.45		
1.45–2.00		
2.00–2.15		
Total (10 possible)		
Total for day		(22 possible)

Name ....
Day ....
Date ....

Morning	No warning	Notes
8.45–9.00		
9.00–9.15		
9.15–9.30		
9.30–9.45		
9.45–10.00		
10.00–10.15		
10.15–10.30		
10.30–10.45		
10.45–11.00		
11.00–11.15		
11.15–11.30		
11.30–11.45		
Total (12 possible)		
Afternoon		
11.45–12.00		
12.00–12.15		
12.15–12.30		
12.30–12.45		
12.45–1.00		
1.00–1.15		
1.15–1.30		
1.30–1.45		
1.45–2.00		
2.00–2.15		
Total (10 possible)		
Total for day		(22 possible)

Name ....
Day ....
Date ....

Morning	No warning	Notes
8.45–9.00		
9.00–9.15		
9.15–9.30		
9.30–9.45		
9.45–10.00		
10.00–10.15		
10.15–10.30		
10.30–10.45		
10.45–11.00		
11.00–11.15		
11.15–11.30		
11.30–11.45		
Total (12 possible)		
Afternoon		
11.45–12.00		
12.00–12.15		
12.15–12.30		
12.30–12.45		
12.45–1.00		
1.00–1.15		
1.15–1.30		
1.30–1.45		
1.45–2.00		
2.00–2.15		
Total (10 possible)		
Total for day		(22 possible)

HOME PROFILE:
QUESTIONS TO ASK PARENTS

Name of child ....   Date of birth ....

How is s/he at home?	
Does s/he respond to your directions, requests, desires?	
Does s/he show s/he cares about your feelings?	
Does s/he respond to anyone's authority?	
Does s/he go out?	
With whom?	
What does s/he do out?	
Does s/he come back at the time s/he is told to?	
If s/he is told to stay in, what does s/he do?	
If told to go to his/her room, what does s/he do?	
Where has s/he got in to trouble most? Home, school, out?	
Describe the trouble s/he has been in?	
Were there any other children involved?	
Who were they?	
Do they have a reputation?	
Has s/he ever been in trouble with the police? If so, how?	
What are his/her main treats at home?	
Does s/he get pocket money?	
Has s/he any way of earning money at home/or a job?	
What is s/he like with his/her brothers and sisters?	
Who chooses what TV programmes to watch?	
Who chooses the meals?	
Describe meal times: seating, order of serving, etc.	
Does s/he go and get food from the cupboard?	
Are food and mealtimes an area of conflict? If so, how?	
Do you feel s/he dominates you and your life?	
Do you get time away from him/her?	
How do you feel towards him/her?	
How do others in the home feel about him/her?	
On a scale of 1 to 10 (10 = most) how happy would you say s/he is at the moment? Can you explain your reasons?	
On the same scale, how happy are you about your relationships with him/her at the moment?	
If you could change things, what would you change and why?	

Never, never, never give up

Winston Churchill

You are now entering a NO PUT-DOWN zone

PROBLEM SHEET

Name ....   Class ....   Date ....

I am upset because	Other people involved	This is what I said

This is what they said	This is how it happened	This is what I will do to fix things

Pupil interest audit

Name ....   Form ....

Best friend's name	Age	This school	Yes/no
....	....		....
....	....		....
....	....		....
....	....		....

My favourite music   Album   ....
                           Group   ....
                           Music style ....

My favourite film or DVD   ....
My favourite TV programme   ....
My favourite TV channel   ....
My favourite game   ....
My favourite food   ....
My hobbies include   ....
The person I most admire is   ....
Reason   ....

The job or career I would like when I leave school is

....

If I were marooned on a desert island, I would want to take the following

Book   ....
Food   ....
Person ....

What my teachers did last year that I enjoyed the most

....

What my teachers did last year that I liked the least

....

If I could change one thing about school to make it better, it would be

....

TO TEACH
IS TO LEARN
TWICE

Joseph Joubert

INDEX